MW01062670

# THROUGH
# The
# CURTAIN

By

Viola Petitt Neal, Ph.D.

and

Shafica Karagulla, M.D., M.R.C.P.Ed., D.P.M.

DeVorss & Company, Publisher
Box 550
Marina del Rey, California 90294

ISBN: 0-87516-517-6

Library of Congress Card Catalog Number: 83-071171


Printed in the United States of America

VIOLA PETITT NEAL, Ph.D.
1907–1981

On August 7, 1981, the gates of Shamballa swung open to receive the returning Pilgrim from the world of Form.

# Shamballa*

Shamballa, Holy City of our dreams,
To which we journey,
Knowing that its gates,
Swing open,
To receive returning pilgrims
From the world of Form.
Home city of the Self,
Whose pilgrimage through matter and
    through Form,
Throughout long eons,
In the realms of time and space,
Bestows Divinity.
And we become His Co-creators,
In God's City of Creative Life.

From *Fragments of Experience—A Spiritual
Journey by* Viola Petitt Neal

*A Senzar or Sanskrit name for the Holy City

**NOOHRA FOUNDATION**
18022 COWAN ST. • SUITE 100B
IRVINE, CA 92714

*Dedicated*

*to*

THE DISCIPLES OF THE SPIRITUAL HIERARCHY

*and*

AWAKENING HUMANITY

*that they may know the source of*
*their inspiration and knowledge*

# CONTENTS

### III
### ESOTERIC EMBRYOLOGY AND PHYSIOLOGY

### IV
### HEALING

## V
## CRYSTALS

# X
# CONSCIOUSNESS

# INTRODUCTION

Little did I know that the year 1930 would bring a friendship that would last for over fifty years. That was the year that I met Viola Petitt Neal. She was first my teacher of physics and mathematics at the American School for Girls in Beirut, Lebanon, and later a colleague and collaborator in reasearch and writing.

During the first twenty-five years, although we remained in constant correspondence, each of us went her own way—she to Egypt to teach and later to Oxford and London to obtain a doctorate in philosophy (Ph.D.) from London University. Her thesis for her doctorate dealt with secret religions of the Middle East.

In the meantime, I completed my studies as a physician and went to Edinburgh University, Scotland, to receive further training as a neuropsychiatrist. My basic interest was the study of the human mind in both normal and abnormal states, trying to find an answer to the hallucinatory experiences of the insane.

Dr. Wilder Penfield of the Montreal Neurological Institute assisted me in obtaining a Research Fellowship from McGill University to study hallucinations in temporal lobe epilepsy and electrical stimulation of the brain in conscious patients during surgery. The data was published in the British Medical Journal and received special favorable comment from the editor. The research had led

me to believe that all of man's experiences were limited
to the physical brain and the five senses.

In 1956, while visiting my old friend Viola Petitt Neal
in Los Angeles, I was challenged to read with an open
mind a few books about the lives of Helena P. Blavatsky,
Alice A. Bailey, and Edgar Cayce—men and women
whose integrity is unquestionable—indicating that they
had had experiences that were neither normal nor abnormal. But how was one to classify such experiences, for they
were not included in my training!

For the first time Dr. Neal revealed to me her own personal experiences, one of which was that as she was falling asleep she would see in her mind's eye, in a miniature
form, frames like a moving picture of beautiful flowers,
places and people in very sharp, bright colors. These had
no particular significance in her own personal life.
Reference to this ability and its true meaning is discussed
in one of the night classes.

A second experience was that when she went to sleep
she was aware of being on another dimension attending
lectures on many subjects dealing with both science and
philosophy. She referred to this experience as *Night
Classes*. Upon awakening, she could recall the lectures the
following morning if she so wished.

Thirdly, she was a student of the ancient wisdom
teaching and an accepted disciple in the Master Jupiter's
Ashram. She had been aware of this since early childhood
and in 1978 dedicated her book of poetry *Fragments of
Experience—A Spiritual Journal*, to Him ("M.J."). She
could both perceive at a distance and communicate
telepathically with the Ashram of the Master Jupiter, a
department of the Spiritual Hierarchy of our planet whose
head is the Christ. These abilities were never discussed or
shared except with a handful of her very close friends.
Since her passing I am permitted to disclose this
information.

Needless to say, her confidential disclosure stunned me. As a researcher of the human mind, I asked for verification of some of her experiences. I was allowed to question her during her sleep, if I happened to be awake myself, and if she were attending "night classes." The following morning I would try to see if she could recall the class which I had taped the night before. To my utter amazement she was able to recall the lecture which she had attended while asleep, almost verbatim, as the tape confirmed. In other words she had "continuity of consciousness" during the waking and sleeping states. As the accuracy of her recall of night classes became evident, the taping at night ceased because it was physically strenuous on both of us.

In my book, *Breakthrough to Creativity—Your Higher Sense Perception*, brief reference was made to some people who had the ability to attend "night classes." Letters were received from readers confirming and describing similar experiences.

*Through the Curtain* is the result of the research that began twenty-two years ago. Only the secretary, Dr. Neal, and I knew of this research.

Before she passed on in 1981, Dr. Neal had agreed that the time had come for presenting the data to help students understand their experiences during sleep. It will also help the scientist to realize that when he says "I want to sleep on it," and wakes up with the answer which he did not have in his full waking consciousness, perchance he is attending scientific classes during sleep and obtaining the answer to his problem from sources other than himself. How else could one explain the common phenomenon of a person not being able to find the solution in his full waking consciousness suddenly finding it after "sleeping on it!"

She chose the title *Through the Curtain* because each time she went to night classes she had to pass through a "curtain of energy" to the concrete mental plane. When

I asked a question while she was apparently asleep she had to move in consciousness to the center of this "curtain of energy" and then back to the concrete mental plane, ask the teacher the question or listen to what was being said in class, and return back to the curtain of energy to describe what the answer was or what her personal impressions were. This shifting back and forth from the physical plane to the concrete mental plane was physically strenuous.

The number of lectures she attended in any one night varied from one to three. The number also varied from week to week and month to month depending on her physical health. Each lecture in the text is identified as to date, marked "taped by SK," meaning the lecture was obtained during sleep, or "recalled by VPN" the following morning. The text contains the letters "SK" standing for Shafica Karagulla and "VPN" for Viola Petitt Neal.

During the taping of the night classes, she was able to retain three states of consciousness: She was aware of me as the person asking the questions, could give my name as well as who she was and her name and the class she was attending, and who the teacher was and what the lecture was about. Thus she was aware of her own identity at all times as well as my identity and that of those on the mental plane of the various departments of the Spiritual Hierarchy of the planet.

I observed that the nights she went to "night classes," her eyes seemed to be focused inwardly as though her consciousness was already tuned in. She herself was never aware of any change before going to sleep. On rare occasions when a few close friends were present I pointed out my observation about her eyes, which they were also able to confirm.

This experimental period was permitted in order to enhance her continuity of consciousness between the waking and sleeping states.

Selection of the lectures is being presented according to subject matter. Letters such as "Z" or "X" were used in this book in order to cover the identity of the real people referred to.

It will be noted that Viola Petitt Neal's night classes had influenced her poetry. A selection of both published and unpublished poems is included. Some were written after her book *Fragments of Experience—A Spiritual Journey* was published in 1978; others were found among her personal papers and signed by her.

Following in the footsteps of the ancient wisdom teaching, the reader is asked to read the material with an open mind, contemplating upon the concepts presented, neither accepting nor rejecting them! It is hoped it will spark an inspiration and a more meaningful awareness as to other sources for our creative endeavors in science, philosophy, archaeology, art, and music. It may also help to explain why so often discoveries are made almost simultaneously in different parts of the world (see reference to the neutron bomb) and the healing that we may receive from sources undreamt of.

Shafica Karagulla, M.D.

December, 1982.

# A Condensed Outline of the Constitution of Man As Given in the Ancient Wisdom Teaching

## *The Seven Planes of Our Solar System*

| | | | | |
|---|---|---|---|---|
| I. | Divine | — | First Cosmic Etheric | |
| II. | Monadic | — | Second Cosmic Etheric | *The Spirit* |
| III. | Atmic | — | Third Cosmic Etheric | ) |
| | | | | ) |
| | | | | ) |
| IV. | Buddhic | — | Fourth Cosmic Etheric | ) *The Soul* |
| | | | | ) |
| | | | | ) |
| V. | Mental — | Cosmic Gaseous | | ) |
| | a. Abstract Mental | | | ) |
| | | | | |
| | b. Concrete Mental | | | ) |
| | | | | ) |
| VI. | Astral or Emotional | — | Cosmic Liquid | ) |
| | | | | ) |
| VII. | Physical | — | Cosmic Dense | ) *The* |
| | | | | ) *Personality* |
| | a. First Etheric | | | ) |
| | Second Etheric | | | ) |
| | Third Etheric | | | ) |
| | Fourth Etheric | | | ) |
| | | | | ) |
| | b. Gaseous | | | ) |
| | c. Liquid | | | ) |
| | d. Dense (Solid) | | | ) |

The causal field or body links the Soul or the Buddhic plane to the personality unit and envelops the etheric, astral and mental fields.

There are within the three major fields of energy in the personality unit twenty-one major vortices or chakras; seven of these in the etheric field, seven in the emotional or astral field and seven in the mental field. The seven centers in each body are related to the glandular system thus:

| *Center* | *Gland* |
|---|---|
| 1. Top Head Center | Pineal |
| 2. Ajna or Brow | Pituitary |
| 3. Throat | Thyroid |
| 4. Heart | Thymus |
| 5. Solar Plexus | Pancreas, Stomach and Liver |
| 6. Sacral or Sex Center | Gonads or Ovaries |
| 7. Base of the Spine, Root Center or Kundalini | Adrenal |

I

Night Classes

# Anticipation

*I have a rendezvous with joy*
*Along the turnings in life's way*
*New vistas in the world of thought*
*That lift the heart with glad surprise.*
*A mocking bird that sings all night*
*For pure joy of beingness.*
*A newborn foal, a child of life,*
*Who stands bemused with wonderment.*
*The golden joy of aspen trees*
*Against a blue October sky.*
*The still white joy*
*Of falling snow.*
*The rippling gold of desert sand*
*Blue shadowed in late afternoon.*
*I have a rendezvous with joy*
*That gladdens all life's winding ways.*

# Mechanics of
# Attending Night Classes

September 17, 1960
Night Class of Viola Petitt Neal
Taped by SK

*Duration of Night Classes*

SK   How long do the classes last?
VPN   Sometimes twenty minutes, sometimes an hour.

SK   How many lectures does the student attend each night?
VPN   Sometimes two or three, but often just one.

SK   Are you going to another class tonight?
VPN   No, I don't think so.

SK   Can you see "X" anywhere now?
VPN   No.

SK   Is the class of "X" still going on?
VPN   It is finished now.

SK   So nobody is there?
VPN   No, there are some students in the room. I think they are asking questions — no, it is finished, they are leaving.

3

SK   Which Ashram is that?
VPN   This class seems to be the Will Ray Ashram. I think it is "J's" Ashram, but I think the teacher is from the Third Ray Ashram.

SK   You mean the one in which "X" is?
VPN   No, the teacher in mine had the symbol of the Master "R" (Third Ray), but he was in the classroom of the Master "J's" Ashram.

SK   Is this the end of the lecture tonight?
VPN   I think so. There is a *hallway with a curtain of light* at the other end.

SK   What does that mean?
VPN   Some of the students are going through it. I think it means they are leaving—I kind of got *stuck* tonight.

SK   Where?
VPN   In the *curtain of frequency.*


September, 1960
Night Class of Viola Petitt Neal
Taped by SK

*The Nature of Night Classes and Their Effect on the Student*

SK   How long do the classes last?
VPN   I don't think it is so much a time sequence. Actually, the classes are on the mental level. It is a period during which very specific intent and design—I will just quote the teacher:

"A certain type of knowledge frequency is directed to a group of disciples. This frequency finds a resonance on the mental body and is recorded in the mental body, almost like a disc of a Victrola. Like a magnetic tape.

"The magnetic tape is very much the principle. In fact, it is interesting, it is really taken from the type of thing that happens. So . . . if you have a magnetic tape recording, figuratively speaking, in the mental body, when the right stimulus occurs on the physical plane—the need or something else—the mental body can play it back, so to speak.

"People who have very disturbed astral bodies are not too good at playing back. You have to have a very steady astral body and very well-adjusted physical body and etheric. You may remember it in waking consciousness entirely or it may come to you as flashes of ideas."

SK  What happens to the student who is going to class in the evenings before he attends the class? Why does he tense up? Or does he tense up? What happens?

VPN  *His mental body is tuned to the frequency of that body of knowledge which will be given in the class.* In other words, it is adjusted to resonate like a dial on a radio. So his attention is partly directed inward and this creates, not so much a tension, as a focus. The focus affects to some degree the astral and physical-etheric bodies until the recording is made. The recording is made when he goes to class.

SK  Does he get tuned into it?
VPN  He is tuned in to a resonating cycle. I feel tired. This is very tiring.

SK  What is tiring?
VPN  *It is that frequency—the curtain. It is like a curtain of rain. You have to kind of stand in the middle of it and it is tiring.*

SK   What does it do?

VPN   *It tunes out the physical body and astral body, and tunes in the mental.* You have, by analogy, to sort of stand in the center of it. When you are doing this, it is tiring.

SK   Why do the muscles feel tired? Does it affect the etheric?

VPN   It affects the etheric body and the muscles of the body.

SK   How does it affect the etheric?

VPN   The etheric is an energy pattern that resonates to the mental body, which affects the physical structure — the actual cells of the physical body.

SK   Is this the thing that makes the student tense?

VPN   It is not exactly tension, in the ordinary sense. It is tuning up.

SK   Is there anything that could be suggested that would help to ease this for the student?

VPN   It does not have to be eased. It won't hurt him. He has to learn to handle it.

SK   Are the classes that are being held — are they held at the time when the student goes to sleep or are they registered in his mental body when he is asleep and then he merely plays it back?

VPN   No. He goes to a class. *Recording is done when his consciousness is fully focussed in the mental body.* This has to be done in a class.

SK   The thing is recorded on his mental body when he is in class?

VPN   Yes, that is it.

SK   But he has to go to a class?

VPN   Yes, going to the class means his whole consciousness is focussed in the mental body.

SK   But sometimes the student does not remember being in class?
VPN   The recording is played back to him when he needs it. When there is a stimulus in the outer world it activates it. But more and more the disciple remembers what he has been told when he wakes up. To go to class one has to pass through a curtain or shed of energy. Classes are held, not in a place, but in a frequency band—a dimension of frequency which one has to attune or resonate to.

This is the end of the class.

March 1, 1962
Night Class of S. Karagulla

### Viola Petitt Neal's Ability to Recall Another Student's Night Class

This morning during the discussion of the night class the question was raised as to whether VPN could recall the presence of other students. VPN said that SK was not present in her class which dealt with healing, color and form, but that she had attended another class.

SK could not recall such an experience and asked VPN to try to obtain the night class that SK had attended. We are not certain whether it was obtained from the record made on the mental body of SK or whether VPN tuned in to the original record of the class which is on the concrete mental plane.

VPN described it thus: The subject dealt with *the nature and quality of the substance of the etheric body*. A thoughtform was projected to the students in SK's class, which VPN saw as a motion picture in her forehead. She described it as follows:

Different grades of etheric substance could resonate to certain defined and limited bands of frequency of energy. The experiment was set up like a tuning fork, with other tuning forks set around so that when one struck a specific tuning fork others with similar frequency resonated to it.

It appeared that every human being was connected by frequency with the etheric centers of the planet. Energy radiates from each etheric center of the planet which is picked up by the etheric centers of humans and animals. The etheric energy man or animal receives in the centers is channeled via the etheric centers of the planet.

Individual etheric centers of a human being resonate to these frequencies. Some can resonate to a wide band of frequencies; others to a narrow band. There are gaps in the bands of frequencies they can resonate to because people have substance in their etheric bodies of different planes. For example, one person may have substance of the seventh, sixth and third etheric planes, while another person may have fifth, fourth and first planes substance. Each would resonate toward frequencies that correspond to their planes of etheric substance. The quality of the etheric body determines the quality of the personality.

This is a broad subject. It will also include certain types of people and planetary types which would show special qualities of substance, which would be characteristic of the place where human individualization took place.

Present in this class — about ten students.

On March 1, after VPN had tried to tune in to the class that SK had attended, an attempt was made to see if VPN could tune in to a *week* previously. The following was the impression obtained:

Apparently, SK had attended a night class a week ago which dealt with the throat center and the thyroid and parathyroid glands. A huge thoughtform was projected into the classroom, several feet in diameter, in order to discuss and demonstrate the structure and mechanism of any center; in particular, the throat center. The lecture dealt with the function of the core and petals in different conditions, indicating a state of health or disease.

The first thing pointed out to the student on this throat center was the core and its movements. The movements of the core in the thoughtform showed that the energies came into the core in a clockwise manner and gradually spiralled down in a cone-like manner, moving inward into a point where it entered the spine. The energies appeared as extremely fine hair-like lines, and were luminous and pale blue in color. The movement was rhythmical and symmetrical in a state of health. The petals had a web-like pattern that was symmetrical and harmonious. It appears that the constitution of the centers is different.

The energy flowing into the petals came from the spine as though spurting out like a fountain in the shape of a bell-like flower. In other words, the energy from the outside flows inward via the core and moves outward via the petals and is dissipated at the periphery of the petals.

The lecturer said that the petals are *bounce-back signals* that tell how the energies are being received and used; in other words, by analogy, how the petals are functioning. The petals are like the bounce-back signal on radar. They are in a sense like an aura around the central whirl of energy which is the core. The petals are the outlet for energy that comes in and it is dissipated from the edges of the petals like the dissipation of electrical energy around a wire.

A thoughtform was projected where there was a disturbance in function of the thyroid in order to illustrate the mechanism. The thyroid was functioning too fast and the energy in the petals spurted out in irregular and too rapid spurts. This was clear in the closeup of the model thoughtform. When one stood back it appeared like a crack or a break between the two petals and in the petals. This was because the symmetrical pattern of the petals had been somewhat broken up by these irregular spurts. The lecturer pointed out that a break between the petals and in the petals showed that the parathyroids are involved in a certain way also.

Lack of flow of energy into the core showed a serious-enough condition that there was at least a beginning of pathology in the physical cells of the gland itself, indicating a hypofunction state.

Energy leaking out at the core means all energy is not moving into the spine as it should and therefore not into the area energized by this center. This could mean any part of the body which the center supplies could be starved for energy. For example, in the case of the throat center, it may be the vocal cords which would show low vitality which eventually could result in a diseased condition.

VPN felt tired and further comments were terminated.

# II

# Extrasensory Perception

# Reality

There is light behind the world of seeming,
Our shuttered house of sense and time and space,
Through all the chinks and cracks of daily living
It penetrates to stab us wide awake.

There is Reality behind the world of seeming
This mundane world in which we come and go
Our infant consciousness securely cradled
Reaches to meet its destiny
And know.

# Mechanics of
# Extrasensory Perception

February 17, 1961
Night Class of Viola Petitt Neal
Taped by SK

SK   Are you in class now?
VPN   Yes.

SK   Which class are you attending?
VPN   There are several classes. I can go to whichever
one I want to.

SK   Which one are you going to?
VPN   Goodness, the subject — it has so much to it that
I guess I had better go to the elementary class.

SK   What are the different classes?
VPN   This whole section is on those abilities and possibilities of the supranormal — what we call extrasensory
abilities or higher sense perception. I think I will go to
the beginning class. The professor — the teacher — is just
going to start this class. Perhaps he gave it before, but
I haven't been in this one before. I think I should stay
here. He is a very nice person.

SK   How many are in this class?
VPN   About fifteen or sixteen, I guess.

13

SK   Do you recognize anybody in this class?
VPN   No. Well, there is someone who comes to classes.

SK   Who?
VPN   He comes from Europe somewhere. I don't think
I know him ordinarily except here. He is German. He
looks German to me.

SK   Is he a doctor, a physicist?
VPN   He is a student — an esoteric student. The teacher
is going to begin the class, I think. He says:

> "In the development of humanity on this
> planet, there are many possibilities of awareness
> which we are not particularly encouraged to
> develop in the long, slow, process of evolution.
> There was a period of encouragement in Atlan-
> tean days that proved very disastrous for
> mankind. Therefore, this knowledge was with-
> drawn from the consciousness of the race, or
> better — held in abeyance, is the word. And to-
> day, there are many members of the human race
> who are developing greater awareness and a
> more sensitive apparatus of response to the world
> in which we live. Many more people have abil-
> ities beyond the normal range of the five
> senses — more than we think have these abilities."

VPN   He says that we are all having impacts made upon
us at many, many levels, from many directions. And that
the people who are a little further along the way in evolution are more sensitive to these impacts of energy, and
that many types of abilities are developed. We are confused about these types of abilities. As a human unit, we
are all mediums for the Light and Life of God — or bridges
between our own kingdom and other kingdoms and in our
own kingdom from one level to another. That we might

use the word "channels" instead of mediums, because the word medium has a very limited concept in our present society—the outer world. That perhaps if we talk about people as channels for energies, we are closer to the real picture. From time to time, people who have this greater ability for being channels—work in certain ways to help mankind. He says:

> "A man like Edgar Cayce had a very good alignment between the etheric, physical level and the mental body, and if the alignment had been as good with the astral body, he could have done his work in full waking consciousness. In this case, he could have seen himself what was wrong with people while he was in waking consciousness, but there was a gap in his development in spite of the very excellent align-ment between the mental and etheric level— the centers and the bodies.
>
> "He didn't have as good a development in the astral body control, so he worked with a group of doctors on the mental plane—healers. These healers on the mental plane could contact pa-tients—know what was wrong with them, and then they could contact Cayce and tell him what was wrong. But he couldn't do it in full waking consciousness, because of this gap. The astral body was the gap.
>
> "And so—to be fully conscious in such ex-periences as these—he could have been in touch with the teachers, the healers on the mental plane, but there must be a good alignment in all three bodies, which he did not possess.
>
> "The group of healers on the mental plane who wanted to work with Cayce in order to help

people had to do it when he was in a state when the astral body was 'damped' down—almost disengaged from the personality unit. There was a fine point where this disengaging was sufficient to come through straight from the mental to the etheric level. It took a certain point and sometimes he wasn't able to achieve it. When he endeavored to be of help and to get a diagnosis from someone he tried to withdraw and, if he could do it just the right way, it was satisfactory. There was a sufficient disengaging of the astral body so that the mental could come straight through. The group of healers who were very wise and very helpful disciples on the mental plane could get through— give the information and make suggestions about what would help the patient."

### Trance-mediumship

VPN   I was asking a question—just a minute.

SK   What was the question?

VPN   I wanted to know how Cayce was different from the ordinary trance-medium? I think the others would be interested in that one too. He says:

"Ordinary *trance-mediumship* is a casual type of mediumship. Usually in these cases the person steps out of his physical-etheric vehicle. There is a little separation between the physical-etheric and the astral and mental unit. The separation is there like a split. (He shows a thoughtform.) A split between the two bodies. And the entity on the astral plane steps into the physical-etheric body of the trance-medium.

This is what damages the etheric body. These people in astral bodies slip in between the astral-mental unit on one hand, and the physical-etheric on the other, that have been separated a little. (He shows a thoughtform.) Then they are in control of the physical-etheric vehicle. They speak and give information which they know and have in their astral level. They are just most of the time curious people who have passed on to the other side or those who want to get in touch. They are not the higher level of teachers or helpers. Sometimes even the entity is functioning on the very lower mental plane and he slips in through the etheric mesh and it disturbs the etheric web badly. It always leaves it weaker and more loose. He gives the message about things he knows or talks about things he knows about. This is the kind of trance-mediumship that is harmful to the medium and not good for the entity."

VPN   The kind of trance Cayce went into was different. The mental unit stayed connected to the physical-etheric body, the astral body was "damped" out or slightly disengaged — not really.

SK   How did he do it?
VPN   He did it by making contact with a certain point in his brain. Cayce knew how to do this. What happened was — this group of healers-helpers were really disciples working on the mental plane. They could talk, they could give their information, but they didn't speak in their own voices, they gave the information to Cayce at his mental body level and then affected the etheric and physical brain and he spoke. But because his astral body was "damped" out, he had only a very slight memory once in a while,

but usually no memory of what was said. Ordinarily you
have to have a continuous stream of mental, astral, etheric
and physical brain consciousness. But because he had a
disalignment there—a gap, because of a poor astral body,
not properly aligned—an entity could not slip into his
physical or etheric body. No entities ever occupied his
physical-etheric body. The healers protected him from
this, and worked with him. He had a very peculiar alignment of the mental to the etheric. The mental brain, we
might say, the mental body had its own connection to the
etheric brain.

SK   Would you say that what he did was a form of self-
hypnosis? Ask the teacher.
VPN   He says:

> "It is an incorrect term. Quite definitely
> incorrect. He didn't hypnotize himself. He vol-
> untarily partly disengaged his astral body by
> focusing on a certain point in his brain. He knew
> how to do this—it wasn't even self-hypnosis. He
> was not hypnotized by anyone outside. He did
> it voluntarily with the intent to be of assistance
> and he knew what he was doing."

SK   How did he obtain the records of the patients and
the records of their previous reincarnations? Was that ac-
curate or was that given by the healers on the mental
plane?
VPN   This was given by the healers on the mental plane.
They have the records there. Occasionally, while he was
in this rather unusual state of awareness, he could see the
records himself. But usually they gave him information,
the teacher says.

   I was just listening to some things. He says that people
who are channels can be channels in a number of different
ways. He says:

"Take Tal-Mar for example. Tal-Mar is working from the level of the causal body. He contacts the causal body level. He has a better astral body than Cayce had. Better aligned, pretty steady. The alignment is good between the astral and the physical-etheric, but he has a poorly aligned mental body. The mental body isn't as well developed as it should be. In the beginning, in his early experiences when he seemed to be in a trance state, there was a cleavage between his physical-etheric and astral self and the mental self. And there were disciples on the higher mental plane who spoke through him. It wasn't the ordinary type of trance. They didn't really occupy his physical body. Again in the ordinary trance-mediumship, which is not so good, the entity from the astral or lower mental planes steps into the physical-etheric vehicle. In the case of Tal-Mar this is not done. There is a disengaging of the mental body."

VPN    I am trying to understand this disengaging of the mental body. This is why he does not remember what was said. The ideas from the higher mental plane — a group of disciples, one disciple particularly — were impressed on his astral brain, his physical-etheric, enough that he himself spoke, but he spoke in his own tone of voice, not that of an entity, because an entity steps in and controls the vocal cords of an individual. He doesn't use his brain really — mostly his vocal cords. But in this case, he was being given ideas directly from the higher mental planes, causal and Buddhic, which had an effect on the astral and the etheric brain and he spoke those ideas on the physical level. Because his mental body was disengaged he wasn't conscious. It wasn't really a crack or break, just disengaged.

SK What does he mean by being disengaged?
VPN Not functioning. Pull the plug out. He shows a thoughtform. He says this is by-passed—it is out of the circuit.

However, over a period of time, several disciples from the Buddhic or Soul level were working to make a connection through the mental body. The centers are not badly aligned in Tal-Mar's mental body, but he has just got a poorly furnished mental body. He has not used it as much as he could—or else something happened along the way about it. I am not sure. It looks better than the other one. But over a period of time it was possible to establish telepathic contact with him. This other was a conditioning procedure. It wasn't important for its own sake, when he wasn't conscious. They are trying to establish a telepathic contact; therefore, they have to use the mental body too. Because he has a poorly furnished mental body he doesn't really understand a lot of the ideas; but he records them faithfully and does what is explained to him—carries out ideas as they are explained to him. He says:

> "There is no time or space on the mental plane, and Tal-Mar has proved to be a very resilient and adequate instrument channel for receiving ideas from Space Intelligences, who are people of a higher frequency, or higher stage of development. Tal-Mar was prepared in this life for this kind of thing."

VPN Somebody is asking a question.

*Telepathic Contact with Space Intelligences*

SK What are they asking? Are there other people who make this contact?

VPN   A great many people are making such contacts —
most of them intermittently — only to some degree,
*telepathic contact with Space Intelligences.* He says:

> "There are a great many people; they all do
> it the same way from the causal, Buddhic level
> to the mental body, to the astral, to the etheric
> and to the physical brain. This is not clair-
> audience at all. It is a transmission of concepts
> and ideas which we translate into our own lan-
> guage — like one of the electronic translators.
> The brain has this mechanism, but one gets the
> ideas and concepts direct, not in language, but
> concepts are translated into one's own language
> immediately."

SK   Is that from the causal body? Is the causal body of
Tal-Mar being used?
VPN   No. No, I don't think — I don't know — I'll ask.
There seems to be a bridge between the causal or Bud-
dhic level of the transmitter to the mental body of the
receiver. A special bridging in a case like Tal-Mar.

### The Conscious Disciple's Contact with the Ashrams
### of the Spiritual Hierarchy

VPN   Contact can be made from the causal level with
a person who has a good deal of awareness of himself as
a Soul. It is a little different kind of contact. He says:

> "Where an individual is a conscious disciple
> on the Path and working with an Ashram, the
> causal body is involved also. The individual can
> either make a contact with the Ashram or the
> Ashram with the student by the mental body
> directly to the astral, to the etheric, to the
> physical brain. Or if the disciple not only hears,

but goes to the place, the causal body is in the
circuit too.

"Also the disciple uses the causal body. One
can ask questions in his own mind and know the
answers often, because he first contacts the
answers on the causal plane about lots of things.
He knows the answers right away, often because
he contacts them on the causal plane through
his causal body."

VPN   There seem to be a number of combinations here
of ways in which people channel. The so-called trance-
mediumship is quite a different thing from being a
channel. This other type, he would call it mediumship,
except the word has been limited to mean people in a
trance state, where an entity actually steps into their
bodies for the time being. An entity that is not necessarily
in a good frequency resonance with the person and,
therefore, can disturb his etheric body badly. He says that
there are a number of other things to be discussed about
this.

But tonight he just wanted to clarify some of the points
about some of them. I think it is a good class to be in.
He seems to give some good information.

SK   When is the next class on this subject?
VPN   Regular classes—whenever one is keyed for it—
these courses kind of rotate. They give them regularly.

SK   Is he giving any more information?
VPN   Just paused a bit here. Someone was asking a question. Cayce had healing ability himself. That is, he was
a channel for it. This was because of his alignments and
his attitude of good will. He wanted to help humanity this
way.

SK   Could you ask a question?
VPN   I think so.

SK    Ask why it was difficult to arouse Cayce, if somebody passed their hands over his body after he had gone
into this kind of sleep.

VPN    He says:

> "This was such a delicate balance, this disen-
> gaging of a body, that it disturbed the magnetic
> currents of the astral body, sort of made this
> disengagement more complete, which was not
> good for Cayce. It carried it too far. It was in-
> terference with the magnetic field there con-
> nected with the astral body—it was better not
> to. This was a very delicate balance that had to
> be established to achieve this. Cayce tried his
> best to be very reasonable about all this and was
> good."

VPN    He says that he will discuss other things of this type
and try to give us a little clearer picture next time. He
says:

> "Remember disciples are channels for the life
> force and you are channels for energies at all
> times. Be aware of this and keep a positive and
> constructive outlook on life so that you direct the
> energies wisely."

VPN    I think this is the end of the class.

SK    Can you ask one question?

VPN    Yes.

SK    Could you ask him what kind of state someone like
"H" goes into? Is there a disturbance in the state of consciousness or mediumship?

VPN    He will discuss that in the next class. It is a little
different type of thing. Not exactly like these other two
that we are thinking about in this class.

SK    Can you ask him if he will be discussing mental and
astral hypnosis next time?

VPN    Yes. He will discuss these things, he says.

SK    Could we ask one question? Could we ask the question about the man who wrote the book about the Third Eye? What kind of possession or obsession or type of thing was it?
VPN    He says that he will discuss this when he talks about another type of occupation of the human body. Discuss the Devic forces too, in that connection. He is not going into it tonight.

SK    Is Tal-Mar there?
VPN    No.

SK    Is anyone you know there? Is "R" there?
VPN    No.

SK    Does "R" go to this class?
VPN    I don't know.

SK    Do you know whether he has been there before?
VPN    I don't know. He says that this is the end of the class tonight.

### Healing by Angelic Forces

SK    Are you going to another class?
VPN    He says:

> "Go into the Chapel, let the angel give you healing energy."

VPN    Oh! It is a lovely angel.

SK    What kind of an angel is it? White?
VPN    It is blue with a great halo, like a fluffy white powder puff.

SK    Are you inside the chapel now?
VPN    Yes, it is nice — very pleasant light.

SK  What kind of healing is he giving you?
VPN  I think anything that is wrong with us.

SK  Can one ask questions to the angel or not?
VPN  No.

SK  Why not?
VPN  He is very tall and beautiful and remote.

SK  And you can't ask him a question?
VPN  I don't think it would be fitting—I don't think so.

SK  Is the teacher around?
VPN  No.

SK  Are you the only one in the chapel?
VPN  Yes.

SK  What kind of light is he directing on you?
VPN  I have to go back *through the curtain* now.

SK  Aren't you going to another class?
VPN  No.

SK  Why not?
VPN  He says that I'm tired. I need to sleep.

SK  Who is saying this?
VPN  The teacher says so.

February 24, 1961
Night Class of Viola Petitt Neal
Taped by SK

VPN  We are out in the paved courtyard—sort of paved
courtyard, and we are going to—we can go to classes if
we like now. I think I should go and find the elementary
class on extrasensory perception—the mechanics of it.

SK    Are you now in class?
VPN    We were just talking with one of the instructors.

SK    What about?
VPN    About the convocation. He says that we were taken into the temple. Not exactly a temple, I guess, but a conference room, for part of this because we needed to think about it. And that also conditions our minds and helps to build the bridge over so that we remember better. But I think we are free now to go to class. Have to find the class on extrasensory perception. Have to go to where the wheel classrooms are. One of the beginning classes. One of the elementary ones on extrasensory perception, but I think it will help to get some practical information about these things. This is the class I was in before and it's on the mechanics of extrasensory perception. The instructor says:

> "If we know how these different methods work, it is going to help later on to train people — help them to develop some of these things more quickly and more easily and in ways more useful to the human race."

SK    Is it the same teacher as last week or a different one?
VPN    No, I think it is the same teacher as before. He says:

> "We might go ahead, somewhat, with the discussion of some of these things that have to do with some kind of contact with other intelligences. The word mediumship is not a good word, except as it is used often with trance-mediumship — in touch with the astral plane. This is the least important type and not good for the medium."

## Overshadowing

VPN   He is talking tonight about *overshadowing*. He says:

> "Overshadowing may be of a number of different types. It is possible to have overshadowing from the mental plane by some disciple on the mental plane who is intelligent, fluent, and is seeking to work with an Ashram. It is a disciple, not an initiate or an Adept, who may overshadow. Overshadowing is different from these other things. In the case of the mental plane, which is the most simple type, the overshadowing individual moves into the mental aura of the person on the physical plane of life. In a sense, he kind of intermingles with the mental aura of the person so that the individual is thoroughly conscious, aware of his own mental processes and yet also aware of what the disciple is saying. This can also be true with a member of the Ashram. One of the Adepts or Masters actually for the time being moves into the mental aura and the disciple or student can repeat word for word what the Master is saying. He can choose at any moment not to do so, or to return to his own mental processes."

VPN   He spoke to me saying I had a very good example of that in the case of "NB" and to remember what was said to me at that time. To remember what happened and what was said in the interviews that I had with the Master Septimus.

SK   Which Master?
VPN   Septimus. He is a Greek Master.

SK  Septimus or Serapis?
VPN  Septimus. S-E-P-T-I-M-U-S.

SK  What happened?
VPN  He says that I remember it. He said that "NB" was an individual through whom certain Adepts and two or three of the Masters were able to speak through over-shadowing. He says:

> "'H' has an overshadowing, from the mental plane, of a disciple who is very learned and fluent. This disciple is still in the human level, but is out of incarnation. But, 'H' is also open to astral influences at times that are not good. This disciple on the mental plane is intelligent and very learned and is doing a very good job of work. He is not an initiate but he is a good and constructive disciple. He steps into 'H's mental aura. He moves on to his mental wave currents. 'H' is able to speak clearly and he is conscious and aware himself as an individual, but he stands aside—his own ideas stand aside. He recognizes this disciple. He speaks the things that the disciple is thinking through his mind, but he is fully conscious. Only because these are not his own ideas, he does not retain them too clearly until he reads them over and thinks about them.
>
> "This disciple is Third Ray Ashram and he undertakes this work from the mental level with the consent of the Ashram. He is not an Adept or Initiate."

SK  Is 'H' aware of him?
VPN  Through the years he has become aware of him as if he were his other self. Sometimes 'H' thinks this is his

higher self or some better self speaking. Because with overshadowing there is a kind of mingling. This is interesting.
Your own mind becomes the carrier wave for this higher
wave frequency like radio.

SK   How is it then transmitted to the physical plane?
VPN   Same way your own mental processes are—your
mind.

SK   What I mean is—is the overshadowing from the
mental plane, or mental body of the disciple?
VPN   Mental body straight to the etheric brain to the
physical brain. Overshadowing is interesting. Overshadowing doesn't disengage the astral body, it passes through
the astral body, but it does not use the astral body.
   It is a different thing in the case of Tal-Mar. The best
way to put it is that in overshadowing, the person working with the human being steps into his mental aura,
becomes a part of it for the time being, and steps out of
it after. The transmission is on a carrier wave—the mind
of the individual. He says that it acts as the carrier wave.
This is not true in the case of Tal-Mar, where there is
a telepathic conversation back and forth.

SK   Could a clairvoyant see what happens to "H" when
the other disciple is present?
VPN   The clairvoyant would probably see the other disciple standing close by him, in this case. He says:

> "The difference between that and just a well-
> meaning entity on the mental plane is that the
> disciple doing this has the authorization to do
> it as a service to the Ashram. There are prob-
> lems with 'H'—this is a private and personal
> matter to him.

"'NB' is a better example. She had a disciplined astral body, physical body and mental body. She was a clear, disciplined and dedicated person of good education, good will and of serious integrity. She was also a channel for some very good information."

VPN   He was talking to me because I seem to be here for a purpose. He reminds me of this. To remember her as an example that I have encountered in my experience. He says:

"With a very well-integrated disciple who is close in the Ashram, there are occasions which are very rare when the Master or an Adept not only comes into the mental aura, but steps into the vehicle of the disciple more completely. This is with full conscious consent of the disciple who is fully conscious of all that takes place if the Master is speaking through his vehicle."

SK   How is that done?
VPN   Briefly, the Master steps in and uses the vehicle.

SK   Well, when the disciple steps out, what part of him steps out? Does he step out into the causal body? What are the mechanics of it?
VPN   He is in his causal body but he has a link with the physical, etheric, astral and mental and he has not lost his link with them. He remembers what is said and done. This is done in partnership, as a working unit, with the Adept or the Master. This happens only where there is a very excellent rapport with the disciple. This is what is called a Disciple in the Master's Heart — meaning he is synchronized to the purpose and work of the Master with loving cooperation with the Master. This isn't done very often. At least, not at present. He says:

"There will be a great deal more overshadowing of another kind. The Christ is beginning to
overshadow many disciples with the mantle of
His Life and Consciousness. There will be a
large group of disciples who will be affected by
this overshadowing—already are being overshadowed to some extent—so that the Christ
concept of the idea will begin to condition the
thinking of disciples who choose to be dedicated
to His work and prepare the way for His
reappearance."

VPN   I was asking how this would come about—what
the mechanics are. He says:

"It would be from the causal body directly to
the mental through the astral and physical-
etheric. A clear line of energy and concepts.
"There is another type of awareness, of extrasensory perception, where the disciple is more
and more open to the archetypal plane. This is
the Buddhic plane. As the disciple begins to be
aware of his own Soul, he is able to contact the
life on the Buddhic plane and know or bring
back to the personality level ideas from the Buddhic plane."

VPN   He says that this is a large subject. There is a great
deal to be explained about it and there will be in a very
short time certain techniques for training these types of
abilities where they had already been achieved to some
extent.
This is the end of the class for tonight.

SK   Could we ask one question?
VPN   I'll try.

SK   What makes the vehicles of certain disciples possible to be overshadowed — such as 'H'?

VPN   'H' is not able to contact the Ashramic level and this is why his work is all compilation. The disciple that works with him has a vast amount of learning, has compiled knowledge — has it all stacked up so to speak. It is useful to get it out. With 'H' it is an alignment. This is interesting. A special alignment of the seven centers of the mental body. He says:

"The astral body is very disturbed. It does not have a very good alignment or there is not much harmony in the astral body. The etheric and physical bodies are mediumistic and in 'H's case the mediumistic aspect helps to transmit from mental over to the etheric and physical brain. This is not a good thing necessarily, but is being used for a good purpose.

"He has problems in the etheric body too, and the physical. This alignment in the mental body is from several lifetimes of great mental discipline and development but he got involved in the left-hand path for a while. Now, he is making a great effort to work on the right-hand path."

VPN   He is not a good example of this overshadowing except that he is one of the people we have been asking about. He said that I particularly asked about him, so he discussed him. 'NB' is a better example.

SK   What about Benny?

VPN   He is different — Venusian — different thing entirely, he says.

SK   Is he going to have further discussion some other time about them?

VPN There are more classes coming up.

SK Does he say when is the next class?
VPN There are classes all the time. I have to go back *through the curtain* because I am tired tonight. He says that holding a contact with the Ashramic level and holding a contact through the curtain is always a little strenuous.

SK Can he explain how you can hold this type of contact? What are the mechanics of it?
VPN He says: "Another time."
I have to not get too tired with it. It is fine to do it. I handle it better than I did and longer. This is enough for tonight.

March 9, 1961
Night Class of Viola Petitt Neal
Taped by SK

### Clear Seeing

VPN *Clear seeing,* not with the physical eyes, but on these other levels, has to do with "identification." You become identified with the thing seen, then you know it. You can become so identified only to the extent of your own development. The quality of substance in your different bodies decides what you can become identified with. The modern term is "what you can resonate to." The quality of daily thought and emotions decides what quality substance is in the etheric, physical, astral, and mental vehicles. Like the mason, we are all builders. Daily we build into our different bodies new and better substance or coarser substance. The quality of thought and emotion selects the material.

The disciple is the conscious mason building day after day the temple in which he, the Soul, performs the creative rituals of life. Clear seeing is normal to higher stages of development and evolution.

"Alignment of centers" means the substance of the bodies is resilient and flexible and more homogeneous in frequency levels, so that the energies coming in move in a harmonious manner. Most people's bodies (etheric, astral, mental) have substance of all type frequency levels; rather like a wall with beautiful symmetrical bricks in one section, rubble in another, irregular stones in another part. You can't get one clear resonant note therefore. Each vortex of energy is in harmonious rhythm to every other vortex in a given body and in relation to other bodies.

Professor Aitken of Edinburgh University has a mental body so perfectly aligned that he has instant access to any knowledge he chooses on the mental planes. His astral body is almost atrophied because it isn't aligned as it should be, so the mental body just by-passes it to the physical etheric brain.

More of this in next night class.

> March 10, 1961
> Night Class of Viola Petitt Neal
> Taped by SK

SK   Where is this class being held?
VPN   I think it is Third Ray Ashram. We have to take our places.

SK   How many are present?
VPN   Seventeen or eighteen.

SK   Is there anyone there you recognize?

VPN No. This is the college on these things. I think the teacher is about to begin now. He says:

"This is another discussion on extrasensory perception or higher sense perception.

"Extrasensory perception is perfectly normal. It is the beginning of another octave of development in the human kingdom and people everywhere will be developing these extrasensory abilities in all countries and nations. Another octave of seeing, hearing, tasting and feeling. It seems unusual to us because we haven't seen those people who have that type of development.

"Yet the next level, the Sixth Root Race, will show much more of this development as a normal part of their growth of these gifts. They come with the perfecting of the personality instrument. There are many different types of extrasensory perception at the present time, but actually all types of extrasensory perception should be normal, rhythmical development in the next root race. Today we find this development unusual, but it is the promise of another stage of evolutionary development.

"There are a number of things regarding this extrasensory perception that we probably want to know about, but first of all we need to realize that those who show these gifts often show only one of them or maybe two, possibly three things. People seem to develop a little unevenly so that they find themselves with one thing developed and not another.

"The personality vehicle should be a much better instrument for expression for the Soul. Therefore, we need to think of the personality

vehicle as made of parts and yet working as a
unit. But at times this type of development is
more marked in one body than in another. It
by-passes or jumps across or, at times, uses other
bodies.

"For example, Aitken of Edinburgh has
uneven development. A very well-developed,
well-aligned mental body in the higher level.
The mental and causal bodies are well
developed. He has instant access to knowledge
from higher levels of life, which is quite normal
for this type of development, but unusual to us.
But his problem is the astral body which is not
so well developed; actually, he didn't use it
enough in past incarnations. So he has instant
access to all knowledge on the mental plane. But
he is handicapped to some degree, because the
emotional body is not so well developed. It has
to be by-passed, so that the knowledge comes
from the causal to the mental to the physical-
etheric level. Once in a while his emotional body
makes a feeble effort and in doing this it interferes to some extent with his use of his mental body. Therefore, he has some problems —
being depressed about emotional problems.

"The Sixth Root Race should have this instant
clear contact with the mental plane of knowledge and be able to pick it up instantly and be
aware of it. Have a good memory for it."

SK   Can you ask the teacher what he means by the fact
that he has a good alignment of the mental body and the
centers? What centers are in alignment?
VPN   The teacher says:

"All of his centers are in alignment, beginning
with the kundalini or root center in the mental

body and right on up the scale. They are all in a harmonious ratio and the brightest one of these centers is the one that is the most active — the ajna (or brow), the head center and the kundalini.

"But on the other hand, the centers of the astral body are not arranged so that they are in a harmonious octave of frequency. This is the fault of the indwelling entity which is the Soul. This person will have to develop his astral body, because he has to have a more perfected vehicle."

SK   Does the same hold true for the development of Aitken's brothers too?

VPN   They have the same type of development. They chose to come into incarnation together in order to give each other a little bit of encouragement and moral support. He says:

"As it has worked out, this man has not been able to do too much that is important to the welfare of humanity, although his knowledge and his ability have been useful.

### Clairaudience

"Many people who are *clairaudient* are simply using the astral body—remember this; but there are several ways of tuning in to the higher knowledge."

### Telepathy

VPN   Sometimes it is *telepathic*, in which case the disciple is in contact with, usually, some disciple or student

in the Fifth Kingdom, and he receives instantly the knowledge or information, through the causal body, that he
needs or asks for. He says:

"This is a personal relationship between an
Ashram and the disciple, where the disciple has
the capacity for this kind of communication.
There are others who have special abilities but
it is mostly a matter of alignment. Sometimes
it is an alignment with gaps in it, in a given
body, or else one of the bodies is not well-
aligned. The physical-etheric has to be pretty
well aligned and then there can be an alignment
of the mental body or the astral body or both.
When you have a pretty well developed alignment of all three bodies then you get more con-
sistent, truer and clearer reception.

"This whole business of extrasensory perception is really a matter of the mechanics of the
bodies and the centers, and the frequency of
energy and substance. A person who has a symmetrical development has these vortices of force
or energy pretty well developed in each body and
moving at a harmonious rhythm and speed. This
is what is expected; this is what is a part of the
development of humanity.

### Precognition

"Many people have many more abilities than
they know. They happen to stumble on one ability, such as, say, precognition and they don't
know they could do other things too. In the case
of *precognition* many events are really set
because of intersecting lines of force that are
about to meet at a certain point in time and

space; and it is possible to see this ahead of time, although once in a while some intervening force may change the direction or line of events. But usually in the case of precognition, the line of events is already established."

VPN   He says that Ouspensky's illustration of the men on top of the building who see more of the parade than the man down in the corner, is a very useful one—a good way to explain it. He says:

"Some of the class have questions in their minds and those who wish to can ask questions about things.

## Instant Clear Knowing

"*Instant clear knowing* is an intuitive perception from the Soul level that comes through as a conviction of clear knowing at the instant. It flashes through from the Soul level, the causal body, to the physical-etheric pretty quickly, without much interference on the astral level. But a person who has a very disturbed astral body has a problem about getting through these flashes of instant clear knowing.

"*Telepathy* in future development will be a normal means of communication and it will be a matter of thinking thoughts which create an electrical field impulse which makes an impact upon the brain of the person who is receptive and he responds likewise.

"The Space People know how to do this. They know how to reach the brains of the people on earth in this way who are receptive. A few are receptive to these things; others are not. Some people can be conditioned very quickly to it, but

to others it is too disturbing, so they get a little
of it, but not much. Remember this is along the
line of normal development for the future, but
it is unusual right now at this stage. It is sort
of sporadic here and there."

VPN   There is a lot of energy in this class. I don't know
why.

SK   What kind of energy?
VPN   Energy of ideas. I think you feel that there are so
many things to know and understand. You only take in
a little at a time.

SK   Are they asking questions?
VPN   I think the students are fighting the energy. It
takes a little adjusting to. Most of them.

SK   What are the various potentials of "A"?
VPN   This is a personal question.

SK   You can't ask it?
VPN   No. I can ask him. Some of the students want to
ask him a few questions like this. He will talk to me a
little later when the class is dismissed. A few of us can
ask questions then.

SK   What is the main subject being discussed?
VPN   The things we have been talking about. I am trying to get what is being said. It is a sort of conditioning
to help one understand the vaster, quicker reception of
ideas, I guess it is. He says:

"In our present civilization it is a little difficult
because lots of things you know you can't use
because people aren't ready for it."

VPN   He said he will talk to several of us now individually. There are three of us who wanted to ask some questions. He says:

"The substance of the bodies and the centers makes a lot of difference in receptivity and if you don't allow the outside world of Form to disturb you too much you are much more receptive."

## The Beam

VPN   He says to me that I am cautious. That I could use the *beam*. Putting out the beam to observe things in different parts of the world — it is kind of like a . . . He says that we don't have anything much to explain it yet in the physical world, but you put out the beam from the ajna center and that it is in alignment with the alta major, the ajna and the head centers. There is a triangle. The beam goes out to different parts of the world. If you need knowledge or information about something for the purpose of helping in the Plan, you can often do this.

SK   Is this alignment on the etheric, astral and mental? On what level is the alignment between these three centers?
VPN   He said that in this case it is a special alignment on the physical-etheric level. That in a sense, you are photographing almost like etheric photography. Oh, it is interesting. There is a triangle of energies in the physical-etheric. Then the beam goes out, and it comes back to the mental body. Then there is a flashback to the physical-etheric again.

SK   What is the relationship between these three centers? When they say it is alignment, is it frequency-wise or the harmonics between these frequencies? What does he mean by "they are in alignment?"
VPN   The three of them become a closed circuit. The top head center has the highest frequency. The ajna (or brow) center — it doubles each time. The alta major center

is the frequency level. It would be in ratio of one—two—
four (1:2:4).

SK   What do you mean: The alta major would be one,
the ajna would be two—one to two to four?
VPN   One—two—four (1:2:4). He says:

"It really begins with the head center. That
way it would make it a little clearer. The frequency relationship 1:2:4 means—it begins with
the head center. In the others it is octaves. The
ajna center is twice the alta major center in frequency. The head center is twice the ajna center
in frequency.

"This frequency or relationship is established
only during the time of putting out the beam.
At other times they settle back to some other
type of frequency relationship."

VPN   One of the others is a particular type of concentration. Of course, there is the intent to do it, but you
seem to—something seems to "click" somewhere in your
head. It is not easy to observe. You have to think about
it when you do it; then you will see how you do it. At
other times other frequency relationships may be established. He says:

"The   frequency   relationship   3:4:5
frequency—alta major, 3; ajna, 4; and top head
center, 5—gives one of the best all-around
alignments for mathematical and telepathic contact and for other types of extrasensory perception abilities. In this case it is a greater triangle:
ajna, head center and kundalini center at the
base of the spine. They will show to the clairvoyant as all being of the same color: golden
yellow; that is, top head center, ajna to base of
the spine."

SK   Would that be observing them on the etheric level?
VPN   Yes. It also shows golden yellow color on the astral level. Higher octaves of golden yellow color—more pastel, more ethereal, not pastel; that is not right—more ethereal. 3:4:5 octaves.

It is the thing Pythagoras talked about—it is the . . . He says that not only telepathy and ideas but pictures too, like a mental television, go with this. Sometimes you just kind of idly see pictures going along, because if you have the capacity to, you could tune it and see more definite pictures of a more specific kind.

SK   Does this relate to the past as well as to the present?
VPN   Yes. It is telepathic contact with the records. He says:

> "This is a kind of alignment that gives you a certain amount of telepathic contact with the records of the past of the planet—in the etheric level not the astral. Although you could see the astral level, it's not as clear there. The etheric level, one of the higher ethers. Some can see the past—historically hear it and understand the ideas connected with it."

### A Devic Incarnation in a Human Form

SK   Could you ask how?
VPN   If it is a question I can ask it.

SK   How does the deva work, seeing clairvoyantly—what is the mechanism?
VPN   He says:

> "The deva or angelic kingdom naturally sees the life force. The energies and the frequencies work much more closely than the human unit or vehicle. It is just like exchange students. Once in

a long while a disciple on the Path wants to
know more about the deva kingdom and has the
permission to do so; otherwise it is very
dangerous. Such a disciple may lend his
vehicles — physical-etheric, the astral and mental bodies — to some reliable member of the deva
kingdom who is on the level of the human line
of development in the deva kingdom. He has an
opportunity to understand, learn certain things
in the deva kingdom, and the deva steps into his
vehicles at birth. He has to have pretty well-
disciplined astral, mental and physical bodies.
He isn't allowed to do this, officially, unless he
has. The deva takes on the karma of the bodies
for that lifetime and works in and through the
vehicle in the human kingdom. In which case,
you have very remarkable abilities of many
types.

"The deva still has the ability to see in a way
that all members of the deva kingdom see. They
are very interested in the life aspect, especially
in the growth of plants and animals and human
beings. They are always terribly impatient with
inanimate objects because they are so heavy and
dull to them. Although there is an atomic life,
it sort of depresses a deva. They don't know why,
but they don't like to try to observe inanimate
objects too closely, too long. Because the heavi-
ness of substance depresses them. But they like
to observe human beings and animals and plants
and they can be very reliable observers. There
are very, very few in the human kingdom, ever.

"Such a deva is like a window into the life
aspect. He sees so clearly and easily some of these

life aspects that the human being struggles to
see through many incarnations of discipline and
effort."

SK   What happens to the disciple who gives his body for
such an experience for the deva?

VPN   He says that the disciple is in the deva kingdom
during that period. He is learning a great deal in the deva
kingdom. When he comes back into incarnation the next
time, the deva willingly relinquishes the vehicle so that
there is no hold on him. Usually, the deva wants to go
back into her or his own kingdom. Where he has worked
in the deva kingdom, he has left an imprint in the human
kingdom that is helpful. His bodies will have the imprint
of the karma which the deva has given him, which he
must accept. Where it has been permitted, it is usually
good karma, not bad. But practically always he will have
a healing ability and a prophetic sense because the deva,
being a part of the Life aspect of the Form, is constantly
giving harmony to the form of growing things or living
things. That is really what healing is.

Healing is allowing the Soul life to express, because
there is harmony in the vehicles of expression. And so,
the deva gives out harmony and helps to establish more
harmony in the vehicles of expression and the person finds
that this healing energy flows through him more easily
after such a devic occupation.

Also, the deva has the ability to see how the lines of
life energy are moving and so he knows what is going to
happen next.

It is simple, he shows us a thoughtform of energies moving up to a point of intersection where certain events take
place and so the individual will have prophetic and healing abilities sort of normally established in his vehicles.
This is an advantage.

SK   How does the deva who sees clairvoyantly use this? What centers are developed? Are they independent of the development of the centers? If the disciple who gave his body did not have clairvoyance, how does the deva use that vehicle to see clairvoyantly?

VPN   The deva can see with or without the vehicle. He does not have to be bothered by the vehicle. He is limited to some extent by the vehicle he is in. He may have some physical karma that bothers him. He needs a good astral body, because he is in the feeling line of evolution. He doesn't use the mental body much. So, primarily, he has to have a steady astral body in the vehicles of expression — one that is not too disturbed — one that has been brought into alignment and harmony.

Now, when the disciple has a physical body, that is, when he comes into incarnation, he will find that he has to get used to using his mental body again. He will find that he will just be blank for a while and he has to get a grip on and use his mental body. It is kind of like some piece of equipment you haven't used for a while and sort of get down and oil it and work with it. So the disadvantage is in the next life. He has to get his mental body working again.

The deva can see clearly in or out of the body, but he can express better through the human vehicle. He says to me:

> "Relax and be more aware of the Life and the Form and use as much of these things as you can wisely and well. Be more aware of the angelic kingdom. They can give you joy and beauty. The angelic kingdom, the joyous messengers and servants of God, have beauty and life and joy.
>
> "The more you are aware of these higher frequencies the more you can be a little sad about the people who go along with their feet

in the mud and their eyes to the ground. You can't wake them up. This is why you need contact with the angelic kingdom. They keep you cheered up."

VPN  He says to two disciples that they both have some of these abilities too and they are trying to learn to use them. He says:

"We will talk again. Come to another class in a day or two. But there is some kind of tremendous thing happening on the planet earth tonight and it is better if we dismiss the class so that you are functioning in your regular consciousness."

VPN  I don't know what this is that is happening. But, he says:

"I think it better for a normal consciousness level."

VPN  We have our consciousness focused entirely on the higher levels of the mental plane when we are in class like this. There is no danger in this. It is just something that is happening on the physcial plane of the earth. It could cause terrific upheavals, but these in themselves are not too important although they seem to be at the moment. He says:

"Let the Grace of God be around and about you to deliver you and to protect you. For the time being the class will be dismissed, but we will talk again in a few days."

VPN  He says to me that I should come back to class in the next few days. I'll do that.

SK  Which day?

VPN  He says that I will be going to class more often for a little while, but it won't disturb me because I have been adjusted to it. I don't think it disturbs me, really.

So, he says that I live such a strenuous life, but things will be a little bit easier in the outside world, so that I can — oh yes — there will be more opportunity for some classes in education and other things that interest me that I could use in constructive ways. He says to the three of us:

"Remember that you have been appointed as disciples in the Ashram."

March 20, 1961
Night Class of Viola Petitt Neal
Taped by SK

SK    What class did you want to go to?
VPN    Class on extrasensory perception. I have to find it. He says:

"Basically, extrasensory perception has to do with a kind of alignment of the centers: the etheric, the astral and the mental body centers, and their relationship to each other, their interrelation within the system. The centers have varied harmonics to each other when they are really functioning correctly and this is especially true in cases of extrasensory perception. The centers can have rhythms that are not necessarily harmonious each to the other. But when they have harmonic intervals like music or where they are interrelated from one body to another, har- monious rhythms, you will find various types of outstanding extrasensory perception ability."

SK    Does he say what these harmonics are?
VPN    He says:

"Usually the interrelation of the centers in the same body or from one body to the other, in the average person is not too harmonious; where it is, especially in the etheric body, we get these different types of extrasensory perception. You can't force these centers and when you try to, you get into trouble. You affect the nervous system or the brain or some part of the body very unfavorably or even in a way that could cause an illness. Any person who has a truly harmonious development will show some extrasensory perception."

VPN   He shows a diagram of the centers in the etheric body; the relationship between the sacral center and the throat center is 1 to 2. He says:

"This person is very creative and contacts the higher source of knowledge, especially in his sleep when he attends classes where creative ideas are discussed."

SK   Is that in the etheric?
VPN   Yes. He says:

"Sometimes there is a very harmonious relationship between the throat center and the ajna center and the person then has great ease in creativity on the outer plane of life — creative expression of manifestation."

SK   What is the ratio between the throat center and the ajna center?
VPN   It is one of harmonious relationship. We could call it a first triad.

SK   What would be the proportion of harmonic between the throat center and the ajna in that case?
VPN   He says:

"It could be one of two or three different harmonious relationships."

VPN   He says, well, that I am not supposed to be in class tonight.

SK   Why?
VPN   However, it is all right.

SK   Why are you not supposed to be in class?
VPN   Because I have been working with some conditioning energies. It will help me achieve clearer alignments of the centers.

SK   Where?
VPN   All of them in all of the three bodies.

SK   What kind of sensitivity would that give you then?
VPN   Better alignment.

SK   For what kind of extrasensory perception?
VPN   Telepathic and contact with the world of archetypal ideas.

SK   What made you go to the class?
VPN   He says that I have it on my mind—these questions. It is a little strenuous to hold the contact.
It's the end of the class.


December 10, 1961
Night Class
Recalled by Viola Petitt Neal

*Manner of Reading the Akashic Records*

This is a discussion on the akashic or planetary records and an explanation of what they were and their value in the future. The lecturer pointed out briefly that there was a great deal of nonsense about the akashic records and that every report of clairvoyants and mediums able to read the akashic records and give individual life readings, was nonsense.

All the members of the class knew this. There were four members in this class on this particular evening. I presume there are others and larger classes at different times. I seemed to be scheduled to attend this class. After the other lectures were over on the political leaders of the world and vortices of evil on the planet, I went into this class on the akashic records. The teacher of this class was a person of very profound knowledge. I would say he seemed to be a very high-level individual. These are inadequate words. His discussion seemed to be that of a person far more learned than most of those who are in the college here. He explained that the akashic records of the planet were the recordings in the seventh ether of every event on the planet. That in a sense this recording was like having a moving picture camera taking pictures of events that go on—like a television camera taking the newsreel, only there was a complete recording of everything; everything that ever happened on the planet, without exception. That there was an automatic built-in moving picture camera, if you would like to put it that way, that continuously recorded all events. They were imprinted on the seventh ether, the highest ether. If you think of the first ether as being the physical plane, the second ether liquid, the third ether gaseous, the fourth ether light, and the fifth, sixth, and seventh, then it is the seventh ether. If you think of it looking from the top down, then it is the first ether. It is the highest ether then. If I designate it that way it will be clear. Always, automatically, the recording went up on the highest physical ether of the planet, so that all events were recorded.

In the future there will be people who could read these records or see them. By reading, he meant seeing and interpreting. These recordings would also help us to see the principles behind them; what the events of history meant, why they happened; how the human race made the actual historical events that affect the planet insofar as history and society and culture go. Also, the physical events of the planet recorded the earthquakes, tidal waves, the animal life, the plant life—everything that has ever happened on the planet and its physical manifestation. And all that has happened on the astral plane is recorded in the astral ethers.

That this is a recording of the mental, the astral and the actual physical events of things that happened. The astral plane affects the astral events; the mental plane, the thinking and mental life of humanity; but this high physical ether brings together and records all of these. It is like having a talking movie. You might have a silent movie in the old days and then you have the talking movie.

The record on the highest physical ether is a complete record. Actual events as they happened, the emotional and mental reaction of mankind to them, and what ultimately produced history. An interesting moving picture, no doubt.

In the future, the sixth root race would have more of this at its command or useful and available to it. There will be quite a number of individuals who will have access to these planetary records; and I use "planetary records" rather than "akashic" as all clairvoyants do, although he used it.

He said most of the clairvoyants and mediums were merely seeing sections of the astral plane, which were true or not true, confused or not confused. None of them are reading the akashic records because they are not read in that way.

In order to read the akashic records, the individual has to have a good polarity relationship between the lower center at the base of the spine (root center or kundalini center) and the top head center with the ajna or brow center acting as the exit point of the triangle, or the point of focus.

That is why VPN could see moving pictures when going to sleep at night. VPN sees from the ajna center as if it were the screen on which the pictures were projected. This is one method of describing it.

When we will have access to these records of the planet we will know history as it truly happened. We will see the principles involved between the forces of good and evil; the forces that produced a certain culture.

Also any kind of architecture is a projection of the energy patterns of the consciousness of the people. Art is the projection of the energy patterns of the consciousness of the people. The religion and the political systems are a projection of the energy patterns of the life of the people — their physical, astral, mental and spiritual life.

We would see more clearly and precisely how these were projected, as we would see a mathematical problem when we could read these planetary records. Previous to this time, it was not particularly useful to the human kingdom to have access to the planetary record, but at this point as we begin to have an emerging of the beginnings of the sixth root race and since the sixth sub-race of the fifth root race is in America, there will be a beginning of obtaining the record which will explain the why and wherefore of history and give mankind for the first time principles which they never really understood before.

After the class, there was a discussion by the teacher with individual students — talking with these students to some degree about their own work. This very seldom happens and in all the time that I have attended classes through the years, there have only been a few times that there has been any discussion with me about my own particular work or what I am trying to accomplish. This is only done when the student's work is useful in the great overall Plan and not in order to make the student feel good or in any way to assist the student with his personal problems. He is supposed to handle those himself and have enough discrimination to do so. So this discussion was more or less impersonal with me as a student—the work that is my obligation, which I choose to do.

No student is forced to do any kind of work unless he chooses, as we say, to "join the army," and then he accepts the command of his superior officers. Unlike the army, he can get out at any time and refuse the commands of his superior officers, if he so chooses. This is understood also. I can't imagine a student who understands what is going on ever doing that, but I know that the student is free to do so. My free will and that of any other student is in no way infringed. If we choose not to do the work assigned to us, we can make that choice.

The teacher sat down with me and said I had a certain amount of development of the two vortices of force that makes it possible at times to see some of the planetary records. The moving pictures I have seen at night all my life were just a "tune in" on the planetary records as I went to sleep. They were not in themselves too important, the things I saw. In a sense this was an exercise, like finger exercises when you are learning to play the piano, to keep me in practice in this particular ability.

In order to see the planetary records of history and events, you have to have a certain harmonious frequency between the vortex of force that has been designated as the top head center, the Spiritual polarity, and the vortex of force that has been designated as the center at the base of the spine, the kundalini center, which is the matter polarity. There has to be a certain amount of synchronization between these centers on all three levels in the vehicle of expression, the personality. That means the etheric center, astral center and mental center.*

In each case this was simply a pattern of energies which produced the kind of focus which made it possible to see or read the planetary records. In the same way that you adjust a telescope to look at the stars, you have an adjustment of the energy pattern between these two. This is not any special gift of God. He says:

> "You could think of the two centers as two
> lenses that had to be adjusted so that they came
> to a focus at a certain point, which was the ajna
> center."

VPN   This was a symbolical description here but a very good analogy. This had to do with the type of choice an individual had made through many incarnations in his interests and development. The person through many incarnations had an interest in both the spiritual aspects of life and two other things — mathematics and science. An interest in science and mathematics developed and brought about a certain frequency in the kundalini center, and an interest in the spiritual aspects of life, meaning and purpose, brought about a development of the top head center so there was a frequency established between these two. I mean a frequency relationship. You had to have a more or less equal development of the two — the interest in science and mathematics and the interest in spiritual truth and the spiritual realities. In one lifetime you might develop more of the mathematical and physical sciences, and in another lifetime the spiritual.

He said that in my last incarnation I moved over more to the Spirit polarity, but I still have an interest in science

*A clairvoyant observation of VPN by an independent person who had no knowledge of this information did perceive development in the top head center, ajna and base of the spine. They were brighter than all the other centers in the body.

and mathematics. When you reach a certain point of development, when the frequency of each center has reached a certain stage, you can see the akashic or planetary records.

In an ancient incarnation in Egypt, I wrote a manuscript on conical sections, worked with mathematics, and at the same time worked with the mystery school teachings trying to relate mathematically the spiritual teachings. In this life, I had picked up the same thing working both from the mathematical and scientific point of view, and the spiritual point of view. He said that I would remember in college that I was torn between the two things. I did an equal amount of work in the sciences and mathematics, and in philosophy. At times, I was very active in college mathematics and physics and put on a chemistry exhibition. At other times, I veered away from that and I went out and sat in the woods to think about why man exists on the planet. Actually I was trying to achieve a balance between these two energy patterns and this was all right in line with development.

He said that my life pattern had led me all over the world to contacts with many people and many ideas. I had to pick up again things I had known in the past. I have had quite a number of years in evaluating human beings for this new method, which is a revival of the laws of Manu. These laws of Manu were known in the early appearance of the fifth root race on the planet and down through the ages have been known, corrupted, known and corrupted again.

Although I had felt all along that my work at the Biometric Research Foundation was my basic work, actually it was a preparation for something else. Again, although it was very valuable to those people who received it and was helping to produce leadership which was important to the country and important to individuals, it was like the finger scale in learning to play the piano. I had to learn to evaluate people clearly; to know what was in their consciousness and what was not; to develop the ESP (or HSP) that gave insight into poeple as well as into the principles. That the "Y" project is the beginning and often when you are in the midst of one activity you are preparing for the next one. It was the beginning of preparation for a time when I would have more leisure to look into the akashic records and point out relationships and principles in history and write on these subjects.

He said that the human race would go through this very bad period which was mentioned in the previous class discussions, but we would begin to be ready for an enunciation of principles. Man was graduating from the old superstitions of religion, although the basic truth of religion was there and it had been overlaid with superstition and authority. True religion would be based on principles—the understanding of principles of life in the universe, which will bring us to the heart of understanding who and what the Christ is on this planet.

He said the time would come when I would be doing a different kind of work. It would be possible to write very quickly and easily because I would have clearly in my waking consciousness all of the concepts that I have had through the years from attending classes. These would rise to my consciousness—outer awakening consciousness, with clarity and precision—and I would hardly be able to write fast enough to get the information down. I would probably do a lot of it on tape recordings and correct it later.

There are other people in the world doing work like this, doing work in other fields, so I am just one of many who will be doing this work. It will be possible for people who are waking in their consciousness to have teaching

in this area, taking concentrated courses of principles that
would be very helpful in the new approach to life, economy, culture and government.

He said that although it seemed very difficult right now
to establish and earth this work, it was being done through
any of the people who chose to participate or felt an urge
from their own inner awareness to help with the establishing of this.

March 21, 1961
Discussion — VPN and SK

*Method of Contacting Archetypal Ideas*

We were thinking of the ability to contact the archetypal level of ideas on the Buddhic plane. Usually we
are so busy with routine and little details of daily living
that we don't take time to do it even if we could.

VPN   I have been trying to be a little more aware of this
kind of thing and, after discussion, I went to bed and was
lying quietly and I began to realize there was a point between sleeping and waking when you have quieted the
outer mind, but you are wide awake still, when you can
move into the world of archetypal ideas, much as you
would walk into a library. Somewhat like a library. You
move into this world of the akashic records and archetypal
ideas — and because your ordinary outer mind is quieted,
the concrete mind or the personality mind, you are able
at the Soul level or the Buddhic level to contact these ideas
much as you walk into a library and open the books and
look at them and, perhaps, choose a book on the subject
that interests you.

Actually, this kind of technique is far simpler than we think. Perhaps it is difficult at first until you learn to slip into it; and you can do it in a full waking state of consciousness. Of course, your mind needs to be alert. If you are sleepy and tired and go to sleep, you go past that point of alignment or point of awareness. It is like a door. You pass by the door and don't enter and go to sleep. Then you don't make such a contact in full waking consciousness as you might otherwise do. I think this type of technique could be acquired by people who have a pretty good integration.

During that period of contacting the world of archetypal forms there was a little further illumination on this concept of life and form. If we could become aware of the Life within the Form, we would have command of the form world — an effort to understand this a little more clearly. The realization that such ideas could transcend the world of material disturbance and confusion to such an extent that if you knew and understood these ideas and concepts you would be able to overcome the outer destructive forces without any way of fighting them or making a point-blank attack on them. It would be a matter of transcending them.

I am still trying to understand what the real principle is with regard to understanding the Life within the Form or becoming identified with it or being able to see it and therefore having in a sense a command of the form world.

SK   Could you describe the technique of becoming aware of this library of archetypal ideas?
VPN   My mind was very alert; we had been discussing a number of interesting ideas. We had several questions on our minds and finally concluded that since it was three o'clock in the morning, we should go to bed and forget about the discussion until another time. So, I went to bed

and my mind was still on the discussion. I was still wide
awake and still very mentally alert. I became very quiet,
lying very still with my mind quiet and alert. Now, many,
many times I go to bed and I am tired and I go to sleep
and I try to make myself stay awake to think and I don't
seem to have too much interest in what I am thinking
about and after awhile I drift off to sleep. But this particular time I remained mentally alert, wide awake, and
so I got very quiet physically. By that, I mean lying very
still, achieving first of all a physical stillness. I felt a little tense when I first went to bed. Simply because I was
still, perhaps, steamed up with all of the discussion and
ideas, but I became very, very quiet physically, still not
really relaxed in the ordinary sense in which you talk
about relaxation, but poised and alert, quiet and what
I would describe as a neutral point in that there was no
reaction to the outside world as such. It was as if one
withdrew all reaction to physical environment. Perhaps
it would be easy to slip into the world of archetypal ideas
or into that frequency level. I can do it when I go to sleep
at night when I go to class. And I can remember it the
next morning, but I am asleep or in a sleep state when
that happens and I remember our class where certain discussions have taken place or certain knowledge has been
given by the lecturer or teacher.

I can remember it very clearly, or I can relay while in
a sleep state, what is being said and remember the next
morning that I have done so, but I thought I could do
something different — remain conscious, so that I was just
on the razor edge between the archetypal world and waking consciousness, and then it was as if I walked into a
library, but I was fully conscious. It was like a fourth-
dimensional experience, and there was someone there who
actually talked with me some. But I contacted the ideas
almost immediately telepathically in the brain consciousness. I wasn't actually taking a book and opening

it in my hand and yet these records existed in a vibratory frequency and I seemed to receive them directly in my brain, which is like telepathy.

SK   How did you focus your consciousness?
VPN   Pulled in my center of focus or center of consciousness some place in my head. But it wasn't a place where I had usually focused it for an Ashramic contact. Now, that is curious because I hadn't thought of that until you asked me the question.

SK   What was the difference between the two contacts?
VPN   Well, when I make a contact with the Ashram — I pull into a central point in the center of my head which must be about where the pineal gland is, and it is a pinpoint of focus or pinhead of focus — a short point of focus. In this case, I simply seemed to move in consciousness inside my head, and to a chamber inside the head, or a cave in the head rather than a point of focus. Maybe it was a large area which I was pulling into focus.

Oh, I think I know what it might be. I would like to explore this technique a little from time to time and see just what it is and how it is done and then perhaps I can be a little more helpful in the process.

February 25, 1962
Night Class
Recalled by Viola Petitt Neal

*Dimensions of Consciousness*

We are one of the mental root race, but we are going slowly and we are thinking in terms of abstract concepts, which is not easy. We are coming into the development of abstract thinking. We have to learn the method of approach to truth whereby we can tune in to knowledge with an instant clear knowing and then examine this knowledge with the concrete mind. The above method is different from the approach to knowledge by the concrete mind.

Another method of tuning in to knowledge is a fourth method of using the mind. You put out a mental antenna and pick up the frequency of the knowledge wanted. Focus on the knowledge you want or need. This is simple, but not easy because you have to have a clear and precise awareness of what is wanted and what is being sought. It is surprising how confused people are about knowledge which they are seeking.

An instrument was shown with thousands of antennae. Each antenna picks up a certain frequency. It is like tuning in or switching to the right station. This approach to knowledge requires clear step-by-step asking by the individual. It is different from the other methods such as analogy. The fourth method is possible for twenty per cent of the people, but it requires a certain amount of development of the mental body. It requires the ability to attack a problem step-by-step, and to tune in to the problem so that the problem itself will tell you what is next that you have to know.

Remember the logical procedure of concrete mind will not necessarily tell you what the next step is and often it hinders you. The concrete mind applies the knowledge and is needed.

When this fourth method of using the mind can be used with any facility, there will usually be enough contact with the Soul and personality to censor the use of this knowledge for constructive purposes only. The destructive person is not able to use this method or approach to knowledge and feels blocked about it. He is very alert to try to find the people who he thinks are creative and use them. Some totally new things will come to the human kingdom through this method for obtaining knowledge.

When we are properly tuned, the knowledge comes clear and strong.

The fourth method is really the basic approach to exploring the universe. The other three methods are preliminary steps and amateur states of mental development. Training in mathematics, especially geometry, is an excellent preparation for this approach to knowledge. The method used in geometry of giving the problem and setting out to solve it, step by step, is an illustration and a training, of course, in this approach to knowledge and the use of the mind.

We do not understand yet, because we have not seen the whole picture, that mathematics is the basis for the universe and for all knowledge.

Culture and civilization are man's application of this knowledge and if we look back over past cultures and civilizations we see new relationships and make new combinations. We are still working within the framework of the knowledge we already have. Modern scientific methods develop the use of three methods to knowledge: (a) inductive reasoning, (b) deductive reasoning and (c) reasoning by analogy.

Mathematically any knowledge exists on its own frequency band which is innate to that knowledge. In fact, the knowledge is the frequency band. By asking the right question you tune in on the frequency band. Underline this in your thinking. This is how the Masters of the Fifth Kingdom tune in to any knowledge they want. A well-developed mental body is essential and a good education is helpful for this type of mental work. Right motivation is automatically part of the tuning device.

Mankind becomes really creative when he can use this method. This is the breakthrough in consciousness which mankind will make. This method will be the basis of the new society and will make it possible. It will automatically establish a hierarchy of leadership and establish a new ideal for development in the human kingdom. Those who will be able to do this will have a radiance and an energy that goes with this knowledge that they contact and present. This is the mental development intended for the Aryan or fifth root race.

SK   The problem to be studied and approached according to the fourth method given was the study about the etheric body as a pattern and web on which the physical body is built, dealing with vortices of energy and what conditions them in the etheric body, and indirectly dealing with things which adjust karmic causes.

VPN   The best approach is the study of the astral effect on the etheric vortices of energy as well as the total constitution of the body. The fourth method could be used to tune in to the etheric body and the astral impact on it and to use psychiatric knowledge and people with special gifts to analyze and observe on the outer plane of life. The etheric body is the foundation of man in incarnation. The physical body is the incidental result and a necessity. Knowledge of the etheric body and its function is essential to helping man in incarnation.


March 17, 1962
Night Class
Recalled by Viola Petitt Neal

*Geometrical Forms, the Key to Tuning*
*in on Specific Knowledge*

Some of you come to a school and remember classwork given, but you must remember that there is a twenty-four hour broadcast on the mental plane and if some people had better "crystal receivers" in their heads they would tune in on these broadcasts. The fact that the fifth root race is to develop the mental aspect means something different from what you suppose. Naturally, concrete mental bodies have to develop. This is, in a sense, a preliminary to the real mental development of the fifth root race.

By concentrating on certain geometrical forms at certain points in the brain, you tune in on organized units of knowledge available at all times to anybody who tunes in. This method can be taught to a student in waking consciousness. Some development of the mental body is necessary and an ability to focus and concentrate. The teaching procedure using actual visual forms will be set up. Those of you who come to class and remember can act as bridges for eventually setting up methods for training many other people to tune in by setting up outer schools. This sort of system is now under an impact of frequencies which will activate a hitherto latent part of the brain which is the caudate nucleus. This is a built-in receiver set for receiving knowledge from the higher mind. This is actually seeing true relationship at once instead of stumbling along and theorizing about facts.

This observation in acquiring a fact has its greatest value in developing the concrete mental body and assisting in outer manifestation of the material world.

A little experimenting with visualizing geometrical forms in the brain in specified areas is helpful as preliminary training. These geometrical forms are keys to tune in on specific kinds of knowledge, at the same time tuning out all others. You start with good-sized forms, such as a diamond, visualizing it as large as a dollar and then eventually using very minute forms at a minute point. You have your whole radio and television set in the brain. This is why mathematics is the key to the universe, as Plato said.

June 12, 1964
Night Class
Recalled by Viola Petitt Neal

## New Alignment of Centers in the
## Sixth Sub-race and Sixth Root Race

The instructor seemed to be an individual from a high level in the Ashram — First Ray Ashram.

Since the Full Moon of Humanity in 1964, the Manu of this root race, the Lord Vaivasvata, has moved into a somewhat closer contact to the human kingdom in a special activity that had been scheduled for this time. At the end of May, the formal beginning of the sixth sub-race as a sub-race was inaugurated and many thousands of disciples graduated into this sixth sub-race. Their graduation was formally recognized by the Manu in gatherings of disciples in their causal bodies and at the causal level. The ceremony may not be recalled by most disciples in the personality consciousness, but all those ready for graduation were formally and individually recognized by the Manu. This particular ceremony did not signify any special assignment of work at this time. This will come later. However, it did indicate a new alignment in the case of disciples which should make it possible for the Soul to reach the personality at the level of the physical brain.

In the present root race, the fifth, the main line of development has been the completion of the mental body and its focusing and aligning. Those who are students and disciples on the Path, for the most part, have achieved this to a degree. At this point a method will be used with the sixth sub-race which will be the method of the sixth root race. Soul and personality alignment is being readjusted on a new pattern. This could only be done after the stage of evolution has been accomplished wherein the astral and mental bodies have been fairly satisfactorily completed. Remember in this connection that there is still work to be done on the astral and mental bodies by all disciples, but the basic work has been accomplished.

The new alignment is of a special type, decided upon by the Manu in Council with Shamballa. This alignment is from causal body to etheric body to physical brain, and then to the astral and mental bodies. Up until now the alignment in the human kingdom has been causal, mental, astral, etheric, physical. With this latter type of alignment, any disturbance in the mental or astral body could block the Soul contact reaching through to the physical brain level. The new alignment removes two of the major blocks, putting them in the line of reception from etheric body to astral and mental. This new alignment does require some adjustment in the etheric and physical vehicles, but this is not so difficult and can be accomplished with the cooperation of the disciple in achieving good health. The disciple will also be receiving specific impacts of energy to help accomplish this. These are energies directed from the Manu's department which will vitalize the etheric and physical bodies and make it easier to achieve a state of health and well-being. On the other hand, too great a transgression of the laws of health will cause much more distress and discomfort.

This alignment will give much clearer impressions from the Soul level into the physical brain. The sixth root race will be characterized by this Soul contact from the higher mind. The sixth sub-race is the pilot group already opening up these channels for future development and bringing changes now at this time into a very confused world.

It has been decided to begin this activity at this time, at least 200 years in advance of the time planned much earlier. The whole life of the planet is speeding up and the implementing of a number of activities is starting ahead of schedule. This means that events will move faster than was at first anticipated. Today humanity is under tremendous impacts of energy from all levels. Therefore, the good and the bad are more marked. You were told at last year's Wesak that the keynote was cleavage — cleavage between the forces of good and evil and in many other ways. This has moved faster than was anticipated at that time. It appears that humanity is moving toward a major conflict in the outer world which will simply be an outpicturing of the major conflict between good and evil in the individual human beings of the human kingdom.

Do not let this unduly distress you as disciples. Keep your focus towards Soul contact, and whatever constructive and creative activity is possible to you.

## Eternal Flame

*Life is a jeweled lamp*
*Forever burning in my heart,*
*Undimmed by darkness in the world of form.*
*My brothers of the lamp are everywhere.*
*A sea gull swinging in ecstatic flight.*
*A forest fawn immobile in the glade.*
*A humming bird with iridescent wings.*
*The jewelled lamp burns brightly in each one*
*My fellowman who sings along the way*
*We know each other*
*Brothers of the lamp.*

# The Wesak Festival

April 30, 1961
Night Class
Recalled by Viola Petitt Neal

## The Wesak Festival, 1961

This year the Wesak festival has very special significance. The place of the festival is within the Crystal
Temple of the Torch. This is a beautiful underground
temple which has held for long ages the archives of this
planet. The great torch above the altar has remained
unlighted through all the ages, until the time when
enough disciples in the human kingdom have achieved the
*Birth of the Christ in the Heart*. When the Soul is born,
then is lighted in the heart of the individual the ever-
burning flame. Each disciple becomes an ever-burning
lamp in the Temple of Sanat Kumara (God). When
enough of these flames are lighted then it is said that the
great torch in the central temple of the planet will be
lighted.

This is a great event upon our planet. Sanat Kumara
came to light the flame of consciousness in the human
kingdom. Until a certain time it was not assured that
enough of our life-wave would achieve this birth of the
Soul. The lighting of the great torch means that enough
of the disciples of the world have achieved this to make

70

possible a new step forward on the planet. The light of the great central flame upon the planet once lighted can never be extinguished. Its lighting at this Wesak festival means that at the heart of our planet the immortal flame has been born and that this will always be a *Christ Planet*. Although the forces of darkness will sweep in toward this central flame engulfing mankind for a short time, they cannot succeed in extinguishing the light of immortal self-consciousness upon the planet. Mankind must still work to evolve, but the immortal self-conscious human being is established on the planet.

This ceremony of the lighting of the torch will take place in the presence of the assembled multitude of disciples, initiates, Adepts, Masters and Kumaras with the Lord Buddha, the Christ, and the Lord of the World. It is the work of the human kingdom as well as the work of all those in the higher kingdoms which makes this great forward step on our planet possible.

This ceremony and all the resulting energies directed to the human kingdom will bring more light, more awareness, more clear-seeing on the part of humanity. It will clear the astral fogs that surround humanity with selfish desires that engulf mankind. The lighting of the great torch—the central flame of the planet—will bring illumination on the mental plane.

The Christ said, "You are the light of the world." We, as disciples, are the ever-burning lamps and we are also a part of the central flame of the planet. By our achievement we make possible the lighting of the flame.

Our candlelight services on earth are a symbol of the lighting of the immortal flame of consciousness. Because Sanat Kumara came to demonstrate light, we who live and move and have our being within His Consciousness faintly discern this truth and outpicture it in all our altar flames in all our religions.

It is said that shortly many more lamps will be lighted as many more in the human kingdom achieve the birth of the Christ in the heart. This will be achieved quickly through suffering and travail as the antichrist "seeks the young child to destroy him." This seeking to destroy all good in the human kingdom will be the last great effort of the forces of darkness on our planet for long ages to come.

Light is the answer to darkness. As humanity, seeing the horror of evil, chooses good with definite deliberation and lights the lamp of immortal consciousness, evil will be dispelled.

When disciples first realize the power of evil and darkness they are dismayed. You do not meet this kind of thing with violence. Light — the light of the lamp of immortal self-consciousness — is the only weapon against darkness. This Wesak will brighten the light of awareness in each disciple. Light has great power. It will show up in sharp clarity the forces at work in our world today. We will begin to know more definitely what we want to choose. The conflict in the world may grow more sharp and more threatening, but in that case it will be resolved more quickly.

The antichrist must answer the challenge of the Lighting of the Torch. He will reveal himself before very long and endeavor to push back the light. Failing this he will endeavor to imitate the light. He will offer humanity the three things which Satan offered the Christ — bread. "Make these stones bread," said Satan to the Christ, "and enjoy all the material things you want. Do the spectacular and make all men praise you." He will do the spectacular to get all men to worship him: the antichrist. He will offer power to all the kingdoms of the world. But all these things are the rewards offered to the sons of darkness. He who is immortal and eternal does not need to grab the material world or power or glory. The Sons of God cannot be bribed or fooled by these things. This is how the antichrist will be vanquished. The Lord of Darkness will be conquered by the light.

As disciples, we must seek to overcome any darkness in ourselves. The only power any negative force has is what we give it by the darkness in ourselves. Let us cast out the darkness that we may walk in the Christ light.

March 25, 1962
Night Class
Recalled by Viola Petitt Neal

*Humanity and the Three Spring Festivals of 1962*

Forces are being marshalled to come to the aid of humanity. Earth humanity is in a sense a colony of Venus and partakes of the Venusian quality. It is basically sound and has an attitude of good will and good intention, but its progress is slow. This, in a way, helps earth humanity and consists of a pattern of approach.

First of all, a frequency impact that began on the 21st of March, 1962, was directed to earth humanity. It will affect the mind and actual physical brain so that earth humanity will start rejecting the negative things thrown at it by radio, television, the press. There will be a turning away from all these things and the Plutonian forces will not benefit. It will baffle them. Venusians and Martians will move in with more positive projects and ideas and earth humanity will move over to these groups and begin to support them. This is so subtle that there is nothing to fight. It is like fighting air. This will hasten the takeover by the antichrist. It will baffle the Plutonian forces and give them cause for alarm.

The three spring full moons will heighten the energy impact and bring what has been a slow deterioration of the planet into sharp crisis—a move up in tempo. This will have several effects on earth humanity: A strong dynamic allegiance to the Christ which begins with Easter. For the first time, an awakening all over the human kingdom at the time of the Wesak festival to the destructive forces. This has never happened before on the planet. They will see that there are forces of light to call on for help. They will see the way to win the battle not with violence, but with the illumination of their minds, and asking for help that is available.

This is being accomplished by the direction of frequencies from the Buddhic plane to the whole of earth humanity. This is the beginning of a widespread opening to the esoteric teaching.

At first, the antichrist forces will not oppose esoteric teaching because they consider religion an opiate for the masses and belief in immortality as utterly stupid.

There is a definite change in consciousness coming about in earth humanity and nothing like it has happened before. It is a matter of weeks rather than hundreds of years. This is a method that has been decided upon in the Council of Shamballa and with the Hierarchy implementing it.

A number of methods were evaluated and this has been under consideration for many weeks. The outer events on the planet of Plutonian origin demanded a change of strategy from the forces of light. The great weapon against the Plutonian forces is the illumined consciousness of mankind. This is really a method of stepping up the light of consciousness in earth humanity and also in Venusians, Martians, Neptunians, Mercurians and Jupiterians. The impact of inspiration on extra-terrestrial planetary groups for good is to help them find forms and methods for utilizing the new illumination of earth humanity.

## The June Festival of Humanity, 1962

This is an extremely important year. It is expected that there will be a tremendous crisis in the outer world involving the whole planet. It could be the establishing of a world government under the antichrist in outer manifestation. It is already established, but not yet revealed outwardly.

At present we are in a kind of "no man's land," waiting for the attack on humanity. Many Venusians and Martians are being forced out of their present ways of life in preparation for having them out of the danger areas and in places where they could give better cooperation when the real crisis comes. Many of earth humanity—the more intelligent group—are very restless and revolting against a meaningless life of economic pressures and jobs that they feel are not honest or constructive. There is a great unrest among earth humanity. The masses even feel a kind of Divine unrest like a person who has eaten too much yet is hungry for the right thing.

There will be an outpicturing of the Hierarchy more definitely and more quickly than it was at first planned. We had to have the impasse for a time because it was the least destructive way to bring earth humanity to a sense of need and, therefore, to respond. Our Planetary Regent, Sanat Kumara, having brought earth humanity to the Lighting of the Torch in the Crystal Temple has been able to ask for extra-planetary help without hindering the growth of humanity on the planet.

Every available person who knows and understands the wisdom teaching is going to be needed to help to instruct humanity because they are ready to respond to the energies of these ideas. Ideas have to be presented without sensationalism and glamour. Remember, earth humanity has a basic soundness.

There were about two hundred students present.

May 14, 1962
Night Class
Recalled by Viola Petitt Neal

*Cleavage—the Keynote for the Wesak, 1962*

This Wesak is focused in Tibet. It is on etheric levels. The political conditions will prevent most of the pilgrims in physical bodies from attending but many will be present in their astral bodies. All disciples of the world will be aware of what takes place at the Soul level. There is an energy focus which will help them to become aware at the personality level.

Each disciple of the world, even aspirants who have any dedication (figuratively speaking) will be a lighted candle—to light the personality and to make them a part of the light in the world. This will give them a more clear awareness of those things and those activities which belong to the realm of light and, therefore, more discrimination to know what belongs to the Forces of Light and cooperate with it. That is why the keynote for the 1962 Wesak is *cleavage*. Because the light they are receiving will show us the darkness. The light they will receive is a protection also because the forces of darkness flee from the light. This inner light will, therefore, conceal and protect those who belong to and have chosen the forces of good. This is referred to in the Book of Revelation as the "White

Stone," and also referred to as the "new name" which designates the Sons of Light.

There is also a focus of negative energy at the same time in the—but this is not so potent. It is powerful because of the concentration of the black forces, but it does not have the power of the Wesak.

This Wesak also marks an impact of the energy of the Avatar of Synthesis coming in through the Christ. The next full moon, this energy will manifest in and through the human kingdom on the physical plane. At this time the whole planetary Hierarchy is focused and concentrated on the energy of the Wesak and all the Ashrams are endeavoring to link up with their disciples and students to reach them with these concepts of ideas and energies.


May 19, 1962

## *The Wesak Ceremony as Perceived by Viola Petitt Neal During Meditation*

The area is surrounded by mountains; no trees are seen. There is a very wide rock which looks more like a flat-surfaced plateau. A formation of people is seen. Many were present.

There is a seven-pointed star formation of people present according to Ashramic position. Within the center of the star there appears to be an inner circle where the Masters seem to be present. On the periphery of the star crowds of people seem to be present. In the very center of the seven-pointed formation a figure seems to be standing, considered to be the Christ by the observer.

At the moment of the full moon, the Buddha appeared on a shaft of Light in the sky and became a channel for energy from Shamballa. He descended into the center of the star and stood beside His Brother, the Christ. Then the Christ moved forward three steps and became the focus for the Wesak energy.

The following ritual was observed to be carried on by the Christ:

> Hands stretched upward as though receiving the higher energies of which he was becoming the focal point. His hands were then stretched outward forming the cross. (Identification with the creative process—Spirit-Matter.) Then He stretched His hands forward and horizontal at right angle to the chest and blessed the crowd. (Outpouring to humanity of the energy of the Spirit.)
>
> The above ritual was done three times. Then all those present did likewise after Him, after completing the three movements each time. The crowd present turned around when they did the ritual as though extending it to all humanity.

The center where the Christ was standing seemed to be over a part of the earth which had a holy ground or a temple beneath it.

A light appeared in the sky, which came to a focus at a point and from there it was rediffused over the surface of the earth. It seemed to cover the whole planet. Gradually it moved in to a more focused circle including just the area. But a certain amount of this light energy would remain from now on, on the planet. One part of the light remained, penetrating to the center of the earth. This is very bright and it is established from now on.

Somehow, the light that seemed to light in the sky was connected with the Avatar of Synthesis.

There was also sound being used at the ceremony of Wesak, but the student who was present could not recall what the exact sound was. "You felt like an electrical frequency was going through you, not too strenuous and yet dynamic." This seemed to last perhaps six to eight minutes and had an effect on the student of opening up of consciousness which will take a few days to adjust to. It seems this was the first time that this type of ritual has been used in this manner.

# III

# Esoteric Embryology and Physiology

# Man

*Eons of time have waited for this son*
*Eternity has held his destiny.*

*And if in infancy he is called man*
*Know this, that he must sleep and wake,*
*And sleep and wake,*
*Through many days and nights of time and space*
*And cherish the clay toys he has made.*

*This child of Matter . . . Maya . . . Mary*
*This child of Will . . . of Life . . . of Spirit*
*Until the day of his majority,*
*When he steps forth knowing his destiny.*

*And in that day shall matter be redeemed*
*And spirit be illumined by that light*
*Which is the splendor we call consciousness,*
*Which is the light of all the worlds that are.*

# Esoteric Embryology
## of the Centers (Chakras)

May 13, 1962
Night Class
Recalled by Viola Petitt Neal

When an incarnating Ego prepares to come into incarnation, his desire and intention (or the Law of Karma and Evolution in unevolved humanity) sweeps into manifestation two great vortices of energy: a) the energy of Spirit, which is the positive or plus polarity and b) the energy of life Substance, which is the minus polarity.

These were shown in a thoughtform intersecting at five major points, which forms the five centers between the base of the spine (kundalini or root) center and the top head center. These two spirals of energy move into a harmonious vortex which forms first the heart center which is a swirling vortex of force. This creates the magnetic pull which begins to attract the physical substance for the building of the physical body. This magnetic center is said to be where the life is anchored. The heart center is often pictured as a radiating sun. It is the first fully established center in this process of incarnating.

As soon as this is accomplished a vortex of energy appears at the top head center and at the base of the spine.

These three vortices of energy establish the three centers and this makes possible the establishing of four more centers —two above the heart center and two below the heart center.

Then the building of the physical body proceeds. The physical permanent atom (according to the ancient wisdom teaching) is simply the pattern on which it is possible for those energies to build the physical body. The quality of substance depends on the stage of evolution and the karma of the individual. The life thread comes in from the top head center, and the energy of substance from the center at the base of the spine. Both of these energies are anchored in the heart center where we find consciousness centered. Figuratively speaking, Christ or consciousness is born in the heart.

The life or Spirit energy is the Father. The energy of matter is the Mother. The two meet in the heart center where the Son is born. This is the magnetic center. The same happens in the two other bodies or vehicles, the astral and the mental.

The important principle is that whenever a positive energy meets with a negative energy in a harmonious union, magnetism results; and where there is a magnetic vortex there is creation and manifestation. In other words, the same process takes place in the forming of solar systems.

Thirty students were present in class.

# Esoteric Aspects of Physiology

December 10, 1961
Night Class
Recalled by Viola Petitt Neal

This seemed to be a survey course with the idea that certain specific points would be taken up and discussed later dealing with the esoteric aspects of physiology.

The teacher began by saying that there were three systems in the human body that correspond to the three planes in the three worlds: the physical-etheric, the astral, and the mental.

The *blood* corresponds to the physical plane. It sustains the actual physical life of the body by providing food and nourishment and carrying away certain waste products. It is Third Ray—which is physical manifestation.

The *lymphatic* system corresponds to the astral plane. It is Second Ray, Love-Wisdom. It deals with the magnetic field of the body, magnetic attraction. If we realized that it maintains the magnetic field of the body, we would understand a little more about what it means in the physical body, for it corresponds to the Love-Wisdom aspect.

The *nervous* system corresponds to the mental plane. It carries the life aspect. It is First Ray or Will Ray.

There is a polarity in the body between the brain and the liver. The *brain* is the positive charge related to the

85

mental plane and, on a higher level, to the Soul aspect; in a sense the focal point of the Soul aspect is in the brain. The *liver* is the minus charge related to the astral plane and, on a higher level, to the personality aspect; in a sense we might say that the whole personality has a focal point in the liver. When the liver is too poisoned, the brain does not work.

There are within the brain plus and minus polarities. There is a repetition in the brain of the seven vortices of force that constitute the whole human being. In the brain polarity, there is a correspondence to the liver in the liver/brain polarity.

*Carotid bodies* in the head/neck correspond to the liver. He did not say the alta major center. The carotid bodies on the physical level correspond to the liver on the physical level in relation to the main structure of the brain which is the top area, the cerebrum.

The *alta major* center as a vortex of force in the etheric body corresponds to the kundalini center as a vortex of force in the etheric body. The discussion was about the etheric body and the alta major center and its relationship to the top head center in the brain. In other words, if we took the top head center in the etheric brain, it has a polarity to the alta major center as a repetition of and corresponding to the top head center and the kundalini center.

The *extra-pyramidal system* will be developed more in the physical brain of future mankind.

The *caudate nucleus* deals with the head antennae — millions of antennae which in the future will deal with the ability of all the extrasensory perception abilities, such as the ability to see events at a distance and the ability for telepathic contact. The sending and receiving station for telepathic contact is located in the caudate nucleus. This nucleus is the mechanism that would be activated and used as the race develops. Some people have a certain amount of development. The ability to read the planetary records (Akashic) has something to do with certain antennae activated in the caudate nucleus. This is the physical mechanism used by the interplay of the top head center and the kundalini center (base of the spine or root center), with its outer focus in the ajna center. This would be the physical mechanism for handling this ability from the etheric to the physical. This physical mechanism is the caudate nucleus. The *ventricles* of the brain act as a screen (like a screen for moving pictures).

SK   Could you describe the caudate nucleus as you saw it in thoughtform presented in class?
VPN   This thoughtform was about three feet long and about two to three feet deep, depending upon which part of it, it was. The teacher projected it in midair but did not discuss it completely because there were a lot of things which were interesting in that large projection. There were innumerable lines like the radiations of the sun. There were different centers for higher sense perception (HSP or ESP).

There were very fine lines, thousands of them, and the caudate nucleus is like a miniature brain for higher stages of development. The centers for higher sense perception were located in different points in this caudate nucleus and the antennae for these were focused at a point. There were certain foci which were pointed out in it that had to do with each higher sense development. In most people the circuits in the caudate nucleus are not connected. This is the best way to describe it.

When the esoteric teaching talked about antaskarana, or the bridge in the brain, it was really referring to a connecting of the caudate nucleus with the rest of the brain — at least the connecting of these antennae circuits.

Each circuit has a sending and a receiving station. With some people, certain circuits are connected. For example, in those who have telepathic ability—the circuit is connected with higher hearing. In those who can see at a distance or can see the Akashic or planetary records, the center is connected with the region of seeing in the brain.

In many cases there are several of these centers already connected in a given human being. For example, those who can hear telepathically, not with their ears but telepathically, and also can see, have the hearing and seeing senses connected.

The higher sense of smell is connected in some people. If this is connected, these persons find the word *nostalgic* has a very powerful meaning to them. The teacher did not explain this. At times, instead of tuning in on the pictures or information they tune in on the feeling tone of something. This, curiously, has to do with the sense of smell, which is odd, but he did not explain.

The antaskarana is built by the student, first, in the etheric brain and then in the physical brain and the caudate nucleus. Naturally, there is a circulation and nerve connection, but the actual use of this caudate nucleus is not known yet and has not been experienced except very slightly by some people who are students, who have gone ahead with their own development.

In summary, it was stated that more will be found out about the lymphatic system, the caudate nucleus and the carotid bodies and their relationships. They have a chemical relationship which deals with the development and use of the caudate nucleus.

Often students who experience a certain amount of this adjustment of the physical vehicle in the caudate nucleus area have *tachycardia* (rapid heart beat) of the type that is produced by a little imbalance in the carotid bodies which disturbs the function of the heart, but it is not a pathological condition. This is due simply to the adjustment that is required for a careful chemical adjustment of the physical body, especially the digestive tract where all toxic conditions begin. In some overloading of the digestive system, he said that certain foods contain those products which are most suited to the physical vehicle and others are not because of the hereditary makeup of the physical body. As we know more about biochemistry, we will be more careful in the selection of food, especially in the case of the disciple. At all times the disciples or students have known that they have to accept certain disciplines in food. For the most part this has been blindly done without a knowledge of the chemistry of which foods are most suited to the physical body of an individual at a certain stage of development. The time will come when we will have a science of the foods most suited to people at certain frequency bands; then we will avoid toxic conditions in our digestive tract, which in turn disturb the liver and the blood stream.

The elimination of disease hinges upon elimination of the toxic condition of the body. The chemistry laboratory of the body in perfect chemical balance would be practically impervious to disease for at least 125 years. The present physical vehicle of mankind was designed to last for from 100 to 125 years without breaking down. We know nothing about the science of the body chemistry. So far our efforts in healing have been primarily directed toward alleviating the pathology or a bad malfunction when it occurs.

The teacher used a lot of medical terms. I think most of the students knew medicine, but I didn't. I think this is why this lecture was for SK. He said the future of the care of the physical body and the overcoming of dis-ease had to do with biochemistry and an understanding of the chemical structure of the body. Many people today are studying biochemistry. They study the protein molecules of the body and the other types of things that he mentioned. One of the scientists who received a Nobel Prize for the study of protein molecules was LP, who is known to SK. But, the teacher said, this is an example of the type of study going on so far. He said it had not crystallized into a system of treatment because the old method of putting foreign things in the body and giving drugs for the alleviation of bodily ailments, especially synthetic drugs, was very well entrenched at the present time. That since no better system is known, it seems to be the best that people can do.

Herbal remedies are excellent; but he said that you couldn't really call them remedies. They are plants provided for the use of mankind to help adjust and re-establish the chemical balance in the body. They should be considered as foods to establish and adjust the chemical balance. The ancient peoples, especially the Atlanteans and the more primitive people, had an excellent knowledge of herbal lore. In some cases it was incorrect, but basically it is a very correct knowledge and could be very quickly adjusted. When the human body needs fluid in the future, it will be administered through herbal teas. The man whom we both know, Dr. B, was attuned to some of this knowledge and was bringing it through. There were many others mentioned — LP, too.

He said a more cleansed and perfectly-functioning physical body or vehicle would make possible a higher use of the brain structure. In this regard, spirituality has a connection with the physical vehicle.

We were quite right about the saints, or the mystics, who were trying to take a higher voltage of spiritual energy in a physical vehicle not well adapted to it. They experienced tremendous functional upheavals, which often quickly disappeared because of the healing qualities of the energies they contacted. But this was not the normal or desirable way of life.

This was a survey of a course that is being given in these classes. He was giving the high points of some of the things to be discussed later.

# IV

# Healing

# Who is God

*The Chinese sage*
*With his ivory balls*
*Carved in beauty each inside each.*
*Seven dimensions*
*Seven worlds.*
*He ponders long*
*And his quiet face*
*Shines with wisdom and inner grace.*
*"Who is God?" I gently ask.*
*"Hold this symbol and look within*
*God is ever becoming more*
*Ever a life in greater life,*
*Worlds without end and lives without end.*
*Each life lives in a life more vast,*
*Until at last the Absolute."*

# The Study of the Etheric Body in Different Centers of the World

September 17, 1960
Night Class of Viola Petitt Neal
Taped by SK

SK  What is the best way of making the study of the etheric body and its centers available to the medical profession or the rest of the world? Is the approach being made at present by humanity correct or should there be modifications?
VPN  Very little is being done, because up to now man knew very little about the etheric centers or anything of this, so not much has been done.

SK  Is there anyone who is studying these things now?
VPN  Yes, several places in the world.

SK  Where?
VPN  In India.

SK  Which part of India?
VPN  Somewhere in the North of India, there are some people but they are clairvoyants. They are like yogis.

SK  What is the name of the town in India?
VPN  Somewhere up in the mountains in a small village. I think this is a mystery school and the name is not given.

They are Initiates of the White Lodge. It is a kind of information like that given by the Tibetan. It is too high, too technical at the moment.

SK   What other places?
VPN   "X" works with it.

SK   "X" works on it? Is "X" working in the correct manner?
VPN   "X" is working under the Ashram too. "X" tries to do practical things in the West — the Western way of approach, which is fine.

SK   Do you think "X"'s approach is correct?
VPN   This is the best approach for the present and "X" knows that.

SK   What?
VPN   "X" ought to know that.

SK   Could "X" improve on the technique?
VPN   This is the best thing to do now. There will be someone else a little later who will and can be of assistance to "X". I think someone connected with the Ashram who will be of assistance in this effort.

SK   Will it be a doctor or a clairvoyant?
VPN   It probably will be a person who has some kind of professional standing. That person has had some training, He has got very clear gifts, like the other person. He will be clairvoyant.

SK   Which other person?
VPN   The Deva.

SK   Is the Deva good?
VPN   The Deva is very good and sees the world of substance and the energies in the world of substance.

SK   What is her name or his name?
VPN   She has the body of a disciple—feminine vehicle.

SK   But it is a Deva?
VPN   Devic being.

SK   Would it be possible to continue the work with the Deva next year?
VPN   Yes, she probably has family problems coming up, but she must be held to the work. This is her destiny.

SK   Do you think she will be away for some time next year in India?
VPN   Well, maybe not.

SK   Is "X" able to study the centers in mental patients or should there be a delay?
VPN   The next step seems to be a glandular problem—-pituitary, thyroid, especially—if possible. "X" gets information in class. The reason "X" is so determined and feels so strongly that certain things must be done and stays with this kind of work is because of the instruction in class. When "X" sees in the class what the work is and what the need is, then "X" becomes dedicated to that work or need.

# Various Types of Healing

September 17, 1960
Night Class
Recalled by Viola Petitt Neal

## *Faith Healing*

This is related to the state of the astral body affecting the physical body. There are certain things as regards this that may clarify the concept. In the class the discussion about the astral body and the lack of its proper alignment affecting the etheric body, is very interesting. It was stated that many of the illnesses of mankind began in a disharmony of the frequencies of the astral body affecting the corresponding center or centers in the etheric body, and then resulting in an effect on the physical body.

Faith healing and the healing at Lourdes and the possibility for an individual to be healed through an act of faith from the Soul level, in which he knew and was sure he could be healed, brings about an almost instant alignment of the centers of the astral or emotional body. This would be so tremendous and dynamic that it would instantly affect the etheric centers in the physical body and bring about a healing such as those recorded in Lourdes and others which are known and experienced by some people.

This act of faith explains what is meant by that term because the person knows suddenly so clearly that he can

# HEALING 99

be healed that there is a flow of energy from the Soul level. You might say from the Buddhic plane which vitalizes, readjusts and re-aligns the astral body and produces this instant healing; or if not instant, a fairly quick-healing process which sometimes takes a matter of days or even weeks. The type of healing which is recorded at Lourdes is one of the most outstanding examples. It was mentioned because over the years there have been records of these unusual types of healing.

## Healing the Astral Body by Symbols or Ritual

This establishes a state of harmony in the astral body and will do more towards a total state of health in the physical body than anything else. For the most part karma is registered in the astral body until humanity has reached a greater sense of development. That is the karmic pattern. The emotional pattern that an individual has when he comes into incarnation is primarily his karmic pattern that he is working with. Through ritual and symbols it would be possible to bring in those energies which will adjust the karmic pattern, which is negative and disharmonious and, therefore, establish a better state of health for human beings and a better karmic pattern to work with.

The symbol mentioned in class was the winged circle of Egypt. We have seen it on Egyptian symbology. It was a white luminous disc; the wings appeared to have colors, but this, I think, is because we think of wings as having feathers.

## Healing the Etheric Body by Sound

With the physical etheric body there will be the use of sound, as a method of affecting substance immediately. In the beginning, the form world was made through sound, and sound at that level, without concept, can be used to begin to establish harmony in the etheric body and in the dense physical. If the imposed rhythm of the astral body continues to be negative and destructive, then the same or similar condition will come about or can come about in the physical and etheric bodies and yet in order to help the individual to find ways to adjust the astral body he can be relieved of some of the problems and pressures of the physical body through the use of sound.

This will have to be a beginning, because it would take longer to adjust the astral body than the physical etheric. So, healing methods will work in the future very definitely with sound to give the incarnating individual breathing spaces to adjust the astral. In a state of health established through the level of sound, the physical and etheric level can be maintained — and this is the beginning.

In the beginning, the Form was perfectly made through sound — but the imposed rhythms of astral and mental levels can destroy the harmony. The harmony can be re-established through sound and maintained if the incarnating individual is able to establish a right emotional and mental outlook.

SK   Why is the winged circle used? To which center is it related?
VPN   The ajna center or brow. This was said last night at some point in the lecture and is interesting because the ajna center is the center of the integrated personality and not the solar plexus, as I would think myself.

SK   Could you see in the demonstration in class how this pulls energy from other levels?
VPN   I was shown exactly what the symbol looked like: a luminous white light. It glowed as a thoughtform in the center of the space in front of us in the class.

## *Healing the Mental Body*

People can be taught to achieve a development of the mental body quickly through methods of teaching mathematics. Today, people are taught mathematics by memorizing it. They do not see it as the science of relationships. Mathematics is the pure science of relationships.

The human race has almost entirely developed the astral body. In the process of doing so it has misshaped and disturbed and warped it, and, now the next step in the human race is through ritual and symbol to adjust and align and establish harmony in the astral body. In a sense it is easier to do this because the astral body is more fluid than the physical. The disharmonies we have brought about in the physical body are in some ways harder to adjust because they are the dense physical body, which is not so fluidic. The astral body could be adjusted more quickly than we think in the overall pattern of adjustment of the human race.

## *Summary*

The following methods will be used in healing:

a. Physical etheric level — sound will be used.

b. Astral level — the use of symbol and ritual to adjust and restore the harmony of all the centers in the astral body.

c. Mental level — mathematics and science; but in an expanding concept of science and mathematics one can be taught to see more quickly relationships through mathematics.

d. Color was discussed as the bridge. It pervades all three methods. Color was the uniting field of force of the three methods, that is of sound, symbol and ritual, and mathematics and science. All three of these methods were unified by a field of color and so color was an overall unifying field of force.

# Alignment of the Centers

September 17, 1960
Night Class of Viola Petitt Neal
Taped by SK

VPN    The astral centers should be in alignment with the etheric. Most of the time they are not. They are all on octaves of frequency that are in resonance and have a harmony like music, or the music of the spheres. First, all the etheric centers have a frequency rate like an octave of music. The astral centers are on the next octave of frequency and then the mental. But it is the astral ones that are always out of tune, like a piano out of tune. They should be on a higher octave of frequency.

If you think of the heart center as middle "C" in the etheric body — this is just an illustration — then in the astral body the heart center should be the "C" an octave above. When this frequency relationship exists in perfect harmony, you have a condition of health. When it is in disharmony you have disease. For example, the solar plexus center is the one in the astral body that gives a lot of trouble. So, also, in the etheric. I think he has something to say about leaks.

## Leaks

*Leaks* are due to disharmony in the astral body causing the leak in the etheric. The leaks are really when there

103

is disharmony between the corresponding center in the astral body. The astral body is anaemic and the etheric body tends to leak all over. The main problem of humanity today is in the emotions, in the astral body.

SK   How could one stop the leaks? Any suggestion as to treatment of the leaks in the different parts of the body?
VPN   Generally speaking, leaks are from the astral body in the sense that disharmonious frequency affects the etheric. But sometimes the leak in the center of the etheric body is simply due to etheric causes. But most of the time it is from the astral body. Leaks can be cured or helped by helping the person change his emotional pattern, if it is from the astral body. Sometimes it is just from the etheric and physical levels.

SK   Is there anything else one could do on the physical and etheric levels to help the leak?
VPN   The Life Force of the physical body comes in to the etheric where it is modified and modulated by the astral and the mental bodies, but mostly by the astral body. Sometimes people are born with damage in the etheric body from other incarnations and then it is hard to do much about it even from the astral level.

SK   What would be the best thing, for example, to treat the leak in VPN's throat? How to treat it and what would be the best way of dealing with it?
VPN   It is temporary, it is partly physical. A little trouble with the physical thyroid from a toxic condition in the body. Also, from all level work.
    It is possible to treat with sound. These higher frequencies of sound will help to establish the right frequency relationship in the different centers in the astral body and also in the relationship of the astral to the etheric.

SK   How do you impose the frequency?
VPN   They are using sound, ultrasonic.

SK   How many octaves above the audible?
VPN   *It depends on the keynote of the person—the triad.*
Each person has his own keynote and depends on what
it is on the scale of audible sound. There is some kind
of mathematical frequency about this, if we knew the
mathematics. You find the person's keynote in the musical
scale.

SK   How does one find that exactly?
VPN   Simply find out which note is most pleasing to the
person.

SK   In one octave or in any of the seven octaves?
VPN   Whichever note in all of the seven octaves he likes
best. Then you take the octave seven octaves above the
audible sound and you find the corresponding note in the
corresponding octave in the ultrasonic.

SK   Seven octaves above the personal note?
VPN   No, there are seven octaves of audible; seven octaves above, inaudible. The note in whatever octave in
the audible sound—find the corresponding one in the corresponding octave of inaudible sound—ultra-sonic. This
is the sound that will help to establish a greater harmony
in the astral body. So, then you treat the etheric with the
audible and the astral with the inaudible octave. There
has to be a way of helping astral bodies of mankind. They
are so confused—cannot reach them.

SK   How long do you play this note or octave?
VPN   Not very long, not more than three minutes.

SK   How many times does one repeat it?
VPN   It could be done three times a day.

SK   How does one know which center would benefit best?
VPN   This kind of treatment is the beginning and
general treatment for a general sort of bringing the
centers, the astral body into alignment. Specific treatment

would also be worked out. It could be worked out in a mathematical scale.

SK    If a good clairvoyant looked at the astral body or astral centers and the etheric centers, could he see these relationships?
VPN    Yes, and it would help if this was done. It could be done—say with the throat center and the solar plexus center. Just start by looking at two centers and comparing the etheric and astral parts and how they are related. This would give a line of research which would be very profitable.

SK    You mean to look at the etheric center and then the astral?
VPN    Let us say the throat center. If you have someone who has a bad physical condition of thyroid, then look at the etheric throat center and, also, look at the astral throat center.

# Photographing the Etheric

September 17, 1960
Night Class of Viola Petitt Neal
Taped by SK

SK    Would it be possible to photograph the etheric body and the centers?

VPN    It would be possible to photograph the etheric and in the distant future, possibly the astral.

An interesting thoughtform is presented to the students — what it would look like. You see the etheric centers very clearly and then, sort of interpenetrating and having a different quality, the astral. The astral centers are larger than the etheric in the thoughtform that is presented. You can see the outline of the etheric centers clearly and the energies moving and scintillating. Then you see the astral centers.

In the thoughtform the lecturer brightens up the etheric centers so that you identify them, then kind of dims the etheric centers and brightens up the astral centers. When he does this you can see the outline of the etheric centers clearly. Next he brightens up the astral centers so that you can see their relationship to the etheric . Then he sort of dims the astral centers and pulls up the etheric and they are brightened. You can see how they interpenetrate.

SK    How do they interpenetrate?

VPN    You know, one is over the other more or less.

SK   Is the astral larger or smaller than the etheric centers?
VPN   The astral centers are larger in this thoughtform.

SK   Some clairvoyants see them smaller.
VPN   They are shown larger in this picture.

SK   Is there any way of photographing the etheric centers?
VPN   There should be a discovery to do with crystals.

SK   What kind of crystals?
VPN   Some kind of thin sheet of crystal.

SK   Any specific crystal?
VPN   Quartz—the crystals are some of the elements which might be useful in this.

SK   How could one photograph through it?
VPN   Just to look through it at first. Try sheets of crystal like those used on radio. Try looking through and photographing through. The secret for this is to be found in crystals, because they have to do with the di-electrical energy which is really etheric energy.

SK   Does one use ordinary film?
VPN   It is not so much the film as what you photograph through. You need a sensitive film, but it is going to be possible to photograph with substances that pick up something more than the physical plane.

SK   Will it modify if one used the crystal with a lens camera or must one use a camera without lenses?
VPN   You can use an ordinary camera and then use crystal in front of the lens. Try it.

# The Astral Body of Disciples on the Path

September 17, 1960
Night Class of Viola Petitt Neal
Taped by SK

This is a discussion of the astral body as it relates you to the world of form. The astral body is your antenna in the world of form. The discussion does not deal with the astral body from the healing aspect, but rather from the point of view of the disciple on the path who has gained a certain amount of control of the astral body.

The desire aspect of the astral body is that dynamic part which keeps humanity moving forward in the earlier stages of evolution. Because we grow and evolve through desire. The desires that attract mankind in the earlier stages of evolution are those desires best indicated to help him achieve growth in consciousness in that stage of evolution that is right and good.

But as he approaches the stage of the Aspirant and Probationer on the Path, the astral body has a different use and purpose. It should no longer be the body of desire in the sense of the desire for things in the outer world, desire for prestige or this or that. It should become a very sensitive instrument for sensing his world, the disciple's world, being aware of the state of consciousness, state of

109

emotions of the world around him, so that he can rightly evaluate his world.

The mental body is the discriminating vehicle in higher levels and should become his discriminating vehicle in the world of form, in the outer physical world. It is like a sensitive antenna giving him the feeling tone of any situation of people in general of the world around him. Very specially it is the instrument for reaching out and becoming aware of the outer world for the disciple on the Path. The mind is for manipulating the outer world. The concrete mind with the higher mind uses those inspired ideas in the outer world.

The astral body is used as an instrument for reacting to the outer world as long as the individual is centered in the world of form—personality centered.

The disciple must not react, but act. If he reacts then his astral body is involved, but if he acts from the Soul level by way of the higher mind, the concrete mind, then truly he changes his world. You do not change your world by reacting, but by acting.

The person who acts from the center of himself must do so without being disturbed by the emotional reaction of the outer world. He must say, "This I must do," and do it and not be involved in what the outer world thinks. So he acts upon his environment instead of reacting emotionally. The astral body is secondary; a reservoir of energy for action in the outer world of form.

Astral energy is related to the Cosmic Buddhic plane and to the physical cosmic. Energy can flow from the Buddhic plane into the astral body when it is rightly disciplined and controlled, in order to give the energy or fuel for action in the world of form. This should be the purpose and intent of the astral body.

In the disciple on the Path the symbol for achieving this kind of use of the astral body is the winged circle of ancient Egypt. This is one of the reasons for the class in symbols of Egypt a short time ago. In the Mystery School of Egypt the student meditated upon the symbol of the winged circle in order to achieve this kind of use of the astral body.

SK   Does the student use the form or the color or both?
VPN   Sort of luminous white as if one saw it illumined with a white light behind it. A thoughtform is shown which is very good — as if it were etched in glass with a white light behind it to give the students a picture as to how to visualize it.

SK   Are you in your own class?
VPN   It is MJ's class in the course I am in.

SK   How many are present tonight?
VPN   Eight or nine students. If the astral centers are really in harmonious relationship it can bring about a humanity where there would be very little disease. But most of humanity has a dis-harmony in the astral centers and this modulates and disturbs the etheric energy in the etheric body. There is a line of cause and effect. Through symbol and ritual the astral body could be directed, trained and brought into harmony in time.

It is interesting, this energy from the Buddhic level, when it comes into the astral body (a thoughtform is shown). This winged circle is like a button or valve that opens a channel to let in energy from the Buddhic plane in small amounts as the astral body can take it. Energy from the Buddhic plane to help achieve this use of the astral body. (A thoughtform was presented — it spreads into this astral body; you can see the color change in the thoughtform.) This symbol can be used by disciples on the Path who are probationary or disciples. It is safe to use it.

SK   For how many minutes a day?

VPN   Visualize it for four or five minutes a day. It would be very helpful. Today, mankind's biggest problem is the astral body in the sense of their emotional reaction to things, especially the great mass of mankind. There will be an effort through ritual and symbol to work with the astral body on the astral level. And with the etheric and physical body sound will be used because you have to work from both aspects. You have to work on the etheric and physical bodies. There is no use working on the physical without working on the etheric. Even drugs and medicines affect the etheric first and the physical second. Their effectiveness is because they have an etheric frequency.

You have to begin the healing field on the etheric level by the use of sound from the physical plane level of modern science, and from the esoteric level using the Buddhic energy through the use of symbol and ritual to treat the astral body.

SK   What about color?

VPN   This will help more on the physical-etheric first. Sound is the key to substance.

### Hot Flashes

SK   What is the cause of *hot flashes* and what could be done to be relieved of them?

VPN   It has to do with unbalance of — a disturbance between the pituitary and the sacral center — ovaries or gonads.

The energy interchange is disturbed in the physical body around 45 years of age. There is often an imbalance of — no it is a lack of right energy exchange in the physical body. It is mostly the physical chemistry of the body. There are diseases due to physical conditions, but this goes back to etheric self structure.

SK    Is it better to handle it with diet or with actual re-
placement of the hormone that is absent?
VPN    Diet and rest and fresh air and normal procedures
are better than medications. They don't solve the problem, that is, medications, but they short circuit it and
cause other problems.

# The College of Healing

March 3, 1961
4:30 A.M. — 6:00 A.M.
Night Class of Viola Petitt Neal
Taped by SK

VPN   During *conditioning classes* energy is directed to
the personality unit, the physical-etheric, the astral or the
mental body, or all three. Sometimes this takes a whole
class hour. It's under the energy impact for a certain
period of time. This helps to improve the memory and
it generally helps to improve the alignment, because some
people don't remember things that are said to them in
the classes. This is not always the reason for the energy.
This energy field is a kind of conditioning energy. It is
a pattern and it is along certain lines of force. The teacher
says:

"We can see a thoughtform of how it works."

VPN   It takes time. It seems very difficult how long it
takes people to wake up, to register impressions from the
Soul level or from other higher levels. They seem to do
it very slowly.

This energy force-field has different colors too — some
are golden-yellow, some are blue, green. There is one
which seems more violet. I think this is one of the more
advanced disciples. It's an alignment for contact with his
Soul and personality and then perhaps Monadic later on.

SK    How is this field created or generated?

VPN    It's hard to say. It seems to have a connection with the centers of the teacher in charge. The different centers are used in the etheric, astral or mental body. It is a matter of different centers in each case, so the centers and the quality of the centers is really what makes the instrument more useful or resilient. That is, the substance of the centers or the kind of energy that goes through is dependent upon the kind of substance that is there in the first place. Those who are more advanced people in the world have a higher type of substance in the etheric or astral or mental body. Sometimes there is conflict with a higher type of substance in the astral and physical-etheric, but perhaps the mental body doesn't have the substance it should and then the person doesn't have the well-rounded development he needs to have. I suppose this is partly a matter of conditioning too. A part of conditioning energy. The teacher says:

"Much of this energy is really sound. Sound and color. But it is higher octaves of sound that affect and condition the aspirant and disciple, so that they can comprehend concepts and ideas."

VPN    There are quite a number of disciples and students who . . . It is interesting that many of these disciples seem to be asleep. They are not aware of being in another dimension. They are being conditioned with their own consent, really, but they show lack of awareness — not all of them, but lots of them act as if they were sound asleep. It's very odd.

SK    What is odd about it?

VPN    I am used to seeing students here aware of what goes on. I have not seen these that are not aware.

SK    How many are present?

VPN    It is a great sort of theatre of people, but each one has a particular beam of energy on him, as if everybody were under a different type of impact or frequency. Each individual is subjected to his own particular impact of energy frequencies, but it seems this energy is a little hard to take sometimes. I am under it too. It is a different kind of energy in my case from that of the ones close to me. It's a kind of energy impact that seems to open up your consciousness.

SK    What is the one you are getting? What is its color?
VPN    It's a golden yellow with some violet. The instructor says:

> "Disciples get this impact of energy whether they realize it or not. Often when they are out at night in the astral or mental body they receive help and energy and conditioning."

VPN    I think this could help the physical body too. He says:

> "Often someone who is feeling ill recovers rather quickly because he is sensitive to these treatments and they very quickly pull him out; but sometimes people are slow to react or respond to the frequencies, so it doesn't seem to make much difference immediately, but the effect is that a change in the bodies takes place.
>
> "'X' has a problem with heat regulation of the physical-etheric body. It has to do with the etheric body and the physical body, and it is due to the thyroid or throat center. The thyroid is activated so that it sends an alarm signal to the physical body and this begins with the pituitary — and the pituitary gland is the governing gland — and there is in the normal process of living the pituitary in the physical body which has control of the physical body. The pituitary delegates work to the different glands — the work they must do.

"If 'X' could get down inside her liver—if she
had that minute state of consciousness—she
would find a liver that is not as harmonious as
it should be. It would look cloudy."

VPN   I can see the thoughtform of this. It looks cloudy
and in some places lots of cells aren't functioning at all
and in other places the function is very poor. In some
places it brightens up. It is like moving around in a cor-
ridor. You see it as if you were a miniature or something.
He says:

"The pituitary sends messages to the ovarian
system and says, 'Work on cleaning up the liver.
Get rid of these toxins.' And there isn't any
ovarian system, and so then the pituitary looks
around for somebody else to handle the problems and he finds the thyroid, the strong fellow.
The thyroid can do its usual job and a little extra. It is kind of like a work group where somebody is absent and the others have to take on
his work. These are absent entirely, so the
thyroid is made to work."

VPN   I was just seeing a thoughtform again.
  The thyroid says, "Well I only have certain avenues to
handle this and I will have to do it the best way I can."
This is a thoughtform and a sort of animated way of
describing this. He looks around at the situation and says,
"Well, the skin is good. There are millions of channels
and the skin is a good way, with all these channels available, for dumping out this trash." So, he sort of presses
a button and the trash gets dumped out through the skin.
He says:

"The liver has to do with the astral body, so
for two reasons the liver has problems with anybody. 'X's' liver is the one we are looking at.

"Maybe things taken into the physical body
have a very definite effect on the liver and poison

the blood stream. The liver reaches up with many hands and takes them out. It is a very self-sacrificing organ; it sometimes kills portions of itself—sacrifices to prevent poison materials from getting into the blood stream too much. The liver is also affected from the astral body. It might be called the astral organ in that people have lots of fears or sorrows or griefs or resentments or negative emotions. These also affect the etheric liver and the physical liver. It is primarily the astral body, not the mental body, that affects the liver. The mental body can affect other organs.

"It is a good thing that the liver is self-regenerating. If the other parts of the body had the same ability for self-regeneration, it would make a great difference in the life and the youth of the physical body. Of course it begins always in the etheric—the etheric liver then the physical liver. A person who has a glandular system that keeps tossing out rubbish is very lucky; he lives longer.

"In a few months 'X' will feel much better about this because the toxic—well, no, there is a lot of rubbish stored in the liver too."

VPN   It is very interesting. I see a thoughtform of it. Rows and rows and rows of rubbish. It seems so magnified, sometimes really the cell has lost its life force, but it is still in the storeroom where the rubbish is stored.

SK   Where is this rubbish coming from?
VPN   It has been taken out of the blood stream and it's also somehow connected with the astral body and this whole thing is very interesting. The liver has a self-regenerating capacity and every now and then it looks at the whole system and says, "Perhaps I can get rid of a

little of this rubbish." And so, it puts some of it out in a conveyor—the blood stream. Then, the pituitary says, "Well, I have to handle this," and it tries to get the ovaries to, but they aren't there, so then, the thyroid decides it goes out through the channels of the skin.

But, "X" is regenerating the liver pretty well. And this has to do with the regeneration of the liver—it's not just food eaten now, but it's an old story, the house has got an attic full of rubbish and the closets full. It is a kind of housecleaning. It means that "X" will live longer and be stronger once the liver can get rid of the rubbish and rebuild. It could go out through the intestinal tract, but the adrenals are not quite strong enough. There is a weakness there; it is not serious, but they can't take on an extra load. If the adrenals were stronger this rubbish would go out through the intestines and colon. The thyroid is kind of busy—a busy one.

SK    Through what center is the liver affected? Which center is related to it?
VPN    The solar plexus center in both the astral body and the physical-etheric.

SK    What does he suggest to help the liver?
VPN    He says:

> "It is pretty far along now, but it will ease off. The liver is getting straightened out. A good diet helps."

SK    What kind of diet does he suggest?
VPN    Just a minute. He is going to tell me something about . . . This is very interesting, because a lot of these people are under impacts of energies to help them with some of these problems too. Lots of disciples. He says:

> "The thyroid has a harmonious frequency kinship with fruit. Also, the whole system of healing goes into herbs. The plant kingdom includes

vegetables and fruits and has a very wonderful affinity for the etheric body and it is the etheric frequency of the different plants that affects the physical body. The Chinese know a lot about old herbal remedies. They are Atlanteans. Different plants have frequencies and they take them into the body. They think we take the herb and it affects the physical body, but it doesn't. It affects the etheric body and then the etheric affects the physical."

VPN  This is very interesting—you can see it in the thoughtform. He kind of puts you inside the physical body, as if you were very, very miniature. Then you can see frequencies that affect the etheric body and then, the etheric body affects the physical and this is how the herbal remedies work. He says:

"This is the principle behind the homeopathic treating. It gets the etheric body first and then the physical."

VPN  Also, the vegetable kingdom and fruits. He comes back again and he says:

"Fruits have a beneficial effect on the thyroid—not to excess, of course, because you have to balance and adjust with other parts of the body. So maybe you need vegetables too. It is a sort of balance.

"Some vegetables have an etheric frequency that is more harmonious to certain parts of the body than others. There are some vegetables that have a harmonious frequency to the liver and this would help the thyroid too, because it would help the liver. If the poor thyroid has got to help the liver, then you can help the liver directly."

VPN   It is this whole College of Healing, really, that has to do with all these things. He says:

> "The reasons why for lots of things are quite different from what people have thought in the therapy."

VPN   I'll ask him a question about 'B'. He says:

> "Somebody else wanted that too. 'B' is a man who is tuned in on some of this and he really sees these things as if he were inside the body. He doesn't admit it, but he has a peculiar type of clairsentience. Oh, it is very different from most. He can get inside the body and feel what is wrong with it. Minute parts — not just a general feeling that there is a pain somewhere. He can get inside the liver and look at it; or he can get inside the kidneys or he can sense what is going on. He even does it with patients quite a different way from other clairsentients. He tunes into this College of Healing. He does it at night — he goes to night classes and he remembers things.
>
> "Well, we will go down the hall and see one of these rooms in these classes."

VPN   Fascinating! Here is one. All students are studying the liver. "B" stays here a lot of the time. This is the class he goes to often. You can see — you are inside the liver — it's as if you were inside a great machine. It is more than a machine — it's a precision instrument. It is a terrific precision instrument and you see what happens. Oh, yes, he says:

> "When people eat the wrong foods and they eat too much — it's not so much the wrong food — some part of the digestive tract isn't working, the food isn't digested, so then it's toxic.

This is the most tremendously vast and complicated system, this digestive system. One little
thing doesn't work, one kind of food does not
digest, so it makes the rubbish like unburned
things."

VPN    Oh! there is a transformation. He says:

"Digestion is a process of transmutation. On
spiritual levels, we talk about transmutation. But
the digestive system is a very complicated system—fascinating—it is very interesting when you
see it that way. So certain things you don't digest, because some little part of the apparatus
isn't functioning. A little faucet doesn't turn on
somewhere for a certain kind of thing that helps
to transmute the food. The food we eat is not
just a matter of the physical aspect, but the
etheric energy we get from it too."

VPN    This is interesting, I didn't know this before. He
says:

"We get etheric energy from it. So certain
foods don't need to be toxic to you, but they are
because some parts of the digestive tract don't
handle it. And so you get rubbish. It gets picked
up and then the liver has it dumped on it. The
liver is really a sacrificial organ. All this rubbish
comes in and the liver has to find something to
do with it. If too much of it gets dumped in the
blood stream, it is going to poison the heart or
the brain, so the liver gets busy quick and stores
it—in its storerooms—hundreds and hundreds
of storerooms. It says, 'Well, maybe I can get
rid of it another time, but we had better not let
it out right now.'

"'Dr. B' is always here studying the liver and the glandular system. He goes to these classes at night and then he gets his ideas and works on them. After awhile, he tunes in on the patient when he comes in and he knows he is really working on a system where he is choosing the fruits and vegetables that give the greatest etheric energy, because it can be helped from the etheric, back to the physical. It is both things. With these people he works with, it takes a long time to get some of that rubbish out of the liver. The patient kind of gets tired of it."

SK   Does he suggest anything for the liver of "X"?
VPN   He says—"fruit juices."

SK   What kind?
VPN   Apple juice is good and, he says, carrot juice and the zucchini juice. The raw will do it quicker than the cooked. Yes, things happen to it when it is cooked. It digests more easily if it is raw—that's curious. The teacher says:

"It is not curious because nature made it that way."

VPN   He is kind of laughing at me. He is right. He says:

"'X's liver is looking better. Soon the load will be off the thyroid a little more. Although 'X' doesn't realize it, it is much better than it was. She doesn't have as bad or as many of these and they are going to ease off in the next few months and get down to very little. Only once in a while."

SK   Does he say there is something else she can do that would be helpful?

VPN   She has been doing a great deal by changing her emotional outlook. He says:

"Fear is one of the things that causes the liver to have a bad time. She doesn't have too much of that anymore. And she has gotten over the grief or the self-punishment. She is getting over the 'hair shirt'.

"She is going through the conflict where the Soul takes over the personality, and she is handling it pretty well. She doesn't need to be fearful. She thinks she is afraid of this or that or something else, but the point of all her fear is the fear of the Soul taking over the personality and all the other fears spring from this. It is the central pivot.

"This is a fear that all disciples have — that students have as they endeavor to come up to that point. It is a fear of losing one's identity. Through many and long incarnations we build up our identity and this is necessary and essential. It takes many incarnations to achieve a focused and well-integrated identity consciousness. In order to be well integrated we have to have a strong sense of identity. It is really the fear of death — death of one's identity — not dying in the physical body, but the death of one's identity. Actually you don't lose your identity — you find it, because the Soul is the True Self. The personality is the Form and you are identified with the personality and you have a fear of losing your identity. So, then, you have the struggle. The Soul seeks to give you Life and an eternal and glorious identity and you refuse it and hide in the corner and shiver and shake. Human beings do. 'X' is going through this stage of her development where she calls it 'losing control'. But, this is what she thinks about it on the personality level. Actually, the Soul takes over the personality. She gains control, so there need not be any fear."

VPN   Oh, he says to me that this is why I don't have fears like that, but I have other problems. When the Soul takes over there is much more vitality in the etheric body—the etheric body immediately begins to be vitalized and it helps the physical too. He says:

"Right diet, especially using the advantages of the fruit and vegetable kingdom, is excellent. It is a discipline that 'X' accepts. She is still working to achieve this union or marriage of Soul and personality. But she has got her astral body much more under control and yet she doesn't wear the hair shirt and punish herself with old hurts and aches and pains—emotional ones.

"The light of love is an illuminating and an aligning energy on the astral body. If she can relax a little bit about letting the Soul take over and get over the fear of losing her identity, it will help. This is something she is working at pretty well. She has a lot of work to do in the field of the etheric body and this is the real field of healing of the future. Others are doing the biochemistry work which is on the physical level. She is doing a very good job about the etheric body."

VPN   This is sort of a privately conducted tour. He says:

"Let's go down the hall. There is a laboratory. They are trying to find out how to photograph the etheric body.

"There are some things being done in pho-tography, some kinds of films that are being brought through. Even with the films we have at the present time, if we could get the right crys-tals—very thin layers to photograph through . . ."

SK    What sort of crystals?

VPN    He says:

"'X' has worked some with this—and it de-pends partly upon the axis of the crystals. She tried some and didn't get much result because she couldn't get the right axis—crystals cut in the right planes."

SK    What is the axis?

VPN    Geometrical planes. I'll ask the question about that. He says:

"You might try also doing a photograph through any kind of a cut stone you have—like an alexandrite."

VPN    I want to ask him a question here. A synthetic stone? He says:

"Try it—even try to photograph through a synthetic stone. Perhaps you could pick up some lines of force if you could get the right axis. This is a precision thing and you would have to get the people who could cut this and know the axis of crystals. It will be done eventually through the crystals."

VPN    I will ask him a question. "What about some natural crystals?" is what I want to know. If I could just get some natural crystals like quartz. Or something that is pretty clear. He says:

"Yes, try this, you might get a crude result that would lead to something. This is mathe-matical and has to do with some precision work,

but there is work being done in different places
and something is going to come through on it
that will help you. Help you to see why. Help
us to see how these crystals can be done. The
key tool will be photography through crystal
forms. Don't be impatient about it, but try experiments yourself. You might hit on something
using some of these—if you got some that have
the right mathematical faces."

SK   Can he suggest what faces it should be, so that we
can find someone to cut one for us?
VPN   He says that this involves a process of knowledge
of how crystals are cut. If we would wait a little while
there would be some things done that we can use. In the
meantime, we could do experiments. In the next few
months, there will be some things coming out. We should
watch the newspapers and scientific magazines. I'll ask
which ones. There are an awful lot of them. He says:

"Some of the electronic things—like the maga-
zine we bought on the light-beam and New
Scientific American—see it—read it—look it
through each time and find some hints in it and
sooner or later it will be in that, and the newspapers, where you will see scientific things. If
we have it in our minds we will pick up the
things that have it and not worry about having
to read hundreds of magazines. Look at the electronic one. That one that had the red light-
beam story in it was a good one. Watch that
one. We will get some information about it from
Scientific American and newspapers we see.

"This is the key to the photography of the
etheric body; and other people who come to
these classes are doing research on crystals. 'X'
is doing this very well. She is finding out all she

can about crystals because she has to know a little bit. She doesn't have to go into the field permanently, but know enough about them so that
she can appreciate and use what other people
do in their discoveries. Let other people do the
minute and detailed research, but know enough
to take advantage of that research. Disciples
should know enough about a number of subjects
so that they can take advantage of the research
that other students do."

"In the meantime, she should find out what
she can about the centers of the etheric body
with her assistant — especially the glandular,
thyroid, pituitary."

VPN   I must ask him a question. He says:

"People come in with different types of
physical bodies with certain things not quite
right or not quite adjusted because of karmic
conditions. They don't have an absolutely
perfect chemistry laboratory. These things have
to be adjusted through life. This is in the future.
You will study what you might call the
hereditary makeup of the physical and etheric
bodies. But really it is your karma which is written in your physical and etheric bodies. It is written there just as it is anywhere else. What you
will be doing is finding out the hereditary or karmic condition as one comes into incarnation.
What kind of physical and etheric body does he
karmically or hereditary-wise possess?

"It is just a word — hereditary — because people in the past did not know better. You come
into a certain family where you get certain
factors — the lines of force crossing to give you
certain kinds of bodies because karmically that

is the kind of body you can have. We will call it your karmic physical body and etheric body. So you will know which things need to be corrected, which things you need to be concerned about and work with. You'll begin to see the astral pattern that is contributing to this. Work on it from the level of the astral body — usually it is an astral problem. This is the whole theory of healing.

"This is why 'X' is so concerned about the etheric body. She goes to classes. She is a very eager beaver. She is one of those disciples working right there in the same college that 'B' is in. He is working on one thing — she is on another. He is really interested in the liver.

"But the whole approach to healing is the use of the plant kingdom — the food, fruit and vegetables to help assist the physical-etheric body. You refrain from putting into the body the things you can't handle, so that you don't poison the liver, while you are giving it a chance to adjust itself karmically from the astral level. Also, you work from the physical level with the right foods, the right herbal remedies and plants.

"All this artificial stuff isn't so good, but some of it helps. All the artificial stuff they give you — shoot into you — is just a stop-gap because they don't know any better. They don't know what else to do so they try. It is not too good.

"You work from the level of the astral body to adjust those astral conditions that cause trouble, and you work the physical-etheric level with the right fruits and vegetables, herbal remedies and things to relieve the strains and pressures on the karmic body that you brought

in. So you work to relieve undue strain and pressure. This requires some discipline. You work
from the astral level to straighten out the conditions that are putting pressure on the etheric
and physical body and disturbing its frequencies, causing dis-harmony and dis-ease.

"Tal-Mar goes to some of these classes in healing. But he also has to go to the classes on some
of the geometry. It is going to be so slow with
him because his mental body is kind of poorly
furnished. Space Intelligences (people of a
higher frequency or stage of development) take
over. They have to talk to him and tell him how
to do some of the mechanical things. But the
thing he is doing is to affect the substance of the
etheric body. The basic substance of the etheric
body brings in a higher frequency. It will have
a rejuvenating effect. But people will have to
straighten out their astral bodies some time
before they can react to this rejuvenating effect.
The materialistic ones wouldn't get anything out
of it."

VPN   This is all the most beautiful pattern. It all works
together like the pieces of a lovely design—like a wheel—a
mandala. Each student in different parts of the world is
working with different interests. He says:

"'X' is the only one doing any really good
work on the etheric body."

SK   Does he suggest any improvement in the method of
approach?
VPN   He says:

"It is all right. Do what you can do now. Go
ahead with the devic clairvoyant. Find out what
happens to the thyroid and pituitary when they

are not in good function, so that when you can photograph you will know what you are seeing. This is very important — it can be done now; the other — even if you could do it — you wouldn't know what you were getting, finding out what the centers look like, occasionally referring back to the astral body condition. Focus on the general etheric body — whether there are pathological conditions in it. What the throat center and brow center look like. These will serve to give a clue for anything else. When you have this information, then when you can photograph something, you will know what you see more quickly. So go ahead."

VPN This is the most fascinating college. It seems to be built like a mandala too. But all the colleges here are in that form.

SK On what plane is this? Lower mental?
VPN No. It's the higher mental plane, because you have to have a good alignment with the causal body to get the information and be able to remember it.

SK But "X" doesn't remember going to class.
VPN I guess it is because "X" doesn't have a good union between Soul and personality yet. He says:

"'X' has a fear of losing her identity. The Soul needs to get more control of the personality and then she could remember. She gets impressions anyway, lots of them. She gets it here, and then you have to put a book under her nose with the information in it to make her remember what she got here."

SK Who puts the book under her nose?
VPN He says:

"Oh, her friends—different people. She gets interested in some book, goes hunting it. The Ashrams work through people. Through her own interests."

VPN    All these colleges are built as a mandala. All knowledge is organized like a mandala. Different disciples are working out on the periphery of the wheel. But eventually all their knowledge fits like sections of the mandala—all together in one central focus. Then you see a whole pattern. This is true with these other classes I go to. Even the colleges on the mental plane are in this form, the form of a mandala. Oh, of course, the mental plane is all mathematical really. It is geometrical. The astral plane has wild, turbulent storms of energy. But the mental plane, especially the higher mental plane, has beautiful precision. These thoughtforms—no, archetypal forms— are often in the mandala patterns. It is very interesting.

## Angelic Forces, the Third Aspect of Healing

I was a little tired when we started, but it is fascinating. I feel much better, you know. He says:

"The *angelic forces* try to work with us very often. This is another source of help in healing too. It is a third aspect of help. The angelic forces are the life aspect and they would help us much more if we would be aware of them and ask for their help. Ask for help from the angelic forces, whose office and joy it is to be of assistance. This is their work and their purpose. Mankind seems to totally ignore the angelic forces, although all his Holy Books talk about them. People act as if they think it is a fairy story or something."

VPN    Then he laughed, and said:

    "Of course, fairies are real too."

VPN    He is a very nice person. He said:

    "Let us go to the chapel before you are fin-
ished for tonight."

## Chapel of the Union of Life and Form

VPN    It is a very lovely place. It is called the *Chapel of
the Union of Life and Form.*

SK    What do you see there?

VPN    I have to see . . . It is very beautiful. It is made
of semi-transparent columns and walls of sort of a milky
crystalline form. Crystalline substance—and through all
this is circulating a very soft, pure, white light. But it is
pleasant. It is not disturbing. You don't feel a busyness.
The total effect is scintillating clear crystal—and that is
the focal point of the chapel. He says:

    "This is why all churches have altars. They
must have a focal point for energy. The focal
point of the chapel is like the altar. It has a sunburst, but it has all the colors—and many other
colors besides—well, more fragile colors, higher
octaves than our colors."

VPN    There is a sunburst that goes out from a central
core of white light. It is the symbol of the manifested universe. There is some kind of ceremony about to begin.
There are disciples and students and others here. It is very
beautiful. The One who is officiating is like a priest—
like the office of a priest from the Nirmanakaya group
line of service. The teacher says:

    "He is a very splendid person."

VPN    There is a great aura of light around him. He is
beginning to speak. He says:

"Spirit and Matter meet in the cosmic union
of eternal ecstasy. There is forever joy in the
meeting of the separated selves. This is why it
is said that the morning stars sing together.

"There is a divine ecstasy and joy throughout
the universe—in the cosmic meeting of Life and
Form—Spirit and Matter. And the flame of consciousness is the crowning glory of this meeting.
Consciousness on many levels. Cosmic consciousness of the cosmic universe. The flower of consciousness is of the human kingdom, on all
planets, in all solar systems.

"If man could only know his destiny as a
Divine Son of God—a son of joy—a son of light.
If he could only realize his divine destiny to join
the suns of the morning, in all the work of
manifestation in creation—then he wouldn't be
so confined within the prison house of his five
senses.

"Be aware of the joy of Life meeting Form.
Basically, desire is Matter reaching for Spirit.
Will is Spirit reaching for Matter. The sorrow
and pain of man is when matter desires matter
instead of desiring spirit. Matter turns its desire
in upon itself and we have man desiring material
things and sensation.

"If desire is turned to spirit, so that substance
desires life as the greatest good, then we have
a right relationship established—harmonious.
But when substance desires substance and it is
turned in upon itself, then disharmony results
in the universe or in the life of man.

"Let your desire be for life. As you aspire to life, life will aspire to you. And you will know the joyous meeting of life and form and you will grow in consciousness."

VPN   This is very interesting—there is a great play of color. This is the end—it is not a service, but a ritual for mankind. It is a center for sending out life and understanding to mankind. It is one of the Chapels of the Nirmanakaya activity. One of the centers of it. The teacher says:

"This is all for tonight. Better *go back through the curtain*."

VPN   And he will walk with me.

## Halls of the Sun

*I walked in a body of light*
*Through the halls of the sun*
*And stood on its parapets*
*Facing the blue night of space.*
*The planets that wheel in obedience*
*Sang as they moved.*
*And the songs of the planets were music*
*That molded the forms*
*Of all things that have been,*
*That are and shall be,*
*In the realm of the sun.*
*Creation was music and song*
*And the splendor of light*
*As we moved on a star-spangled path*
*At the galaxy's rim.*

# Healing By Sound, Form and Color

February 17, 1962
Night Class
Recalled by Viola Petitt Neal

*Sound* may be considered as having a positive charge, *geometrical forms* as having a negative charge. These two have a polarity aspect together which gives rise to *color*. In this particular trinity the seven colors correspond to the seven planes of manifestation. It is the triune form that breaks light into seven colors, which we can observe.

Crystals are the key to this polarity relationship because they are exact geometrical forms. Greater knowledge of relationship between crystal forms and sound will be found in the future than we have yet discovered. At present we use, to a lesser degree, crystal sets such as radios. We will have musical instruments made of crystal forms which will bring in "the music of the spheres." This kind of music could be used for therapy. Platonic solids are the basic forms for studying relationships to sound.

The cone of ninety degrees on four sides is the key pattern — a bridging form. There are two more forms in addition to the platonic solids, making in all seven forms. The sphere is one of these seven forms and represents the top head center. The world of form in its essence means geometrical forms. Dense physical forms are the final manifestation of these geometrical forms. Crystalline forms are the best condensation of this abstract world of form and give us an understanding so that we can picture it. Algebra and arithmetic are derived from geometry.

Audible *sound* is a very small section of the sound spectrum. Light on our planet or any planet is the result of sound frequencies from the sun, intersecting with form frequencies from the earth, producing light and in the lower octave, heat. The angle of intersection determines the degree of light and heat. This is sound in marriage to form—and from this, light is born. This concept of the origin of light is contrary to views held by science on our planet. However, there are a number of scientists moving to this concept.

The reason that a five by seven rectangle is pleasing is because it is a basic form in manifestation and also it is related to the five centers in the trunk, to the seven centers in the whole body.

When mankind learns the correct use of sound combined with geometrical form (seventh ray) activity, he will create an orderly society and a beautiful one on the planet. This is an activity of the sons of mankind in microcosm performing the same rituals that in macrocosm are performed in the Temples of the Sun. These rituals will be centers of frequencies moving out over the planet and bringing the consciousness of man into resonance. They will create harmony where now disharmony exists.

The conquest of the forces of evil will ultimately be accomplished by use of rituals of sound and form. For evil is that which is disharmonious and cannot exist in a harmonious pattern of sound and form. The word "ritual" in its true defining is an orderly movement of sound and geometrical form in sequential patterns.

To digress, even the magicians of the Middle Ages knew this and performed their magical ceremonies using geometrical forms and their so-called "sacred names" which were actually sound. They sometimes achieved actual effect in the material world, as well as the astral world. These attempts were amateurish and for selfish purposes.

The Masonic rituals, builders of the universe, belonged in this same tradition where some knowledge of ritual combining geometrical forms and sound was their great secret. The Masonic order has more of this concept than any group on the planet. They do not know what it means. Some of their more advanced members have spent a lifetime on the *lost word*. Actually if they only knew it, they are seeking to comprehend the correct mantrams and their relationship to correct geometrical forms. Their symbols of the compass and the square are more correct than the religious symbols in religious rituals. This is one reason for the conflict and human jealousy between them and the Catholic Church, because both of them are close to discovering a great truth, a great secret.

Three students were spoken to individually. The student interested in physics was told to apply this knowledge in the field of physics, but that the knowledge should not be given out as yet.

Remember the basic concept given in the lecture that when life or spirit moves outward from a center, it is energy and when energy moves inward to a center or vortex it becomes matter. Matter is a pattern rather than a solid, a pattern of energy moving into a center. As long as the pattern is manifested, we have the so-called solid matter.

February 28, 1962
Night Class
Recalled by Viola Petitt Neal

Healing can take place on the dense physical, etheric, and astral levels. Sound affects the actual physical substance itself. Form affects the etheric body. Color affects the astral body. This is an overall principle, although the three types, that is, sound, form and color, affect all three bodies. The right combination of sound, form and color will bring about speedy healing although any one method shows beneficial effects.

### Herbal and Natural Remedies
### Compared to Synthetic Drugs

The effect of drugs is a physical effect due to the frequency of the drugs affecting the dense physical frequency of substance. *Herbal* and *natural remedies* produce their effect by not disturbing other frequencies of the body. *Synthetic drugs* may have a spectacular effect in one particular area or disease, but almost without exception these have a destructive effect on some other organ or tissue or cell structure. Various herbal and natural remedies — natural calcium in egg shell — could be used instead of sound in combination with color and form.

The mechanism of using sound has to be set up so that the person administering it is not disturbed by the sound frequency which is not good for him or compatible with his frequencies.

A colored lamp could be set up which has colored plates of certain geometrical forms to be used.

The violet circle affects the astral body if placed at the solar plexus center and in turn affects the physical and etheric bodies.

March 1, 1962
Night Class
Recalled by Viola Petitt Neal

The key to the different bodies is the *form*. Sometimes one has to begin with the mental body, but more often one begins with the astral body to get at the originating cause.

The circle is the key to the astral body when used with color. The diamond is the key to the etheric body when used with color. The triangle (equilateral) is the key to the mental body when used with color. The mental body completes the trinity of the personality, and basically it is the manifestation for humanity generally. Should the cause of disease originate at the mental body level, then it affects the astral and physical. With most people the cause of disease originates at the astral body.

For a long-range program for establishing a bettter condition in the physical-etheric with mentally polarized people, one works from the mental body down to the astral and etheric — and the colors most useful now on all three levels are:

*yellow* used in case of low energy, vitality and poor function;
*green* for harmonizing, equalizing energies, normalcy;
*blue* to be used in case of congestion, fevers and tension.

One should begin by using either blue or yellow, whichever is indicated, and then end up with using the color green. The treatment could be given on the same day; that is, the use of blue, yellow and green, or an interval of a few days could be allowed between the use of the different colors.

The individual who is being treated has to be favorable to being helped. It is not possible to treat a totally negative and destructive person who does not cooperate with the forces of good. Most people who are sick are receptive to any help and are favorable to receiving it. People who are more disciplined could use these methods on themselves, but it could also be done for them.

The great treatment that humanity on this planet needs is more of the Soul grip on the personality vehicle and where there is enough development there is one fundamental type of treatment that establishes a state of health in the personality unit. Many more people could be responsive to this at this stage of evolution. It is a long-range program that could be used parallel to any other immediate treatment of the physical-etheric, astral and mental bodies.

If the Soul had the control of the personality vehicle which is indicated for any particular stage of evolution (that is, the degree of control possible at the stage of evolution of the individual) it would be possible to establish a maximum state of health very quickly in all three bodies with, of course, karmic limitations.

The colored diamond form affects the physical-etheric body. Visualize it over an organ and/or over the center which controls that organ. For example, a person with a disturbance in the digestive tract and liver could use the diamond form over the liver area or gall bladder as well as over the solar plexus center. In the first case, you are treating the dense physical etheric organ and in the second, the etheric center itself.

The circle form affects the astral body when used with color. The form automatically directs the treatment to the astral body and you treat the center in the area involved.

In using the colored triangle, it should be placed first on the ajna or brow center, then whichever center is the area involved. The flow of mental energy via the ajna or brow center is to the total personality from the mental plane. Mental energy is the cohesive force which holds a personality vehicle in manifestation. The mind is the distinguishing mark of human man.

Love is the cohesive force that holds Divine man in manifestation. He is distinguished by being "I" conscious, the Soul. The personality has been unified with the Soul.

Etheric energy is the cohesive force for animal man. He is distinguished as "I" the physical being, belonging to a group soul on the astral plane. The cohesive force is etheric energy which comes through the spleen.

The cross is the symbol on the Soul level. There are three colors that could be used. The ethereal scarlet cross, which comes close to rose color is used to energize the personality. It should be visualized on the top of the head or in front of the person. This is helpful if the individual has a state of weariness in the struggle of life.

The gold cross (like the metal gold) could be used for protection at all levels. It could be used for spiritual illumination for establishing better contact of the Soul with the personality—to better use the personality vehicles to carry out the Soul's intention.

The violet cross—(ethereal type of violet) could be used to bring Monadic energy into the Soul-personality unit. It brings in life force directly, without having to bring it by indirect methods. This Monadic energy helps individuals more quickly and clearly to see and to know divine purpose in their own life and for humanity. This is helpful to use when one is way down by seeing negative forces in the outside world and blocks to constructive work and action. It can bring the kind of illumination that shows a student how to override these blocks. It can bring the clear-seeing that gives reassurance that God's Plan will triumph.

Each of these three colored crosses can be used in order: the rose colored cross, the gold colored cross, and the violet colored cross. They can be meditated upon by the student without harm and it is beneficial at this time. Anyone who is too negative will probably block any benefit, but will not be harmed.

The cross should be visualized in color and placed on the top of the head or in front of you. Different people would use different methods according to ray types. The first ray type finds it easier to visualize the cross on top of the head; the second ray finds it easier to visualize the cross through the whole body with the arms being the arms of the cross; and the third ray type would visualize it outside themselves.

The black cross is a symbol of the Eighth Sphere, and should never be used. It is used to invoke the power of substance and temporary guards of substance.

Twenty students were present.

April 27, 1962
Night Class
Recalled by Viola Petitt Neal

Sound affects basically the etheric body and in turn the other bodies.

Color affects basically the astral body.

Form affects the mental body.

At this stage of human evolution, it is possible to set up a system for the development of culture and refinement of the personality vehicles. The people would have free choice to avail themselves of this development. It could not be forced upon them. At the present time, they are having negative things thrown at them, such as pornography and brutality, without any alternative choice for a tangible method that would give them more spiritual development. As soon as possible, it is desirable to start with these methods.

The Catholic Church is the only ritual procedure available to the public that has any merit at all. It is not really available to the general public because of centuries of rigid demands on its adherents, and it is really haphazard in its effects on the vehicles.

There are musical compositions already in use in certain keys that could be used to begin with. In specific chapels, with certain form and color, music in special keys will be used. The sound should be soft, as a general rule. *Violin and piano* will be for general use. *Organ music* helps to establish Soul-personality contact. It breaks up negative astral patterns in the vicinity, and is very helpful specifically in detaching elementals from the solar plexus or other places in a human being. There are occasional people from the time of Atlantis, because of magic practices, who have elementals attached to them which disrupt their whole etheric and astral bodies. Organ music could have helped Mrs. "R" and probably detached the elemental that was present, but a mending process would have been required also.

In the past the church has given mostly inspirational worship services. In the future the church must give ordered procedure for development of the personality vehicles for growth in awareness, healing and adjustment of the vehicles, and their integration in preparation of the house of the personality for the occupancy of its Self or Soul. The church or temple must become the focal center for establishing a new civilization and culture, the culture of the Soul, which the Christ called the Kingdom of God on Earth.

There will be new music specifically designed to get specific effects. The Theremin was a type of musical instrument that had possibilities for producing some of this type of music. Other instruments like the Theremin will be produced where the individual is part of the instrument. Such music produced by highly evolved individuals could be very useful in ritual procedure. The music could be piped into the chapels and synchronized with the form and the color being used. Yellow and blue and clear scarlet could be used for average humanity. Violet, golden yellow and ethereal rose could be used for serious students. Green could be used as a harmonizing color with all groups. It would be used at the end of what is called color treatment to harmonize and equalize the different bodies. Indigo will have a special use. It is not blue; it is a different color. It has to do with Soul/ personality contact. It will be used in special ceremonies, using the OM for disciples preparing for initiation.

With pigments you have substances which absorb some light frequencies and reflect others. For example, when they reflect both red and yellow you get or see orange; but this is not necessarily orange light.

# Adjustment of the Different Bodies in Disciples

September 12, 1962
Night Class
Recalled by Viola Petitt Neal

Seven students were present at this class. The discussion was on the adjustment of the different bodies as we expand in consciousness.

There are three main impacts which bring about these changes in consciousness.

Our experience in the *outer world* which includes the pressures of events in a strenuous period of history as well as the personal and individual life experiences. In every life there is change and always this change is toward growth in consciousness. Whether this is accomplished depends upon the person himself. He may resist growth and achieve only the minimum of growth. But with the disciple on the Path, there is a great deal of cooperation in the process of growth where the changes and experiences of the outer environment are concerned.

*Personal efforts* bring about growth and development—such as meditation, study and a steady effort to grow.

When the student becomes a disciple and seeks aid from his own *higher Self* and the *Ashram*, there is assistance

147

from those in the Ashram which brings to bear energy impacts upon the centers of the different bodies to systematically aid in the adjustment of the vehicles — etheric, astral and mental. With each forward step in consciousness, the vehicle must be adjusted and this must not be done too suddenly or too drastically.

When the centers in the astral body are stepped up in frequency there has to be an adjustment to the whole personality vehicle to the frequencies of the etheric and mental bodies. These adjustments must take place in such a way as not to disrupt the personality vehicles so that the individual can still function adequately in the outer world. Sometimes there is a period of being jittery for a day or so, or a feeling of being in no man's land; or simply a feeling of having no reaction to life either of enthusiasm or depression. The adjustment in the astral body is probably most noticeable to the disciple, for it affects his feeling tone.

When it is the mental body that is being adjusted it is not usually so noticeable. He finds that he isn't as creative or as alert on the mental level for a few days. This passes almost unnoticed.

On the etheric physical level, there may be tension or a low energy level for a few hours or a few days.

In the case of a disciple under training with the Ashram and working with the Ashram consciously, these changes may be more defined and the discomfort more marked because he is a soldier in the army, so to speak, and has to take it. However, it is always a matter of careful supervision by the Ashram so that no harm comes to him.

May 22, 1965
Night Class
Recalled by Viola Petitt Neal

An algebraic formula was presented to the student: the physical is to the astral as the etheric is to the mental.

Mental healers direct their minds to visualizing the physical body in a state of perfect health. This is not the correct way to do it. The mind should be directed toward visualizing the etheric body instead of the physical and seeing it as a web of light with no shadow and no congestion, but as a scintillating field of force. It is via the mind that it is possible to direct etheric energy to the etheric body, thus vitalizing it, and as a natural result the physical body begins to improve, depending upon the karmic possibility.

A thoughtform of the etheric body was then presented showing within it brighter, denser channels which looked like the nervous system in the physical body. Then the splenic center was superimposed where earth and solar prana entered. The seven centers up the spine were superimposed and were finally followed by the alta major center.

The lecturer explained that it should be in the caudate nucleus area that pranic energy should be changed into electrical energy to flow along the nervous system. In average man, at present, it is the carotid bodies that are associated with the alta major center and this change takes place largely in the carotid body rather than in the caudate nucleus. In more evolved man this changeover takes place almost entirely in the caudate nucleus. Eventually, the alta major center will entirely express outwardly through the caudate nucleus instead of the carotid bodies.

In Atlantis, the alta major center was used for purposes of magic and there was great misuse of pranic energy and disturbance of the physical body.

The caudate nucleus is really the organ of a higher type of clairvoyance and perception. It contains millions of antennae to sense higher worlds of frequencies. It is the outpicturing of the alta major center in more evolved man.

After the end of the class, one student (SK) asked the lecturer why the physical body puts on excess weight in the case of many people as they grow older. Was it due to the function of the glandular system, ovaries, pituitary or thyroid?

The lecturer replied that there were different types of cases and some were more complicated than others, but that generally speaking the kind of thing referred to was due to sluggish liver. He suggested:

> "Visualize the liver as a pattern of clear and scintillating white light with no shadow and this will help to establish a better condition in the etheric liver and then in the physical."

Know the etheric body is like scintillating light and try to treat the etheric body with the mind. You don't treat the physical body with the mind.

March 9, 1961
Night Class
Recalled by Viola Petitt Neal

The creative use of the throat center includes three aspects: *The dynamic voice,* using the Will Ray or First Ray energy, shatters old thought patterns and builds new ones, as new ideas penetrate the mental bodies of the hearers. The hearers are receptive in this case.

*The magnetic voice* has the Love-Wisdom quality or Second Ray. It heals, enlightens, lights up consciousness, speaks to the Soul, draws forth the hearer's own Soul quality and Soul participation.

*The creative voice* uses the Active Intelligence energy or Third Ray. It invites the hearers to participate in consciousness, with creative thinking on their own. They are stimulated to explore the world of ideas on their own.

Remember humanity is the throat center of the Planetary Logos.

# The Effect of Man's Emotions on Nature's Upheavals

October 15, 1961
Night Class
Recalled by Viola Petitt Neal

The teacher was discussing the fact that often in a great crisis in the human kingdom there are also great upheavals in nature — extremes of heat and cold, cyclones and winds, earthquakes and volcanic eruptions — and explaining in terms of what we know is true. He said:

"You are all familiar with psychosomatic medicine and its theories that the emotional and mental, but mostly the emotional states of the patient, bring on the physical conditions. This has been a recent development in modern medical thinking. However, the esoteric teaching has always taught this is true. According to knowledge we have, more than ninety-five percent of the physical ailments of human beings are due to the emotional states. They affect the etheric body and then the physical body. An individual who is given to explosions of anger and resentment and other negative emotions will eventually have a bad liver, or he may have a

stroke. The individual who is constantly disturbed by fear and insecurity and worry, which
is a type of fear (you might say that worry is a
mild degree of fear) may find himself disurbed
with heart conditions or circulatory diseases.

"If you indulged in violent emotions you
might eventually have a liver disease and you
might call that an earthquake of the liver, or
it might affect the stomach and the digestion —
stomach ulcers and hemorrhage or vomiting
attacks — which is very much like a volcanic
upheaval in the physical body of the planet.

"Our planet also has its physical, etheric,
astral and mental bodies. Mankind on our
planet is very especially associated with all of the
emotional aspects of the planet. The condition
of all kingdoms on the planet — the mineral, the
plant, the animal, the human and the Fifth
Kingdom — has an effect on what happens to the
planet. The human kingdom on a planet, if constantly indulging in negative and destructive
emotions, eventually affects the astral, the
etheric and the physical bodies of the planet.

"In synchronization with the emotional states
of humanity and the crises that may come
because of this, there are also upheavals in
nature in the physical body of the planet —
earthquakes, volcanic eruptions, cyclones, winds,
violent heat and cold. We might say when an
individual indulges in too long a time of anger,
he has an earthquake in his liver, or he may
have an asthmatic condition, and we might say
there is a cyclone in his breathing apparatus. Or
he may succumb to some disease where there is

high fever and violences and extremes of heat, or correspondingly extremes of cold, in the physical body of the individual, so by correspondence to the physical body of the planet.

"These things take place because humanity as a kingdom is an organic entity, just as the individual human being is an organic entity. As an organic whole, the human kingdom very intensely affects the astral body."

VPN   He said that our period in history on the planet was at a great point of crisis where, after centuries and thousands of years of certain behavior patterns of the human kingdom, we have come to a point of crisis. A point where the energy impacts become so great that something has to give. If energy is poured into certain patterns for a long period of time, in a human life or on the planet in a planetary pattern, there comes a point where those energies are going to produce some kind of a change, which we call crisis. In our modern American slang we say that "something has to give."

Today we have reached such a point of crisis on our planet. There will be a tremendous physical upheaval on the planet as time goes on. Even our exploding atomic bombs have hastened this because they have affected the etheric and physical bodies of the planet tremendously. There will be problems and difficulties in the human kingdom, such as war. This will be destructive to many people in the sense of their going out of incarnation, but to go out of incarnation is not a tragedy. It would be a disaster if there were not a better civilization to come into in our next incarnation.

If one indulged in violent emotions he might eventually have "an earthquake of the liver." Similarly, by correspondence, precisely the same thing takes place on a higher level on the planet. As above, so below, the lesser is made in the image of the greater and the greater in the image of the lesser. He referred also to the fact that we had many circulatory diseases today. The fluids of the body are very definitely affected by every emotional change in the human being. Individuals who indulge in fear and worry and resentment also show problems in the circulatory system.

## Summary of Correspondences

| _Planet_ | _Human Kingdom_ |
|---|---|
| 1. Cyclones, winds | 1. Diseases of respiration, asthma |
| 2. Temperature changes heat, cold | 2. Fevers, subnormal temperature |
| 3. Earthquakes | 3. Liver upsets, violent emotions |
| 4. Volcanic eruption | 4. Vomiting |
| 5. Tides | 5. Circulatory diseases |

# V

# Crystals

# *Illumination*

*Perhaps once in a lifetime*
*Do we know*
*That we are Spirit;*
*For in our house of earth*
*We cannot bear*
*Knowledge so glorious.*
*Naked we stand before the light of lights.*
*We seize our covering of clay and flee*
*Into the darkness,*
*Lest the light destroy,*
*All that we know*
*Of that which we call life.*

# Crystals — A Source of Energy

September 4, 1960
Night Class of Viola Petitt Neal
Taped by SK

SK   What about crystals?
VPN   All kinds of crystals kept in geometrical form.

SK   In which Ashram is this class being held?
VPN   I think Third Ray Ashram.

SK   What are they saying about crystals?
VPN   Because crystals are the highest development of the mineral kingdom they are the key to the fourth ether and also key to "F" energy.

SK   What crystals should be studied in relationship to the fourth ether?
VPN   The five Platonic solids in crystal form are the keys to the energy which is equal and opposite to electricity. They are arranged in an ascending spiral. Let me see what connects them. Because they are parts of a spiral, they seem to be connected with a di-electric substance.

SK   What are the di-electric substances connected with it?
VPN   Now the spiral is like a wire only it is di-electric substance. Crystals are placed in ascending order of a geometrical pattern. Well, when you see the form, the

159

first one and the second turn of the spiral is right in front of me. The spiral makes two more turns. One and a half, I guess, then the crystal is directly on the other side. Next one, here on the side facing me. The next one on the opposite side. This is the arrangement—a crystal, a little larger than the size of the end of my thumb. Oh, they use sound on this crystal.

SK    How do they use sound on crystals?
VPN    Certain sound—it has an effect on the arrangement of the crystals and the "F" energy. But it is energy from cutting the lines of force of the earth.

SK    How does the use of sound on crystal cut the lines of force?
VPN    The spiral movement is the same movement as the earth—if you make a spiral in order to cut these lines of force.

SK    How does one make the spiral?
VPN    Just like you make it with a coil of wire. Oh, it is like an etheric spine. You make spirals like the Rod of Mercury.

SK    Do you make the spiral out of the crystal substance?
VPN    No, you place the crystals at different points of the spiral. It is made of di-electric substance.

SK    What is the di-electric substance being used?
VPN    Silk or glass—something more practical. You take a metal that does not conduct electricity and you make a spiral of it. Actually, the spirals are like the Rod of Mercury, the caduceus with a glass rod down the middle. The crystals—the five crystals—are placed like the five centers on the spiral.

SK    What kind of crystals would you use?
VPN    Quartz.

SK   Small quartz or special quartz?
VPN   As it comes — natural.

SK   Do you place it in different positions on the spiral?
VPN   Simple form in ascending order — the five Platonic solids represent the five centers in man, in the trunk of the body.

SK   Which center does the tetrahedron represent?
VPN   The lowest one. Then in the order of complexity to the top.

SK   What are the five centers? The base of the spine, the solar plexus, the heart, the throat, the head center?
VPN   No, the root center, sex center, solar plexus, heart, throat center — in the trunk of the body.

SK   What about the head center?
VPN   The centers are repeated in the head, but the body is an energy system and is based on the centers. It takes the pranic energy. The centers are like the crystals — it is an energy system.

SK   How does one apply the sound to the spiral with the crystals?
VPN   Certain sounds will affect the crystals and produce energy.

SK   What kind of sounds — sonic, ultrasonic or infrasonic?
VPN   There are several levels: a) below the threshold of hearing — these are dangerous; b) audible sounds — these are useful in mechanical energy, heat, and light as we use energy; c) another octave above the audible — that one has many possibilities in healing; d) the second octave deals with higher forms of energy, especially teleportation. I think it is the fourth octave above the audible, which has to do with teleportation.

SK   Which one deals with healing?
VPN   The first and second octaves above the audible sound.

SK   What about ultra-sound?
VPN   There is a lot of exploration to be done on it. It is dangerous to use. Some of it could be destructive, but it could be harnessed and handled.

SK   Does one produce healing in these centers by sound?
VPN   You will find that certain sounds acting through this crystal arrangement will affect the energy rhythm in the centers and establish a harmonious frequency. The health of the physical body is a state of harmony—a harmonious frequency of the pattern. The physical body is a pattern of energies, although it appears solid. When the pattern is disturbed there is dissonance (a thoughtform of the energies is shown). When you have disease, you have the harmonious pattern disturbed and broken up and it can be restored by sound.

SK   How?
VPN   Sound directed through these different crystals when they are all together or one at a time—even audible sound is the first beginning in establishing the rhythm. The Ego or Soul on its own level directs the orchestra which is the human physical body. But at the personality level there are interferences—the mind and the emotions impose other rhythms. At the physical level you could do a great deal to establish a state of harmony. There must also be change in the mental and emotional self.

   In the future, people will be told about the art of healing. The patient will be fully instructed in how he can cooperate with the healing process so that there will be the will to adjust with mental and emotional states which produce interference in the rhythm and the harmony of that orchestra which is the human body.

SK   How are we able to tell the state of any center in disease and then restore it to its normal rhythm?
VPN   Each person has a keynote and a triad based on the keynote. To begin with, it is not perfect. Begin by finding the person's keynote. It is done by finding out what musical note he likes best. It is a kind of crude beginning by which the first 258 in the sonic treatment, I mean in the audible, could be tried. In the next level above the audible, try the same keynote in the octave.

SK   Do you mean, if a person likes "G" in an octave, then you try "G" above the audible?
VPN   Try "G" and the triad of "G" in the audible first. You could see how he reacts and what the effect is. Then you could try it in the octave above the audible. This must be done cautiously. Too much amplitude is loudness and would not be good. It should be done softly.

There seems to be a class on basic energy — the energy animating the form — all forms, atoms and its equal and opposite polarity, electricity. Electricity is in a sense the physical polarity. So we use the word, di-electricity to convey the idea of opposite to electricity.

SK   If someone has a leak in one of the centers how could we help the person to close that leak?
VPN   You might try his keynote very softly and the triad of that keynote for about sixty seconds.

SK   Do you repeat it?
VPN   Yes, or you could have a sustained sound electronically.

SK   Do you apply it over the center? Or does it matter where applied?

VPN   It does not matter. Use it just in the room where the person is. Only here is the problem. You know the triad for that person — but it might be disturbing to others present. He could have it with earphones by himself and not for more than sixty seconds to begin with. So he hears it. It is not necessary to place it over that center. If he hears it, it goes through the body — the whole body.

SK   Can we go back to the question in which you were describing how to get "F" energy with that spiral? You suggested the spiral be made of di-electric substance and that crystals are placed on different points of that spiral. The lowest one on the turn of the spiral and the next one between the points where you put the first and the second, etc.
VPN   It looks like a one-and-a-half turn — they are put on the positive spiral. There are two, like the caduceus. The one that passes from right to left as you stand in front of it is positive. This is how it is shown in the thoughtform.

SK   How does it cross the earth's field?
VPN   It is like the spiral. The person directs sound lengthwise of the spiral.

SK   What kind of sound? A note or one frequency or what?
VPN   In the beginning if you make one, just work with the octave 256 beginning with middle "C" on the piano to 512.

SK   You mean the vibration 256?
VPN   Yes, the musical sound. You could work with the piano using the notes on the piano.

SK   But how do you get energy out of this?
VPN   I want to find out if I can. This is what happens in the human body — the spleen is not in the circuit of the spine. That is something else on the side. I am trying to

understand this. It is curious. It is just the sounds coming in through the spleen. It is almost like a membrane or something, I don't quite see — sound comes in through the spleen. That is why it is not a center like the others. It affects the centers of the spine. Sound comes in through the spleen. It is like fine wires around each center, but not exactly. I guess the frequencies travel in the ether.

SK    But how do you get "F" energy?
VPN    The spiral is connected in the system. It is like a machine. It is interesting — the second coil or wire is like the caduceus — a secondary coil. The primary coil corresponds to the one that has the crystals on it and the secondary coil is like the secondary coil in an electrical system. The coils are worn like the caduceus. The primary coil is connected with the center of sound. Now I can hear wonderful sound. The secondary coil is connected to the machine or mechanical device.

SK    What kind of sound do you put through the primary coil?
VPN    You can begin experimenting with audible keynote 256 to 512.

SK    Do you pass that through the primary coil?
VPN    Yes.

SK    What kind of machine could we use on the second spiral to show there is energy flowing through it? How is the energy set up there?
VPN    I am trying to see it. It seems kind of simple. You have to put something in the circuit which will give you either light or heat. Something like a copper plate. It is an electrical conductor and, therefore, is resistant to di-electrical energy. At first, I thought it could not be copper, but it was shown that it is a non-conductor of di-electrical energy and is resistant to it and, therefore, should

heat up. This is a simple system like the simple system in electricity.

The splenic crystal, the one that corresponds to the spleen in the human body, is a cone — two cones together. When they are placed together it is a solid crystal. It is shown as if it were taken apart. But if you put the two cones together with the right angle where you have the faces of cones — also a plane passed through the cones will give you a square passed through the central axis of the cones — because the angle at the point of each cone is also a right angle.

SK What type of a cone would you use?
VPN Quartz, glass, but the angle at the tip of the cone must be a right angle one if the plane is passed through it at any point.

SK How are the two cones over the spleen producing the energy?
VPN The spleen has an etheric one. All the sounds of the Universe play upon us, but we resonate to certain ones. If our thinking is negative, the emotions disorganized, we resonate to some of the disharmonies and affect the splenic center and all the other centers. Most dis-ease originates at the present time in the astral body of humanity.

SK Now we come back to the mechanism of generation of "F" energy? What kind of specific crystals should be placed on each one-and-a-half turns of the spiral?
VPN Quartz crystals and beginning with the first platonic solid.

SK You mean the Platonic solids have to be made of quartz crystals?
VPN Yes. That is, you put a tetrahedron on the tip of the lowest one. Then on the next one-and-a-half spiral, the cube, etc. in their ascending order.

SK   Will they all be made of crystals?
VPN   Yes. It is simple. You can make a mold for the crystals, but you could begin with what is called crystal glass.

SK   You mean the crystal glass would also do?
VPN   You have to have the form. Glass is di-electric.

SK   If one of the spirals is made of di-electric, what about the other spiral?
VPN   The spiral wire is made of any di-electric substance. It is the points that are the crystals.

SK   Do you have the two spirals made of glass and also put crystals on them?
VPN   It could be, but it is not practical. Use some other di-electric substance.

SK   Does the instructor suggest any other ones?
VPN   He said just look them up.

SK   Do you apply sound to one tip of this spiral?
VPN   Yes, Platonic solids and you keep it sounding over the highest portion of the solids.

SK   Can it go through the di-electric coil?
VPN   Yes and the second coil acts as a conductor. You close the spiral and that is what the splenic analogy is.

SK   How do you close the spiral?
VPN   At the top and the bottom you bring the ends of the spiral extended together at a point at right angles to each other on one side, the right hand side, and the secondary coil you bring to a point on the other side.

SK   You mean you join the two spirals separately?
VPN   Yes. They are not joined together, but are joined at right angles. In the human body there is a joining of the sushumna. Both spirals join the sushumna on top and

bottom. But you are trying to make a mechanical device. We have to pull it out and look at it and work with it. The sushumna is where the spirals are closed. It is the closing link. It is like the Rod of Mercury, but the sushumna continues into the medulla oblongata. The two energies fuse at the top of the neck. A model is shown as if it were made of wires. Two wires, two spirals, are connected to the rod at the bottom. They are also connected at the top. The rod continues and in a sense, although it is not the same, the rod is a miniature of Sanat Kumara's Rod.

> September 5, 1960
> Night Class
> Recalled by Viola Petitt Neal

Crystals show the highest development of the mineral kingdom and are the key to healing through sound, and "F" energy. Crystals include precious stones. Preliminary work has been done in India using gems for healing. In the future, different gems will be used for the different octaves of sound. For example, a ruby cut in a special way will transmit a certain frequency of sound. Individuals will be able to wear a ruby which will be cut in a special manner and will transmit certain frequencies to that individual but not to others around him. Different crystalline forms of different minerals could be adopted in healing and all crystals transmit sound which may or may not be audible.

*The Hope Diamond* has a special cut and because of that it transmits certain destructive energies. That is why it has been associated with bringing bad luck to those who wear it. Because of its beauty, there is associated with it a great deal of emotional jealousy and envy, the combination of which has always resulted in bad luck to those who possess it. The diamond is at present at the Smithsonian Institution, Washington, D.C.

*The Opal* is helpful to people of high intelligence. It is destructive to individuals with a lower I.Q. That is why it has been considered as bad luck at times. It transmits a number of frequencies. It could be used to transmit the frequencies desired. It has the widest range of frequencies of any crystalline form.

*The topaz* is constructive to "G" because of its cut.

*The ruby and emerald* transmit different frequencies. If an individual loves a stone and has a strong feeling for it, it may indicate a need within him for that frequency.

It would be interesting to look up references dealing with the superstition of gems and jewels throughout the ages.

Before the invention of radio, certain secret societies discovered this process of transmitting sound through crystals and cut the crystals in some form which helped to transmit and receive messages throughout the world.

Sound frequencies, even if they are not audible, will have the same effect on the individual. (Example: the demonstration shown the other day of the use of inaudible sound in water which in turn was transmitted to the physical body of the subject and from whom, through a microphone, we could hear the music played). It is the frequencies which go through the body that are important, though they may not be heard. In future, the manner in which the crystal is cut will modify the frequencies transmitted and will be the key to the keynote and triads of the individual being treated and who needs that frequency without affecting others around him.

Because of the axis of crystals, photographing through them may help to photograph the etheric body. Crystals photograph patterns of energy. It may be advisable to get a very fine crystal film — these are thin sheets of crystals — and photograph through them. Crystals used in radio are the finest available; even rejects may be good for this use.

# Thirty-two Crystalline Forms —
# The Key Pattern

February 23, 1962
Night Class
Recalled by Viola Petitt Neal

The thirty-two crystalline forms are the key patterns for the way the energies are built in the universe; and the key to unlocking energy in a constructive way. The atomic bomb is a destructive way to unlocking energy. It may be called the left-hand-path method.

Knowledge of the crystalline forms may be considered the right-hand-path method for unlocking energy by the use of crystalline forms and sound in the audible, supersonic and infra-sonic, to manipulate and direct forces. Man has not yet become basically creative. His movement into creative fields is close at hand. He will discover how to use crystalline forms to unlock, direct, and control energy and to modify and mold substance. Remember the universe was created by sound. Very shortly the scientists will be saying this.

It is curious and yet not strange that man here on this planet first discovered the destructive method for breaking into creative patterns of matter and energy — the left-hand-path method.

*The Van Allen Belt* is a band of supersonic sound around the earth and is constituted of a depository of tremendous radiatory energy that is related to the etheric poles and axis, which are at right angles to the magnetic poles and axis of the earth. It is radiating. The radiations seem to move in a circular path round and round within the Van Allen Belt. This belt is very powerful and potent radiatory energy. It attracts cosmic rays and appears to confine the energy within the belt. Also it was remarked that it does not trap all the cosmic radiations, but a large portion of them.

There is a pattern in the thirty-two crystalline forms and the thirty-two vertebrae in man. These have patterns of different energy levels, which later on are to be made clear. These different crystalline forms are the control buttons for handling sound of all levels and for directing and controlling it.

The five Platonic solids have a mathematical relationship to the fact that 2 multiplied by itself five times gives the number $32 - (2x2x2x2x2 = 32)$. The cross is for the ajna or brow center. It is the meeting of Spirit and Matter.

February 24, 1962
Night Class
Recalled by Viola Petitt Neal

Present in class were seven students, two of whom were esoteric scientists.

Crystals are orderly arranged molecularly and magnets have an orderly arrangement of molecules also which makes possible the magnetic lines of force. By correspondence: a) the magnet is the Matter polarity and b) crystals are the Spirit polarity. The orderly arrangement of molecules in crystals produces an etheric field. The etheric field is similar to the magnetic field of force. Just as the magnetic field is a key to electricity, so the etheric field of crystals is the key to di-electric energy. (Refer to the magnetic and etheric axis of the earth.)

There was in the middle of the room a beautiful cut crystal of icosahedron which was revolving and reflecting light as it revolved. Almost like moving in two ways at once, like a gyroscope at right angles to each other. In the crystalline forms we have the pure geometrical patterns of the creative process.

Concentrating on a particular geometrical form first at his throat center, then at a point in the brain, made it possible to start the "K" motor. The motor itself required a certain type of construction which was no secret, but once he had started it by this method it continued to operate until he shut it off, either by mechanical means or again by focusing on certain geometrical forms in his brain. "K" happened on this through experimentation. He knew it was dangerous to give it to people and never said how he did it.

Energy systems could be constructed through the use of crystalline forms, and how much energy and the kind of energy could be regulated by the kind of crystals. This would not involve the use of wires as in our present methods. Light produced by such method of energy will be soft and more beautiful than harsh light of electricity and will be beneficial to the physical and etheric bodies of mankind. The basic first product of "F" energy from an energy unit made of crystals will be light and this light could be transformed into heat and mechanical motion.

There must be at least seven people in the world who could make them and use them so that when there was a breakdown in society "F" could be made available for light and heat to assist mankind to survive, without much cost. Such light could be produced in abundance and directed on a small plot of land, producing fantastically rapid growth of food. A family of six could be supported by a plot twenty-five feet by twenty-five feet for needed food, for both light and temperature could be controlled like a spotlight.

The class discussion ended with the following:

"Ask and it shall be given you
Seek and ye shall find
Knock and the door shall be opened unto you."

# The Therapeutic and Scientific Uses of Crystals

May 10, 1962
Night Class
Recalled by Viola Petitt Neal

The jewel in the heart of the lotus mentioned in the esoteric teachings is also referred to as the diamond, and there is a symbolism here which also exists in the physical world. The symbolism is that the black carbon becomes the scintillating diamond of flaming light. All physical life is based on carbon, ordinary amorphous carbon. It is the basis of organic life and eventually through many transmutations, the jewel of the Soul is born, which is symbolically the diamond. Both the amorphous and diamond are pure carbon.

So the diamond is the symbol of the material life transmuted into Spiritual life. Because this has basic truth and symbolism in life, people value the diamond greatly. There is even a symbolism in the fact that only so many diamonds are permitted on world markets by materialists. Actually, this parallels the people in the human kingdom who have brought forth the birth of the Soul. The materialistic people feel that by possessing the diamond they possess something very valuable because underlying it is the true symbolism of a diamond. Usually they in no

174

way possess what the diamond stands for. Even the fact that the diamond must be cut and polished is a symbol of the cutting and polishing of the Soul in experiences of the personality in earthly life. There is written in the Book of Life the evolution of the mineral kingdom. A diamond has a very high frequency and often for people who are greedy, selfish, or evil, the diamond high frequency is such that the wearer cannot take it and may be shattered by it unless he is too insensitive to respond to it.

Those who owned the Hope diamond were more evolved people, but selfish, and some of them truly evil, and so it had a shattering effect on them. People build up thoughtforms around such jewels that may also be destructive to the owner. This is why the crown jewels in England are kept in a museum and only used briefly at some great ceremony, like the coronation, where the power of their frequency is distributed to many people. That is why many people keep their jewels in a safe deposit box and wear imitations. They cannot take the frequency of the jewels, although they do not know this.

Old crystals are symbolical of the higher frequencies in the cosmic scheme of things. They are also in a purely practical level of experience resonant to higher physical frequencies and they have an effect on the physical body. Crystals establish either a more harmonious frequency in the physical body or, if the individual has too negative a pattern in his emotions and mental body, the frequencies fight each other and the result is not helpful; and it is not because the jewel is not good.

Crystals have given man an open door to the contact with and use of higher frequencies of energy to build and to mold his civilization. We are at the beginning of the use of crystals, and on the knowledge of crystals we will build the physical structure of the new civilization. For example, the new discovery of the laser beam, and what has been found so far is the key to "F" energy and uses of all kinds. The secret of the crystal is in its geometrical form, as well as the quality of its substance. The diamond is the most evolved crystal.

As soon as more of humanity brings the birth of the Christ in the heart, there can be a rapid development of consciousness by the use of geometrical forms and also by the use of crystals themselves which the disciple will wear. This is understood to a limited degree in the Masonic order where a certain degree entitles the wearer to a ring with a diamond in the symbol.

The energy flow into the center could be handled therapeutically by the use of crystalline forms in the form of the five platonic solids. These forms could be placed on the periphery of whirling discs and whirled at so many revolutions per second, with the person placed in front of it to help establish a steady rhythm of a given frequency in the etheric centers. This kind of healing will be permanently effected only if the person is cooperating by his own mental and emotional attitude. A person harboring a great resentment could not be permanently cured, if ill, because of it.

The whirling disc would be best made of eighteen carat gold or copper plated with gold. The size should be about six inches in diameter. A crystal form is placed on the edge of the disc which revolves at two hundred times per second for ordinary humanity and six hundred times per second for more evolved individuals. This depends on their development. One crystalline form is used at one time depending on the center involved. The duration must be for brief periods—one minute and up, maybe once a week or three times a week. The disc faces toward the person, in line with the center to be treated and moving clockwise relative to the person.

Crystals can be made of quartz, but with certain diseases other crystalline substances would be more beneficial. The form used depends on the center to be treated according to the platonic solids. The crystals could be in the range of one-quarter inch or one inch in size. Actual size is not too important, but the form is important. One center should be treated at any one time. The effect of this would be to impose a harmonious rhythm on the center and correct and steady the inflow of energy of the right frequency. The individual can disrupt the rhythm by his own negative emotions and thoughts, but such treatment relieves him physically so he can direct his mind to correcting the causes.

Present: Twenty-five or thirty students.

June 21, 1962
Night Class
Recalled by Viola Petitt Neal

We live in an ocean of frequencies as a fish lives in the water. The fish is unaware of the many possibilities of the medium in which he moves. So man has been totally unaware of the possibilities of the vast ocean of frequencies in which he lives. The many energy frequencies move in geometrical patterns. When the geometrical patterns are altered, their manifestation is altered. Crystals are those substances which alter the geometrical pattern of frequencies. We must realize that these frequency patterns are more or less stable, but that crystals because of their strength of geometrical pattern can modify and reform the frequency pattern. In doing so, energy can be released and directed to man's purposes.

Actually, light results from a change in frequency pattern. Emphasis is on the pattern—geometrical form. Light can be produced by using an arrangement of crystals which can modify certain frequency patterns. This does not require solar energy or light. It can be done equally at night as well as daytime. This can be done without wearing out the crystals. Light could be produced in a house with such an arrangement of crystals and turned on and off by a simple button that would arrange the crystals in the right pattern or disarrange the pattern.

Another type of crystal arrangement in a certain pattern could produce heat. This is an access to energy by altering the geometrical pattern of selected energy frequencies. Various crystalline forms can be used to key into patterns of frequencies and give specific types of results. Synthetic emerald is the key to producing light. Quartz crystals are the most versatile of all crystal forms. For tapping a new source of energy the geometrical forms are the key—hexagonal forms.

# The Use of Crystals for Lighting

March 17, 1962
Night Class
Recalled by Viola Petitt Neal

Light does not travel as we think, but there is a band of frequencies which, when intersecting each other at given angles, gives rise to light. Light is an effect of two causes. The two intersecting frequencies have a relationship of ( + ) positive and ( − ) negative polarity. The nature of light is different from what we think. It is produced by positive and negative frequencies meeting at an angle. We have thought of positive and negative electrodes, but we have not yet thought of positive and negative frequencies.

In the "world of frequency" when two frequencies meet each other, you get, (a) the sum of the frequencies; and (b) the difference of the frequencies.

In the case of the two frequencies that produce light: (a) the sum is equal to light; and (b) the difference of the frequency is heat. The angle of intersection determines the intensity of light and the amount of heat. Instead of using electricity to make light, we will use light to make electricity. Not only is there an abundance of light to be used for energy, but we are immersed in an ocean of frequency that could be harnessed in a simple way to give light, heat, mechanical energy.

179

It would be possible to produce whatever climate we desire over an acre of ground. It would be possible to set up a small crystal reflector to cover an acre and grow any kind of food in mid-winter if necessary. It would produce a climate of a certain temperature in a small area.

Just as metals are keys to electricity, so crystals are keys to this new development of the use of energy by man. We will find a vast amount of crystalline forms in the earth. Actually there are diamond forms. The discovery of the laser effect is just the beginning of a series of discoveries.

The secret of the "K" motor was a crystalline form that was used and no one knew. It was under everybody's nose, but no one felt a crystal had an effect on a motor. "K" found out that just by visualizing the geometrical form of the crystal he could get the motor to start. But there were crystals in the mechanism of the motor. Simpler devices than "K's" motor could be made. A simple combination of magnets and crystals could give you all the energy needed to run a house.

The magnet represents the most orderly focus of what we may call the matter polarity. The crystal represents the most orderly focus of what we may call the Spirit polarity. Creativity takes place always between two polarities. Therefore, the right combination of magnets and crystals will produce the creative effect of energy.

We have already discovered in the cutting of crystals how to get certain sound effects at different frequencies. This would also give us a different frequency of energies for use. Light on the crystal and magnet, that is, lines of force from the magnet, are the components of a new energy system. Future lighting will be glowing crystals.

# VI

## Science

*"When we contemplate the* atom, *we stand at the dawn of creation. The creation of the atom is the beginning of time and space."*

—Night Class, February 1980

## How Far

*How far is space?*
*How long is time?*
*This boggled my mind when I was three.*
*"Space is as far as far can be,*
*Time is as long as long can be,"*
*My Black Mammy said*
*When I was three.*
*That seemed as right as right could be.*

# Man — Life — Form — Light

March 29, 30, 1961
Night Class
Recalled by Viola Petitt Neal

With man, seven planes of frequencies are interwoven. In the case of the three higher planes, there are fewer frequencies interwoven. The tapestry that is man has many patterns within the framework of the pattern we call "Man." The more evolved individual has a pattern of consciousness which includes more of the higher frequencies.

The meeting of Spirit and Substance is the beginning of movement — the origin of frequency which moves out on a spiral path. The oscillating circuit in electricity is the pattern of the creative process. It is the pattern of the cosmic marriage from which are born the outward moving spiral frequencies which make up the web of the created universe.

Sound is the frequency which builds the form. The form is a spheroid. This is the basic pattern of form. This is due to the fact that all motion of frequency is spiral — galaxies and solar systems show this spheroidal pattern — so does a raindrop.

When life meets form, mathematics originates. Mathematics can be defined as how life and form interact. It is the Law of Spiral Motion. Einstein said that space is curved. He had in a measure tuned in on this spiral motion of frequency and the spheroidal form which is the result of this motion of the frequencies of the created universe.

The oscillating circuit — Spirit and Substance — is the cosmic dance in ordered pattern, the Dance of Shiva. This cosmic dance, in ordered patterns, which produces form through which the life expresses, is copied by primitive people in their ritual dances. The planets circling in the solar system perform a cosmic dance. Eventually, we realize that all mathematical relationships can be defined in terms of intersecting spirals.

The life aspect being the positive polarity, the first thrust of form outward to matter conditions the type of form that is built. Therefore, we say that life commands the form.

Not only is the universe a pattern of frequencies, but the angle at which frequencies intersect determines what kind of manifestation we have. When certain frequency rates intersect at certain angles, physical light is the result. It, in its turn, is also a frequency. *Light does not travel all the way from the sun—frequencies do, and when they intersect with earth frequencies, light is the result of this meeting. Light is the sum of the frequencies as they beat against each other. Heat is the difference of the two frequencies.* In winter, although we are closer to the sun, we in the Northern hemisphere experience winter, less light and heat. This is due to the angle of intersection. So the angle of intersection of the particular frequencies which make light and heat is the important thing, not the nearness to the sun. The more oblique angle to the sun causes winter.

# The Book of the Universe —
# Correspondences in Patterns of Energy

October 16, 1961
Night Class
Recalled by Viola Petitt Neal

The lecture had various correspondences in the fact that the pattern is endlessly repeated in the universe. The lecturer made several points about these correspondences, some of which we are already familiar with and yet there is a more profound understanding of the meaning. First of all, in this pattern that is always repeated throughout the universe, there are always two polarities: spirit and matter, mind and emotion, masculine and feminine, etc. This pattern originates from the interplay of two polar opposites. This interplay produces other pairs of polar opposites which again produce interplay. This is how the pattern is formed. (There were thoughtforms demonstrating this.)

The two polarities make an interplay — there moves out from this meeting of polar opposites something like the spokes of a wheel. The way this thoughtform was made showed that at the end of each spoke was another circular point, a circle indicating another point of energy. These points of energy were separated and they alternated plus and minus around the wheel. Immediately there was an

185

interplay between these points—plus and minus points, which indicated positive/negative polarity. They seemed to separate from the parent wheel and there was an interplay between them and again a moving out like the spokes of a wheel, until you saw the pattern of the universe like a tremendous globe with points of energy. I could tell there was a tremendous interplay and the pattern was always circular and the lines of force were always spiral.

The whole universe is patterned as solid geometry— spiral—the energy moving out in a spiral form. The geometrical forms are sections of a globe, rather than actual straight lines, although we think of them as straight lines. They are all sections of a great globe or arcs of a circle, you might say, instead of just straight-line patterns. For example, you see a triangle form which is the arc of a circle—three arcs intersecting rather than three straight lines intersecting.

It is true that a straight line is the shortest distance between two points, but in the universe all space is curved. The arc of a circle or of a sphere is the shortest distance between two points. He said that when Einstein talked about space being curved this was the concept he was trying to present. Einstein did not quite clearly understand himself, and he was not able to present a pictorial form so that people really understood it.

When two opposite polarities meet, these energy patterns, the spokes of the wheel that we see when we look at them closer, are spiral not just straight lines of energy. Eventually there is such an interweaving of them in the universe that we get an atom or a solar system where there is a tremendous interweaving of these lines of force.

An atom is where the lines of force curve in on each other and move into an interior pattern instead of moving outward. They cease then to be energy and become substance. If they are still moving outward they are energy.

The interweaving of these energies preserves the spiral form or motion, because all energies move this way as they intersect each other, and continue to give each other momentum which is spiral, circular.

The lecturer said that tonight we are reading the Book of the Universe. There are simple principles which will make it very easy for the scientific minds on any planet to unravel much of the mystery of energy and substance, if these principles are more clearly understood. Because the universe works in this way, then it is obvious that the correspondences would work on the analogy because you know how the pattern works. It works the same way with an atom or solar system. There is a *neutral point* of the opposite polarities — plus and minus, positive and negative.

I am trying to remember what that was — to remember the rest of this lecture, because there was a great deal to it and the lecture tomorrow night is on magnetism, so I have to try to remember what the story was on this discussion.

# Origin of Magnetism

October 16, 1961
Night Class
Recalled by Viola Petitt Neal

This discussion has something to do with the origin of magnetism or what magnetism is.

Whenever there is an interplay of opposites which is the pattern of the universe, the origin of all energy, all substance and all form — this interplay of opposite polarities is almost as if the universe were divided in some way that is beyond my comprehension into a neutral point, or the homogeneous universe, and is made heterogeneous by dividing into polar opposites.

He reminded us of Spencer's definition of evolution: "Evolution is the integration of matter and a concomitant dissipation of motion by which an indefinite incoherent homogeneity passes to a definite coherent heterogeneity and the forces involved undergo a parallel transformation."

This interplay was the origin of all manifestation in the universe. In this great activity there are points of rest, or "neutral points;" for example, in the heart beat there are points of rest and points of activity. We are familiar with this and he was trying to give us analogies. He said that there are neutral points. He went back to the discussion of an atom as being interlaced spirals of energy — they move in on themselves. Whenever these out-rushing great spirals of energy turn in upon themselves and form a pattern, you

188

have an atom, or a solar system, or a human being, a plant or animal, a form through which the life is moving. The pattern is always the same.

The energies move in this pattern — in at one vortex and out at the other — so you always have a slight depression in the top of an atom, or planet, or a sun and a slight protrusion in the outward movement; but the pattern remains in the way in which the spiral energies move in upon each other through the center of every form, whether it is visible to the eye or not. There is a point where these energies move around each other as if they were moving around a rod. Now that rod (and this is a schematic portrayal) is the neutral point. This pattern is ever-moving, but appears to be stable because the pattern is stable. The energies are moving all the time.

All forms, such as an atom through which two polarities express, are patterns of energy. They appear to be stable because the patterns appear to be stable, but the energies are always moving and changing. This was a new concept to the minds of the students present. It was probably a new concept or different concept of an atom. These spirals of energy move in forming the stable pattern, but the energies are ever-changing.

Taking for example a picture of an atom (which he flashed as a teaching aide — although it was three dimensional like a thoughtform) you could see the energy moving. The two energies were making different colors in the thoughtform, the minus ( − ) energy was blue and the plus ( + ) energy was red, he said, simply to give us a contrast. They move in and where they move into an atom, a planet or sun or anything else, there is a slight depression; and where they move out, a slight protrusion. All globe forms are slightly off the globular form. Where they move in, there is this so-called "neutral point" in the center. It is schematically portrayed like a rod. The energies moved across each other. These spiral energy forms moved back and forth around this rod—or back and forth. They really formed the rod—the rod wasn't there to begin with, but the fact that they moved in like this, like the Rod of Mercury that doctors use as their symbol. They move in. Moving back and forth across each other, they move in a spiral form. The Rod of Mercury is a flat form and this was three dimensional. As they do this, they create a "neutral point" in the center of the atom or the form.

This is what held a human being—life in manifestation. Life in a form. This neutral point was really what held an atom in manifestation. The modern scientists refer to this as a "neutrino." They call it a "neutral particle," no doubt for lack of a better way of describing it because it required certain concepts in thinking that were abstract and not easy to give in a concrete form. This "neutral point" is a type of energy and has something to do with magnetism, the binding force of the universe.

These innumerable rods or neutral points of every atom, every form in the universe, were what held it in manifestation. The secret of magnetism is, in this concept, what it is. Although these "neutral points" held the universe in manifestation from an atom to a solar system, or a sun, or a planet; if these points were unduly disturbed it would be very destructive. But it would be destructive to the life more than to the form. In a sense for a time you would produce dead atoms. It is only a way of describing it rather than an actual factual concept.

In a sense the "neutral point" holds the two polarities sufficiently apart to guarantee interplay. It is kind of like a buffer between the two. It holds them sufficiently apart to produce interplay and yet preserve the pattern. He says that you have to produce interplay between these two forces or energies. You cannot produce it—you have to keep it in continuation, is the correct way to say it. You have to keep the interplay in a continuous process and yet held sufficiently apart so that they do not rush together. The "neutral point" is that so-called rod, for lack of a better name. That holding-apart field is related to magnetism. This will explain the phenomenon called *magnetism*, sometimes referred to as the *third energy*. It appears to be static magnetism because it is the "neutral points." It isn't moving like electricity or other energies we talk about. It is the *holding apart* and it is the *holding together* of energies at the "neutral point" of the universe. The holding apart of the two great polarities and the holding together of all of the forms that are made by those two polarities. This is a very interesting concept. Magnetism is the attraction and the repulsion.

May 23, 1962
Tuning in to Knowledge
by Viola Petitt Neal

During a discussion between SK and VPN about magnetism, there was a period of silence and VPN gave her impressions of what she was able to obtain about the subject. These were the impressions, as she tuned in to this field of knowledge:

Magnetism is the creative result or manifestation of the meeting of two opposite polarities: Spirit and Substance or Matter. In the overall concept, the *Soul is a magnet*.

An actual physical magnet is made up of two opposite polarities: positive ( + ) and negative ( − ) electricity held in balance. A magnet can be separated into its component parts of positive and negative electricity by passing a conductor through the magnetic field at right angles to the field. A permanent magnet is a magnetic vortex where positive and negative electricity continue to mix in equal amounts in an eternal pattern.

Passing a conductor at right angles gives us the symbol of the cross. A temporary magnet is set up in a circuit; there isn't a permanent pattern. A pattern exists for the current flow. Example: Electro-magnetism. A wire carrying a current has a weak magnetic field around it because all along its length, while the current flows, there is an equal amount of positive and negative electricity. So you have a magnetic condition which is temporary.

Magnetism on the physical plane is an equal amount of positive and negative electricity held in a pattern either permanently or temporarily. The physical plane manifestation of magnetism is an overall pattern of the whole creative process.

The Soul as a magnet partakes equally of Spirit and Substance and is always described as magnetic.

Magnetism should be described not so much in terms of attracting as in terms of manifestation partaking equally of two opposite polarities, either permanently or temporarily. This type of description of the nature of magnetism could be more clearly understood. In a sense the attracting aspect is incidental to this basic fact.

The *Magnet* (the Soul or iron magnet) attracts what may be termed *imperfect creation* because it is endeavoring to establish the perfect creation of equal amounts of opposite polarities in that which it attracts. Example: The physical magnet that attracts a steel pin for the time being has equal amounts of opposite polarities established in the pin.

Of course, people who are more conscious of themselves as "I, the Soul," have an attractiveness to those still struggling as "I, the personality." This is the mystery of the attractiveness of the Christ to the people of Palestine as the perfect expression as a magnet.

It is interesting to point out at this juncture that some clairvoyants are able to see blue, the Spirit aspect, and pink, the Matter aspect, at either end of a magnet. In a way, these two colors are the polar opposites of the color spectrum. It is a repetition of the polarity pattern.

Crystal is a magnet of di-electric polarities having equal amounts of positive and negative energy, which is equal and opposite to that of electric energy in this relationship. Di-electric energy is Spirit and electrical energy is the Matter polarity.

Dia-magnet is equal charges of positive and negative di-electric energy, which helps in a permanent or temporary pattern. The relationship of di-electric and electric energy, where they are in a creative pattern, is a solar system which is actually a magnet where the two energies, di-electric and electric, are held in equal relationship.

# The Neutron

September 20, 1964
Night Class
Recalled by Viola Petitt Neal

The neutron is the sound binder of substance. The ultimate secret of the atom is not in the electron or proton, but in the neutron. A study of the different elements will reveal what might be described as a harmonious variation in the sound binder (the neutron). If you look at a periodic table you will find there a pattern of how the sound binder works in a pattern of order and one might say harmony. The words *atomic weight* could be replaced by the words *atomic sound binder*.

Kepler's discovery of the ratios of planetary orbits is another example of the pattern of the sound binder. What we might call a cosmic atom scale, for let us remember an atom is like a solar system and a solar system is like an atom. Throughout the universe you will find solar systems that correpsond in their structure to every atom of substance. In other words, a sun with one planet will correspond in pattern and in actual structure to a hydrogen atom, etc. Such things as asteroids will show a faithful correspondence to other particles of the atom. One might say that the music of the spheres is not just poetic fancy.

This lecture is being given at this time because of discoveries that had been more or less accidentally made in the nation of the Soviet Union. The mysterious death of some of the scientific personnel led almost by accident to the discovery of a certain sound frequency which affects the sound binder of the iron atom. This is a supersonic frequency. It is an extremely narrow band of the supersonic scale, but lethal because it affects the red blood cells of man and animals.

In plant life it could greatly distort and disturb our present plant kingdom, but is not as instantly lethal. Fortunately, the method has not yet been discovered for directing and controlling this supersonic frequency so that it would kill only one group of people in one part of the world, say London, and not kill those who send it out. Those who have made this discovery know that the risk and danger is tremendous and it has cost them serious casualties even in very small and controlled laboratory experiments.

With this particular supersonic frequency, the "note" or frequency of the sound binder of iron is changed so that the iron is broken down into another element (transmutation of one element into another) but this is fatal when it affects the iron in the blood stream. Let us remember it will also affect the iron in any object within range. You can, therefore, imagine what man could do to his planet. Those who have stumbled on this discovery do not yet know what they are doing—certainly do not know the full implications. They will not dare to use it because of the fear of destroying themselves or the whole human race, and this is most certainly possible if they did use it.

When the sound binder of the atom is tampered with there is no radio activity—the phenomenon involved is something totally different. In the sound binder or neutron of the atom is the secret of magnetism. The neutron is magnetic. The electron and proton are electrical. In their movement the electron and proton are intensely stable—a pattern of energy is set up which is an atom of hydrogen, or an atom of iron, or an atom of gold, etc. The actual frequency of the sound binder (or strength of magnet) determines how many electrons — how much the proton charge.

It is an interesting fact that in the element iron is a key, or a door we might say, to the secret of the constitution of matter. The relationship of electricity as we know it to the iron magnet tells us how this cosmic pattern works. In the case of iron there is not a completely closed system. In the case of so-called conductors there is not a closed system. By relating copper, for example, to the field of iron of an iron magnet, a trickle of energy which we call positive and negative electricity flows through the gap in the cosmic wall of substance and we have an energy that we can control and use.

We go back to the concept that the sound binder is magnetic as we conceive of magnetism. It is significant that the breakthrough in electricity and breakthrough in the discovery of a sonic frequency that will affect the neutron has to do with the element iron. For iron constitutes this loophole or door in the cosmic wall of substance. The discovery was made in the Soviet Union through a study of the Van Allen belt and the application of Tesla's work. Knowledge of this sound binder could result in a control of energy from the atom which will not involve death or danger to the planet; which will not involve radioactivity and which could give a new energy source.

There is a third method that is neither fusion nor fission. It has to do with sonic frequencies used in a different way from what the Russians are doing with their new so-called weapon. Their discovery can result in a new breakthrough in energy for man which could be beneficial to the whole evolutionary process — could come about hundreds of years ahead of time. These things are not always, therefore, disastrous. Sometimes they force a development for good that would lag behind for centuries. As so often happens, man's danger forces progress.

Every atom is a closed electromagnetic system. The *neutron* is *magnetic*. The *electron* and *proton* are *electrical*. From the outside it presents an appearance and reality of an atom of a definite substance. That is hydrogen, gold, etc. In future lectures, we will discuss other aspects of this breakthrough.

Sixteen students were present, at least five of whom seemed to be English or American. I think they were scientists. I seem to be an interested auditor.

# Time and Space

October 4, 1964
Night Class
Recalled by Viola Petitt Neal

VPN   He says:

"In this discussion we will endeavor to achieve some different concepts from those usually held within your framework of thinking. In order to think of the world which you perceive with your five senses and interpret with your mind and color with your emotions, you must have certain concepts.

"Two of these concepts — time and space — come under our discussion tonight. Let us use a somewhat inadequate analogy and say that time and space are the picture frame and glass through which you look at the universe which is the picture. Time and space are an invention of the human mind as its tools and methods for dealing with what it perceives in terms of thought.

"Tonight we want to think in terms of sound and sequence: sound we will roughly equate with space, sequence we will roughly equate with time. Sequence and sound, therefore, we will equate with time and space moving from accepted concepts to more expanded concepts.

"The visible material universe is put together by sound in an orderly sequence. This orderly sequence is the basis of mathematics. And mathematics is really the science of what you call 'time.' Let us remember here the ordinary concepts of time are inadequate.

"Sequence is a more expanded concept and we must define sequence to mean instantaneous or timeless, and many stages in between.

"We have said that the universe is put together by sound and we speak of the material universe. At this point let us define substance as definitely different from matter: matter meaning material as we commonly think of this word. You are familiar in chemistry with a saturated solution just before a compound begins to precipitate out of the solution. At a certain critical point the slightest change will start the precipitation out of solution. Up to that point it is held in an invisible state.

"Now let us define substance: Substance is that state in the universe similar to the condition in solution just before the point of precipitation and matter is the precipitate.

"In the larger picture of the universe, sound moving in orderly sequence causes substance to precipitate and it becomes matter with the stamp of orderly sequence upon it and a perfect pattern which we call different elements. This orderly sequence is the Time Binder of the universe. We might for the present discussion define *mathematics* as the science of the *time binder* of the universe and *physics* as the science of the *sound binder* of the universe. The two sciences, of course, are interdependent and cannot be separated.

"I want you to think of orderly sequence as something much more than your ordinary concept of time. Orderly sequence determines wave length. In the vaster structure of the universe wave length determines which and what element. A combination of sequence of sound produces a certain element of material matter. Sound moving in specific orderly sequences to a point of intersection precipitates out of substance an orderly arrangement of electrons and protons with the sound binder, the neutron which we call matter. The sequence is the time binder of the atom.

"This time binder accounts for the mathematical and orderly arrangement of the atom of matter. It also *times* its length of life. You can apprehend the atom's orderly arrangement, but except for radioactive substance, you can discover very little about the atom's length of duration.

"At this point let us discuss a new concept of space. Let us admit all these definitions are inadequate; nevertheless, they are used to expand your thinking.

"Space is an infinite web of sound moving in orderly sequence. What you call space is the vaster area in which substance has not yet precipitated into matter. You perceive atoms or solar systems as existing in what you call space. They exist within an orderly sequence of sound. In these concepts are new frontiers of science. Of necessity the perceiver of this orderly sequence of sound and of the material universe stands at a strategic point of vantage. To some extent he becomes a modifier of the pattern. Man can modify to his own destruction or he can modify the pattern so that he becomes more the master of this material environment, extending the circle of his comprehension and achieving higher levels of moral responsibility in an orderly universe.

"The developing in man of moral responsibility in an orderly universe ultimately requires a knowledge of science and an understanding of the world of meaning which you are getting in your courses of study in another department of this college."

VPN    Seventeen persons were present, of whom four were women. One person sitting on the right of this student should have been present at the preceding lecture on sound binder. This whole college is from the First Ray Ashram. The sound binder lecture is from the Seventh Ray Ashram.

# Esoteric Concept of Matter and Energy

January 24, 1972
Night Class
Recalled by Viola Pettit Neal

VPN   This was a scientific lecture in the department of the Fifth Ray Ashram, with over one hundred people present. He says:

"In your scientific world today you are familiar with the statement that matter is energy. This is literally true beginning with the building blocks of all forms, the atoms. The actual structure of the atom is a matter of tight vortices of energy. The pattern of every atom in the universe, or we might say the pattern structure is relatively stable, to all intents and purposes very stable. But contrary to what you may have thought, the energy moves in and out of the area constantly at given rates of speed. These rates of speed are modified to some degree by temperature and other causes which we can go into later. What I want to present to your minds is not a static particle of matter, but a stable pattern with the energies constantly moving in and out.

"The atom is composed of a stable pattern with a tight and dynamic spiral vortex of subtle

202

energy moving into the center of the pattern at high rates of speed. This center you are accustomed to thinking of as the nucleus of the atom. The energy moves out in ever-widening spiral cones from this center of input. The energy is positive or plus as it moves in, and negative or minus in the outmoving spiral cones. Every atom has a field which is produced by the outmoving spiral cone. The pattern of these spiral cones is also a stable pattern. Depending on the element, there may be one spiral cone as in hydrogen or many as in the case of the atom. These spiral cones you now refer to as electrons. The total atom, including the inmoving vortex of energy and the outward moving spiral cones, has a spin on an axis of rotation.

"I would refer to this as the Life Energy of the universe, but the term *life energy* has connotations for you which will make it difficult for you to keep your minds clear to think creatively. Therefore, we will call it etheric energy, meaning 'a subtle, powerful and all-pervading energy.' We might say that all space is an ocean of energy and wherever we find matter or substance we find this energy moving in and out of stable patterns. We could describe a solid object (let's remember solid to our five senses) as a web of energy patterns which are the atoms that make up its form.

"When we come to living forms, and here again I must use a term familiar to you, such as a plant, an animal, a human being, we have energy patterns again. A plant has two fairly large energy vortices similar to the energy vortices of the atom. Again the energy flows in to the center or core in a tight spiral and moves out in expanding spiral cones. In the case of the plant form, the outmoving cones of the two vortices form the field around the plant and the sensitive who can perceive these vortices can describe the conditions of the plants as healthy or diseased (or about to be diseased) by the condition of the vortices and the field. In living plants, animals and human beings many things can disturb the pattern and the inflowing energies, though the pattern again is fairly stable. The atoms composing the form are not disturbed in their pattern or energy. In the case of the plant, as with the atom, the energy flowing into the center core of the vortex is plus and the outward flow of the expanding cones is minus."

# The Hymn of Isis

February 2, 1980
Night Class
Recalled by Viola Petitt Neal

I am Isis the Virgin Mother

I am mathematics

I am science

I am medicine

I am the substance of which all forms are
    built in this world

I am the energy of substance

I build the forms, many and diverse
    through which life expresses

I am the Divine Mother of Consciousness.


Perhaps the mysteries of Isis will give clues to a new kind of energy. (Etheric neutron of the atom — first etheric neutron of the atom — first etheric level.)

Love is seeing and perceiving relationships and relatedness. Wisdom for action and understanding is a result of perceiving relationships and relatedness.

205

The term *Holy Spirit*, used in the Christian faith to signify the matter polarity, is strictly speaking the energy of
substance. The vast intricacies of the form must have an
overall simplifying aspect.


February 2, 1980
Night Class
Recalled by Viola Petitt Neal


Finding the discovery of a new kind of energy, man pro-
gresses by using physical, emotional and mental energy.

When we know the mystery of the neutron of the atom
we will have opened a door or a tube to siphon off the energy that constantly flows through the atoms and we will
catch it as it enters the atom, which will be pure electricity. The atom is an energy pattern which concentrates the
energy which is flowing in and out of the pattern at very
rapid rates all the time. It is the concentration of energy
that gives the appearance of solids. The energy of the
universe is flowing constantly through atoms. Pure energy
flows in the neutron and at this point accepts a plus ( + )
and a minus ( − ) charge, and it is at this point of manifestation of the universe — all atoms of substance have
similar patterns.

We are moving in space in our evolution in consciousness
to the point that we will know how to intercept this energy
at its point of entry and differentiation, and channel
measured and controlled portions (without danger) to uses
in the material world very specifically, but also to the emotional and mental worlds. In a sense we will be intercept-
ing energy at the point of the beginning of all things.

Some of this was known to the Mysteries of Isis in ancient Egypt. The teacher said:

"You are aware of this, of ancient schools in Egypt, and that is why you feel sure there is a kind of energy not yet discovered or being used. We are moving close to the time when this energy will be discovered and used, as there begins to be an externalization of the Spiritual Hierarchy on the planet.

"The knowledge is in the consciousness of a number of disciples in incarnation at the present time. It will come to the surface of consciousness in due time. It is being cautiously manifested by members of the Fifth Kingdom so that the time is right—but be sure it will come. It is possible that it will be handled by a few seasoned disciples, initiates and adepts without the total process being revealed to the masses or greedy materialists."

# VII

## Education in the Future

## The Book of Life

*Life speaks a language*
*Through its myriad forms.*
*A firefly*
*Joyful in the summer dusk,*
*A hieroglyph of life.*
*A rabbit*
*Listening in a daisy field,*
*The word made flesh.*
*My fellow man,*
*A lyric of the Lord.*
*The book of life is open*
*To be read.*
*I am a child in kindergarten*
*Learning words.*

# Ritual and Consciousness and
# Their Effect on Education

September, 1960
Night Class
Recalled by Viola Petitt Neal

Correct ritual is the educational method of the future. Defining ritual in its broadest sense:

*Ritual is an ordinary sequence of words, movements or acts performed in right and correct order in order to invoke and direct energies (physical, etheric, astral, mental, and spiritual) toward definitely-intended purpose.*

For example, in modern advertising, the purpose of a ritual mantram with an accompanying picture on television such as "Winston tastes good like a cigarette should," is to get people to buy this type of cigarette. Many of these in modern advertising get results, but are hit or miss.

There is a science of ritual by which the desired results can be accomplished. The religions of the world know something of this science. The armed forces of the world use the principle rather effectively. The secret societies — Masons — have bound their members most effectively to purposed activity through the use of ritual. However, the secret of ritual has never been known to mankind on this planet. The fact is a certain simple procedure performed

211

in correct order could change a civilization almost overnight; on the other hand, wrongly used, could be very destructive. In a sense, ritual is drama; the drama of the solar system; the drama of the life process; the drama of the dance of Shiva. We might here further define ritual as man repeating God's processes — in symbolical action. Ritual implies symbolic forms — symbolic words or mantrams — and symbolic acts. The mass of the Catholic Church can be observed as an example of this. For at least fifteen minutes to six hours after attending the mass, the individual has a raised or expanded state of consciousness.

The ritual dance performed in correct order as some of the ritual dances of India, Java — religious dances — can put both the audience and dancer in resonance with tremendous spiritual energies for a short time. The dancer can become "divinely possessed" by spiritual energies he or she is interpreting. What must be emphasized is the exact and precise ritual which can make an individual or a group resonate to an exact and precise energy and force, producing calculated and purposed results in consciousness and subsequently in behavior. Rightly used, such ritual in no way interferes with free will but promotes the normal process of growth as sunlight promotes the normal growth of the plant. On the other hand, there are rituals which invoke the forces of evil and produce destructive resonances in individuals and groups. Some of these rituals are known and are being used in the world today. It was such ritual discovered and widely used which brought about the destruction of Atlantis.

Remember, humanity on this planet can resonate to the widest range of frequencies of any humanity in this solar system. The time has come when the disciples of the White Lodge and its initiates and adepts are being prepared to put out in to the human kingdom rituals of the White

Lodge to which humanity can and will resonate, thus producing constructive growth in consciousness very quickly. This ritual must and will emerge in the center and in the midst of countries and civilizations today—like the blooming of flowers of light that have been hidden and unnoticed buds. These rituals can change the resonance of humanity from the material aspects of life to the consciousness or Soul aspect.

Here and there tentative approaches to this use of ritual have been made. The Biometric program is one of these tentative approaches with a simple but very useful ritual for an adjustment in the astral body. The three symbolic forms bring in the energy of the three rays for achieving a certain type of adjustment. This is given in passing as an illustration.

As you can observe, the growth of plants, types of marine life, follow certain logarithmic spirals and mathematical proportions such as the golden section (golden rectangle) and all rituals have a mathematical foundation. Harmonious sounds have a mathematical foundation. Mathematics is the basis of sound and creation proceeds from orderly mathematical relationships to the sounds that arrange all matter, all substance in orderly pattern. We might say in overall concept, mathematics is the archetype and the creative universe is the manifestation of that archetype. Mathematics is the purest expression of relationships, and creation of a manifested universe is a series of orderly relationships. In the human kingdom the scientist is simply discovering these relationships.

To come back again to the ritual, there is a basic principle involved. If, and as, man follows through in his rituals on the pattern of the creative process, he will tune in to the energies of the universe or resonate to them because he is working in the same mathematical pattern as the energies. For example, in the field of education, to pour facts into the child's mind is not truly education at all. Education must successively by ritual processes put the child in resonance with the energies of the world of ideas. In this way his consciousness is *led out* into the recognition of new relationships, which is true growth in consciousness. The education of the world today gives him dissociated groups of facts and it is almost by accident or chance that he truly sees relationships.

In the field of religion true access to Spiritual energies can be achieved through right rituals, and in the future these rituals will be graded series like classes in a school, designed for each state of consciousness. Such rituals can promote an orderly growth into the next succeeding state of consciousness.

Specific rituals will be given to accomplish certain types of resonance. These could be used first with smaller groups and later with much larger groups of people.

# The Purpose and Future Methods of Education

March 5, 1961
Night Class
Recalled by Viola Petitt Neal

The teacher said that we had been totally confused about the real purpose of education in the human kingdom. We have thought it was a case of cramming a child's mind with facts. Other people have had the concept that education was a *leading out* of the mind, which is not too bad a definition. But, as we come into a period of greater understanding we will have a new concept of what the purpose of education is.

First of all, the real purpose of education is the alignment of the bodies, especially the emotional and mental bodies and an integration of the personality unit. When we come to an understanding in the human kingdom that this is what we want to achieve in education, well-integrated personality units so that the individual is able to register the impact of the Soul, we will have a true definition of education.

Some people are at the level where primarily the astral body needs to be adjusted, integrated, aligned. Others need to concentrate, primarily, on integrating and aligning the mental body and, ultimately on the synthesis and integration of the total personality unit, which should be the object of education.

The second purpose is to assist the individual in the ability to see relationships and, in this regard, certain principles could be taught. First of all, the great and outstanding principle of analogy which was first given in the Hermetic teaching in ancient Egypt — the principle of as above, so below, the lesser is made in the image of the greater and the greater in the image of the lesser. But actually man is a self-conscious individual seeking to discover new relationships in his world and in the universe. He should be taught to think of himself in this way.

Thirdly, to train the individual to recognize the sequence of cause and effect on every plane. This is very simple on the physical plane. The laws of physics and mathematics can be pointed out with this understanding on the physical plane level. On the emotional and the mental plane we are beginning to approach this concept with our very, you might say, elementary approach to psychosomatic medicine. But there are many other aspects of the law of cause and effect on the emotional and the mental level.

So, the educational concept at which we start is: man is an immortal self-conscious individual seeking to perfect his vehicles of expression — physical, etheric, astral and mental; seeking to become more aware of relationships in the world in which he lives and on all the levels: and intelligently aware of the law of cause and effect on every plane of life. Schools of the future will be dedicated to this concept of education.

The method will not be so much the cramming of a child's mind, or an adult's mind, with facts, as it will be a method of pointing out relationships, and the mechanics or technique of this method of education is one that is best described by the word *ritual* using it in its broadest sense.

There are certain rituals that will impose upon the personality unit — physical, etheric body, astral body, or the mental body — right rhythms and frequencies; or we might say harmonious rhythms and frequencies.

The Masonic ritual is one of these key rituals. The teacher hastened to explain that most of the people who are in the Masonic order today do not really understand the meaning of ritual, are not able to profit by it and, in fact, often take it very lightly. But in the inner Masonic order there are preserved certain ritual procedures — concepts and movements within the lodge and the use of geometrical form that could be very valuable in an educational method. At least, it is an example of this.

Of course, he went on to say that there are both constructive and destructive people in the Masonic order and this has always been true. The French Revolution was largely the result of certain procedures within some of the Masonic groups and orders, because they used the secrecy of the society as a cloak under which to produce revolution and sedition. But this in no way invalidates the value of the ritual or method, nor is it in any way a criticism of those constructive people who have been in the order and still are in the Masonic order.

He said that the fact that the square and the compass are the symbols of Masonry is very interesting. In its ancient and esoteric origin the Masonic order had to do with the building up of the personality unit.

At this point, I will go back a little bit in the lecture of last night to explain that the two symbols of Masonry, the compass and the square, are two of the basic mathematical symbols. It was said that with the compass and the square the builder could build the universe. Those two basic concepts, the compass and the square, give us unity and duality. So, we move from unity to duality to the trinity of manifestation. The white and black pillars in the Masonic order symbolize the two opposite polarities, the positive and negative—light and darkness.

It is possible to study the Masonic ritual and find a number of interesting principles and relationships. And to do this, disassociating myself from any feeling of approving or disapproving, the present Masonic order has unconsciously preserved a very ancient ritual which means very little to the average individual in the order. Nevertheless, it is something that should not be lost, in the same way that a great many of the esoteric principles were preserved in the Tarot cards only to eventually become playing cards for games.

He said that the building to be built was the personality vehicle through which the Soul or Life would express. This is the real symbolism. Both the Catholic Church and the Masonic Order took their ritual procedures from the very ancient lodge of the Master Jupiter, one of the very ancient esoteric lodges. Certain things used in the Catholic Mass have a very definite effect on the astral body and to some degree on the mental body.

He said that the personality units—physical, etheric, astral and mental bodies—are mathematical patterns. The use of certain geometrical forms, both in actual physical movements and in concentration on these forms, has a definite effect on these energy patterns. This is a principle we will become more familiar with as we go on. There will be certain orderly, rhythmically, harmonious procedures in the school of the future that will produce certain effects upon these different bodies. Remember again, that the purpose of education is the perfecting of the vehicles through which the Soul or Immortal Self expresses.

He said that there had always been an interest in a school or college that would produce the greatest amount of expansion of consciousness in the least time with a harmonious development that would be in no way one-sided or disturbing to the individual. Such a system of education could be achieved through the use of certain ritual procedures, through the use of certain geometrical forms, sound and color. In the future we would decide what school a person was in, rather than what grade he was in. What school he was in would be a matter of whether he had a problem in the astral or mental bodies that needed solving and adjusting. The grades in school would be our grades and stages in evolution in consciousness.

With the eighty percent of people who are not yet doing much to develop the mental body, the primary study would be in the law of cause and effect, especially in the physical and the emotional worlds. This is basic and is the only principle upon which any morality or ethics can be built that is stable and lasting.

For those people who are in the upper twenty percent, it is very important to teach them to see relationships because they have the mental equipment with which to do this. Usually, they will be working on the mental level, although if there is some lack in the astral vehicle of stability or alignment, there will also be classes for this.

People would get a lot of facts in their process of education, but the emphasis would not be on them. However, the value, the meaning and the relationship of the facts, would be emphasized. Incidentally, we will get the facts that we need without too much difficulty. There could be a graded order, ritual, and the use of mathematical or geometrical form to affect the patterns in the mental, astral and physical etheric bodies. Sound and color will be used as well as music and color.

Primarily, the lecture seems to be important because of the new approach to the purpose of education. As an illustration of the use of geometrical form, he said that the Biometric use of the circle, the cross and the triangle is an example of a formula for making an adjustment in the astral body of the individual. This is just one little thread of the principle of using the geometrical form. Primarily, it adjusts the energy level in the astral body as well as bringing about a better alignment in the astral body and its centers. There are other specific formulas that will achieve other types of things. But in the future we will be able to use these.

Our educational system will be something totally different from what we now conceive of as education. Our present concept is very superficial. It is primarily aimed at equipping the individual to fight the economic battle in the world. Most parents think of education in those terms. A child must be educated so that he can make more money and get a better job; generally, fight the economic battle and struggle for economic goods and establish some prestige in his society.

He said that the new form of education will establish, of course, a different kind of society automatically. This could start with one school using these principles. It does not have to be a whole system imposed upon a whole country or any one country at one time. It can begin with just one school that uses such a method.

He mentioned some of the educational principles of Steiner as being an approach to this type of outlook, and some of the methods he used. Rhythmics for the physical body are very good, and were inspired from this level of concepts in which we were in contact in our discussion.

I asked him about Professor Aitken of Edinburgh University who has such a tremendous memory — incredible beyond any ordinary human ability — and who also has the ability to instantly tune in upon the answer to the square root of some long number and give the answer more quickly than he could by using a calculator. He said that this type of ability would be discussed in future lectures. He and two members of the Aitken family (I think this was what was said) came into incarnation in the same family in order to give each other moral support. These three people developed a very amazing alignment of a type that would be discussed in another one of the night classes. Otherwise, they would have found it a little lonely and disturbing to be totally alone in such a capacity and ability.

He said this had nothing to do with heredity. That heredity was a concept we had for the lack of anything better. You do not inherit anything from your parents. You came to certain parents because they had the combination of genes and physical characteristics to give you the kind of vehicle which karmically you were entitled to or deserved to have. These three brothers did not inherit anything from their parents. The kind of physical bodies they had were the physical bodies which they could achieve through these parents. He said it was just like going out to buy something. You find what firm has the quality product you want and you go and buy it from them. So, you go and look for the parents who have the quality product you can afford to buy from the point of view of the physical etheric vehicle you are going to get.

He said that the child gets his physical body from his mother, and during the time that his body is being built he is getting most of his etheric vehicle from his father. It doesn't matter if the father is present or close by or not, he can be on the other side of the world and the child is still getting the early building blocks of his etheric vehicle from the father and the physical from the mother.

The three individuals in Professor Aitken's family, came into a family where they could get the type of physical vehicles that were suited to the ability they had. They came in together in order to have some moral support and, also, to see how useful their particular development of facilities could be to the society of their time and age. There were other aspects that they had not developed. It was a one-sided development, but one which they would need to develop and that this particular type of alignment which produced this particular type of special ability would be discussed in future lectures.

The teacher suggested that I look up my books on magic squares and on other mathematical concepts and, also, the books I have on Masonry and I would discover relationships I hadn't seen before. He said that the magic squares had concealed in them some of the secrets of this method. Other types of mathematical games, you might call them, also had certain ideas that were valuable. This whole concept had to do with mathematical or geometrical form. He mentioned the Platonic solids and he said it was quite true that Tesla achieved a lot of his concepts by observing these five Platonic solids — thinking about them. They had an ability to stimulate the mind to see relationships and in the future such forms as these would be used. He said that the ancients were correct when they put such an emphasis on the study of mathematics and by that he especially referred to geometrical form and pattern as well as to numbers.

Pythagoras said that he who understood the meaning of the 3-4-5 right triangle — the square of the hypotenuse is equal to the sum of the squares of the other two sides — would understand the secret of the universe. He said this 3-4-5 right triangle did have a very important principle and we were to think about it.

The three of us in this class were interested in education. Especially an education that would produce an orderly development, instead of a haphazard development of the human personality.

# VIII

## Planetary Types

## Halls of the Sun

*I walked in a body of light*
*Through the halls of the sun*
*And stood on its parapets*
*Facing the blue night of space.*
*The planets that wheel in obedience*
*Sang as they moved.*
*And the songs of the planets were music*
*That molded the forms*
*Of all things that have been,*
*That are and shall be,*
*In the realm of the sun.*
*Creation was music and song*
*And the splendor of light*
*As we moved on a star-spangled path*
*At the galaxy's rim.*

# Planetary Types and Their Psychological Patterns

The term "individualization" is used in the ancient wisdom teaching to indicate the time when animal man became human man. At that moment self-consciousness was born. It is believed that not all of our present earth humanity attained this stage of evolution on the planet earth. The teaching states that some of present earth humanity had individualized on other planetary schemes. For example, it is said that the Lord Buddha had come from the "moon chain" evolution — and that the ensouling Life of our planet came from the Venusian scheme. Others might have come from the Martian scheme, or the Mercurian scheme. Some of those souls incarnated in a physical body on the planet earth millions of years ago, yet retained some of the characteristics of the scheme on which they had individualized. This section may explain the various basic characteristics found among our earth humanity. They may become our future psychological types.

The sections were left as they were given at various dates of the night classes. (Editor's Note — S.K.)

225

January 3, 1962
Night Class
Recalled by Viola Petitt Neal

The Eighth Sphere is begotten of two parents: The Life of Substance (Father) and Substance itself (Mother). There is no spirit aspect as such. This life of substance is a black light. The progeny of this union are the misbegotten demons of darkness, the *Soulless* spawn of evil because there is no spirit aspect. It is a hopeless sphere.

The Eighth Sphere had its origin on Pluto. Its creators are powerful and integrated human beings denying spirit and integrated at the matter polarity. The ultimate end of this sphere is annihilation because it endures for a time along with its creators. It is an evil center of power.

Denizens of this sphere are on the planet earth with some of the creators of this evil. These demoniac beings are totally evil whereas their creators can never be totally evil. These demoniac beings are a temporary creation. They do the work of their creators in demoralizing and corrupting and terrifying mankind. These soulless beings will be more visible to mankind in the time ahead when the forces of evil will come into full manifestation with the appearance of the antichrist. These are some of the terrors mentioned in the Book of Revelation. Today these demoniac beings are like anchor points for a great network of evil on the planet. Once and for all mankind, especially earth humanity, will truly experience what evil is and choose. New Guinea is a focal center for the Eighth Sphere.

The sign of the cross is a great protection against the demoniac beings for it is a cosmic symbol of the divine marriage of spirit and matter. Before the symbol of the cross the demons flee, for they have no part in the divine creation. The symbol should be used thus: Throat, right shoulder, left shoulder, heart. Ajna, right eye, left eye, throat.

*Jupiterians* are conscious on many levels, aware of the psychic world around them. They are mediums in a sense. They are conscious mediums. They are able to see the elemental life on planet earth and may be considered as scouts. They are fuzzy because they see too much. They can see the Deiros — the elemental life and how they feel.

Jupiterians practically always use the etheric body as the vehicle of experience. Ordinary psychics use the astral body as the vehicle. They are slow to learn, but when they come to earth they learn quickly and also learn about evil. Jupiterians incarnated on the planet earth are more easily contacted by so-called "saucer people." Jupiterians are receptive to the Soul or Buddhic plane, to physical etheric and by-passing other bodies; thus they are not precise.

*Martians* who have been to Pluto develop the ability to sense or "smell" the Plutonians. Smell is discrimination on the spiritual level. Mars is the lower octave of Pluto, because they pursue scientific knowledge and truth — the material world. They are militant defenders of truth. Warriors. They carry the banner of truth into the far frontiers of the solar system.

*Mercurians* are observers on the planet. They collect knowledge and can be good teachers. Mercury has a Fourth Ray energy which is Buddhic, intuitional and expressive of the Christ, as Mercury and Sun are One.

*Neptunians* are vague — fuzzy in their thinking, not aware of the evil forces; aware of the mental plane and other planes. They have instant clear knowing from the mental plane.

March 17, 1962
Night Class
Recalled by Viola Petitt Neal

*Neptunians* have a connection from the Buddhic to the astral plane fairly-well established. They have a tendency to bypass the mental body. They have a capacity for *instant clear knowing* in a situation as to what to do or say. They often say things that are correct without really knowing what these things mean in terms of clear mental analysis. They have the capacity to inspire people with the energy of certain ideas without giving them the mental tool with which to work. They could carry the energy of certain ideas and use it to stimulate others who have the mental equipment to earth the ideas.

If they develop the mental body, they will have more access to the use or earthing of their ideas. Classes for Neptunians would encourage this Buddhic-astral contact, but also develop the mental body more. They tend to have a mystical quality, an intellectual vagueness that is exasperating to the more trained mind. Because of their Buddhic-astral channel, they have a spiritual quality that is attractive — a type of magnetic attraction. They have some of the joy of the Soul coming through to the personality and do give out energy to other people. They have an energy coming through which gives them vitality. They usually recover quickly from an illness. The mechanism of their quick healing is Soul or Buddhic energy coming through since the astral body in present humanity of any planetary type is ninety-five per cent of the cause of illness in the dense physical body via the etheric. This Soul energy very quickly establishes harmony in the astral body and consequently in the etheric and dense physical bodies.

*Eartheans* are responding to mental stimuli in a speeded-up manner. There is a waking up to the mental plane.

Earth humanity is basically sound and with its present intellectual response the time has come for the opening of
esoteric schools that would have at least four departments:
basic true teaching about God and the Universe, evolution, reincarnation, and karma; esoteric mathematics,
numbers and geometry in their true sense and science;
thoughtform building and manifestation; and a new approach to art, drama, and sculpture. Earth humanity is
reaching a state of need where it would flock to these
schools.

Colleges of Healing would be associated with these
esoteric schools, training people with special gifts. There
will be graded series of instructions at different stages of
development. The above applies to other planetary types
also.

*Jupiterians* have a somewhat different type of etheric
body, which expands a little farther beyond the periphery
of the dense physical. The etheric body is more of an instrument than in other planetry types. It serves as an instrument for contact with the whole etheric world around them
and to some degree with Monadic energy to the etheric
body.

Usually they do not have a too-well developed mental
body. They do not use the astral body as most people do.
They are constantly sensing with their etheric body — the
condition of things, especially the forces of nature. They
are good earthquake barometers if they only knew it.

> March 22, 1962
> Night Class
> Recalled by Viola Petitt Neal

*Jupiterians* do not use the mental body as much as some.
They tune in and have etheric instinctive awareness which
helps them to deal with the world. They tune in in this

way on human society and make right moves for their material welfare. In investment, they do not reason it out but sense it on the etheric level and act. They often have a rigid mental outlook because they don't think much. They are not possessive or materialistic, but have a feeling that the abundance of life belongs to them. Depending upon how evolved, this may be just on a pleasant material level, or it may have a more spiritual implication. They give out a lot of etheric energy to people around them.

*Neptunians* are devoted to the goals of the human race, ideals and people who seem to be the embodiment of those ideals; devoted to creative activities. Their focus is more on the ideal activity and creativity for themselves and humanity than on the value of humanity itself. Their attitude is devotion rather than love. Humanity is important because it is an instrument to produce the idea, and people are incidental to creativity.

### The Three Aspects of Trinity

The Martian has love of truth—First Ray.
The Venusian has love of humanity—Second Ray.
The Neptunian, love of creativity—Third Ray.

# The Plutonian Control of
# Earth Humanity

June 10, 1962
Night Class
Recalled by Viola Petitt Neal

Present in a large auditorium were members of the Fifth Kingdom and disciples of the Human Kingdom. This was a convocation abstract from the lecture recalled.

The speaker seemed to be a being of great authority — one of the Council of the Seven from Shamballa.

*The Planet Pluto*, the invader planet, eighth sphere, within our solar system, constitutes an integrated and hard core of evil. The invader planet chose the planet earth to take over because the humanity on this planet is at a great point of crisis in its evolution. Therefore, the planet earth is the most vulnerable planet in the solar system.

*The Planet Pluto has a deification of matter* or substance which is the pull-back on evolution. This deification of matter anywhere in the universe in some small degree holds the great creative process, which is the interplay of spirit and matter as creative forces and sets up a small abortive kingdom by using substance and the dark light of substance as the creative polarities producing a *cancer* in a solar system or a universe.

231

The planet Pluto was thrown off from another solar system and moved into orbit around our sun. It seeks conquest of the planet earth to extend the kingdom of darkness. The Plutonian forces are *Herod, the King, seeking the Christ Child to destroy him.* This is the basic problem with the planet earth.

The means of control of earth humanity by Plutonians are: communication, including radio, television and the press; education of children; governments of the world; money of the world.

The Plutonians do not want earth humanity to get into space. Since they follow expediency in any situation and go along with what they cannot prevent until they find a way to use it for their own advantage, they go along with the space program because it is a way, in their thinking, to bankrupt people and government with taxation.

Because the planet earth is important in the whole solar system and because its Planetary Logos comes from the planet Venus, at this time special assistance will be given from the planets Venus and Mars. Unfortunately, it is necessary for the humanity of earth to be more uncomfortable and distressed than they are now, in order for them to get their eyes open to what evil does to them and therefore enlist their own free choice, their desire for good in the work of liberating them. You cannot liberate people who do not know they are enslaved.

The forces of evil do not have the wealth of the planet earth, but they have set up a control of the wealth through money. As soon as the people of the planet really know their predicament and ask for help, the frequencies for cleansing will be directed on the planet. Those who are too materialistic will go out of incarnation and not again be incarnated on this planet.

Earth humanity will at first be bewildered with no efficient Pluto to manipulate its wealth (wealth means food, clothing, shelter, etc.). A Government of the Planetary Hierarchy will be set up with the Christ in outer physical manifestation as its Head, until several generations of humanity have been educated and human disciples and initiates prepared to direct and govern the humanity of this planet.

Apparently there was an intermission and the second lecture was given by another member of the Hierarchy, probably the Manu, but it is not certain.

August 26, 1962
Night Class
Recalled by Viola Petitt Neal

The following is a summary of what VPN was able to remember of the lecture on the motivation of planetary types. This was from a First Ray Ashram.

The upper twenty percent of the intellectual range of humanity is composed of the following percentages:

Plutonians . . . . . 6%
Martians . . . . . . 4%
Venusians . . . . . 4%
Mercurians . . . . 2%
Earthians . . . . . . 2%
Jupiterians . . . . . 1%
Neptunians . . . . 1%

The lower eighty percent are mostly earth humanity.

It is important to understand the motivation of the different groups.

*Plutonians* came to the planet earth to invade and exploit and take over. Scattered throughout all ranges is the "X" group of the previous Third Ray solar system, remnants who did not achieve the expected development and were given a second chance in the Second Ray solar system.

*Martians* came to help earth humanity by the conquest of nature — scientific advancement, implanting love for truth and recognition of law and order in the universe.

*Venusians* are interested in assisting and helping humanity seeking growth in consciousness. They are often altruistic and love to serve.

*Mercurians* are the observers and recorders of the solar system. They are often teachers, historians and collectors of knowledge. They collect and impart knowledge. They do not get involved in the turmoil of earth humanity.

*Jupiterians* tune to the etheric level and have a great understanding of the forces of nature around them.

*Neptunians* are the mystical group and endeavor to give mystical comprehension of God. Some of the Saints during the Middle Ages were Neptunians. The better types of Neptunians tune in, in a vague way, to the Buddhic plane and register this as feeling at the astral body level.

*Other Types.* Very few have come from outside our solar system, strayed in so to speak. And a very few are a demoniac group.

# How and When the Planetary Types Came to the Planet Earth

August 27, 1962
Night Class
Recalled by Viola Petitt Neal

At the time when animal man became human man on the planet earth, over twenty million years ago, Venusians of high development came in to help start earth humanity in its development. The number of Venusians who came with Sanat Kumara were few.

During the Atlantean period of the *third sub-race*, Venusians and Martians incarnated on the planet earth. Some actually came in physical form by space ships to help earth humanity. During the *fourth sub-race*, Neptunians, Jupiterians and Mercurians incarnated on the planet earth. During the *fifth sub-race*, Plutonians came en masse and invaded the planet earth. Some came in space ships from Pluto. During the *sixth sub-race*, the Martians and Venusians who had come during the third sub-race had presented to earth humanity a very highly cultured civilization. It was felt that by giving earth humanity the gift of a type of civilization they would be inspired to make the effort to evolve themselves to the point where they could produce such a civilization themselves. (These were referred to in the lecture as the gifts of the fairy godmother

235

in folklore.) This would have worked out had it not been for the coming of the invaders from Pluto.

The Plutonians used a frequency band which affected the physical brains and astral bodies of earth humanity in such a way as to inhibit and delay their growth and development. We may call it the first great "brainwashing." Brainwashing is exclusively a Plutonian invention. It is often spoken of in the fairytales of the world as the "evil jinn" who comes at the christening of a child. For example, in the *Sleeping Beauty* story the princess pricks her finger with a needle and falls asleep for centuries. The fairy tales and folklore of the world tell the whole story of humanity over and over again.

The frequencies used by the Plutonians had little or no effect on Martians and Venusians, and very little effect on the other three groups. But earth humanity has been bewildered and confused and has been in the wilderness ever since. The time is close at hand when, as in the fairy tales, the "spell will be lifted." The Plutonians use a first ray energy and the antidote is first ray energy wielded by the Christ of this planet. Earth humanity will begin to make up for its long sleep in matter. Venusians and Martians will give knowledge and assistance which can be quickly received and assimilated by earth humanity.

(Other parts of this lecture cannot be recalled at this point.)

Plutonians, instead of achieving individual soul development and individual immortal self-consciousness, developed a very strong, powerful race group soul on the concrete mental plane. Each individual is like a finger of this monster race group soul, which because of its very nature, is very powerful, integrated, one-pointed and one-purposed for long ages of time; to all intents and purposes it is immortal. This is why the highly intelligent Plutonians have a feeling of being invincible and immortal, an attitude which impresses and awes ordinary earth humanity.

The "X" Group of the Third Ray Solar System are despised and expendable tools of the Plutonians. They consider earth humanity sturdier stock and more useful slaves.

The caudate nucleus in the brain of earth humanity was inhibited in its growth and function by the frequencies the Plutonians used. This had a direct connection with the thymus gland which has a direct relationship with the heart center. So both the intellectual development of man and his love aspect were inhibited. Therefore, both the caudate nucleus and the thymus, which have a direct connection together, were inhibited. Humanity will begin to use the ability latent in the caudate nucleus. This development will bring energy into the heart center of humanity to bring about the development of wisdom and compassion along with a telepathic ability to contact the world of knowledge. The caudate nucleus is a latent radar system which will make possible very amazing direct contact with knowledge and the environment of man.

The band of frequency which was directed by the Plutonians to humanity at the time of the Fifth Subrace of Atlantis inhibited this development in earth humanity and largely directed their motivation toward the material things and sex. It did not have this effect on the Martian and Venusian groups as far as motivation and direction goes, but it has prevented their use of the caudate and thymus because there was no response from earth humanity.

Today Venusians and Martians are under a strenuous impact of energies to prepare them also for a change on the planet and in the development of earth humanity. Those members of the human kingdom who remain in incarnation after the upheaval incidental to the removing of the Plutonians will very quickly begin to develop those faculties latent in and symbolized by the caudate nucleus and thymus. This is really a polarity established between the heart and top head center. The Plutonian polarity is between the base of the spine and the alta major center.

The Venusian, Martian, Neptunian, Jupiterian and Mercurian groups will even more quickly begin to function through these two centers: the top head center and the heart center. In that case, it will also be a matter of the use of the top head center and the heart center in the brain which are located in the region of the thalamus.

In passing, the pineal gland is the activator of the caudate nucleus, but this function has been latent and dormant.

There were other parts of this lecture which could not be recalled.

# Psychology of the Future

November 16, 1963
Night Class of SK
Obtained by Viola Petitt Neal

The psychology of the future will deal and be based on the following three aspects: planetary type, motivation and evolution in consciousness.

The *planetary types* determine the overall direction and the line of endeavor of the individual. It might be called "a point of orientation toward evolving consciousness." In our present period there are present some of the following planetary types: Egos from the Third Ray solar system belong to our present Third Ray solar system and should be differentiated from a previous Third Ray solar system which existed before our present universe.

In the present Third Ray solar system there is the evolution of the Intelligent Activity aspect, especially in regard to the mental substance. By contrast the previous Third Ray solar system developed the physical etheric and astral substances; thus the desire and the sentient aspects are prominent in our present solar system. There are at present over one thousand on our planet earth who are from outside our solar system and who belong to the Third Ray solar system.

(The night previous to the lecture, "D," a member of the First Ray Ashram, indicated that the Third Ray solar

239

system developed the mind aspect and formed the ajna center of the Great Being of Whom Naught May Be Said, just as our solar system is the heart center of that Great Being.)

Individuals from the Fourth Ray solar system are constantly developing the ability to balance the polar opposites. With every equilibrium further equilibriums have to be established because there is a constant new inflow of energy. They have a high development of the arts because all creation takes place because of the interplay of polar opposites. Therefore, in a solar system where this interplay of polar opposites is the chief emphasis, as it is in the Fourth Ray solar system, there is great creativity and true art is a creative process. There are around one hundred of these persons at the present time on our planet earth. They are attracted because we have a great deal of Fourth Ray activity on this planet.

There are about five hundred individuals on our planet from the Seventh Ray solar system. More will be incarnating as the Seventh Ray energies flow in. They will have exceptional organizational abilities.

Second Ray solar system (our own): there are two planets which are the polar opposites—Vulcan and Pluto—both of these First and Seventh Ray frequencies. Vulcan has achieved a balance between the top head center and the base of the spine center. It is a Will Ray humanity, functioning in etheric bodies, but able at will to control the substance of the three worlds—that is etheric, astral and mental on this planet earth. They are an extremely vital humanity and their frequency is not too easy to take on our planet earth.

Our Second Ray solar system holds a unique place because it is the place of birth of the Cosmic Christ or Consciousness and is the heart center of the seven solar systems which form the body of that Great Being of Whom Naught May Be Said.

*Motivation* involves a line of development through many incarnations of the individual, of his attitude toward the human kingdom and responsibility to it, of his understanding of the great process of the universe — the plan and purpose on this planet, specifically, and his relatedness to it. Motivation deals with the relatedness to plan and purpose, and man as an individual with his own free will accepts this relatedness and responds to it.

*Evolution in consciousness* may be defined as that level of "idea frequencies" to which the individual can respond. He can, therefore, be put in an educational grade where ideas in the frequency band to which he can respond can be presented to him.

# Thoughtforms of Planetary Types

June 12, 1964
Night Class
Recalled by Viola Petitt Neal

This class was a discussion on thoughtforms in the department of the Seventh Ray Ashram: the power of thoughtforms, and the projection of thoughtforms into the outer world of manifestation. Why some thoughtforms produce manifested results and others do not. The instructor began by saying that when the planet was invaded by the Plutonians in the Atlantean period certain things happened. This Plutonian invasion was both by a type of spaceship and by simply incarnating in this human life wave on the planet. Since the *Plutonian* humanity is governed by and resonates to a group soul there is less conflict in the Plutonian personality, but also very little understanding of spiritual truth or reality. The Plutonians are geared to the frequencies of matter or substance and do not really understand love-wisdom or Spiritual aspiration as a humanity. The Plutonian is basically first and seventh ray, using the concrete mind as the vehicle of expression.

At this point the instructor went into a discussion of thoughtform technique on the part of the different planetary types in our life wave on this planet.

The Plutonian is very alert and focused, always seeking power; first, over other human beings and also over form.

Because of the dynamic quality of the first ray and the organizing ability of the seventh ray they have achieved control in high levels of practically all human institutions. Their thoughtforms are clearcut, well organized and focused, energized by will energy.

At this point the instructor showed the class a moving picture projected from a well-focused projector and said, "This illustrates the clearness of the Plutonian thought-form."

He pointed out that *earth humanity* is characterized to a large degree by the fourth ray of harmony through conflict. The thoughtforms of earth humanity are vague, fuzzy, changing. Earth humanity can be swayed to change its point of view over and over again. Then he showed us a vague, fuzzy pattern on a screen which changed with different impacts of energy that hit it.

The instructor explained that the *Venusian* type has beautiful patterns of an end result—people living in harmony, a state of goodwill, idealistic forms of government—these are fairly clear pictures, but they fail to have a clear picture of how to bring this about. Definite, detailed plans and definite, detailed thoughtforms are all too often lacking. Usually the Venusian is not aware of the organized, dynamic power for materialism which he is up against with the Plutonian. This is almost incomprehensible to him. He also has a respect for the free will of man and does not feel it right to overly influence or coerce humanity.

The *Plutonian* has not the slightest qualm about over-influencing and coercing humanity.

The *Martian* type is in search of truth. He knows that truth is important to humanity, but he has been very little concerned with the application of truth in human society. He builds clear thoughtforms energized by the will ray with regard to his own search for truth, but this does not affect human institutions and society directly. Others pick up the truth and apply it. All too often this is the Plutonian.

The *Jupiterian* believes in God's abundance; that he lives in a universe that could and should abundantly supply all his needs. He can get pulled into a materialistic interpretation of this concept, especially if he comes under the influence, as he does, of Plutonian institutions and individuals. Occasionally the more evolved Jupiterian will have a clearcut thoughtform regarding some undertaking for the welfare of mankind, and carry through on it. However, on the whole, the Jupiterian group as such sees the end result of abundance without being clear about the means to that abundance.

The *Neptunians* are idealistic and devoted to beautiful ideals, but their thoughtforms are vague and nebulous and appear in the mental realms more as lovely clouds of color, energized by sixth ray energy. They do have an effect on the astral bodies of humanity in a general and helpful way.

The *Mercurian* is the collector of knowledge, the teacher, the recorder, the historian. In this case, by teacher we mean the hundreds of teachers who teach in schools and educate the children in that knowledge which is the heritage of man's experience. We are not referring to the great spiritual teachers. He has clearcut thoughtforms that have to do with imparting knowledge, and with educational procedures. He often has a tune-in on history and sees it like a moving picture. He is doing the job he should be doing in society, but the material offered him for the educational procedures needs to be different. He is an observer and does not pass judgment on events or material.

Now to an analysis of the present problem in the human kingdom. The Plutonian invaders have almost complete control of the human kingdom. One of their techniques has been most effective in gaining and holding power over the human kingdom. They observe and know that most of humanity is "I" conscious at the astral level. They, therefore, constantly and incessantly stimulate the astral bodies of mankind by desire for things (modern advertising, for example). They set up standards of status — value — importance — and constantly stimulate earth humanity to achieve these graded standards of status and value. (Make of car you drive, job level, kind of house you live in, etc.) They keep humanity so busy measuring up to these and so harassed by debt in doing so that people have no time to analyze, think or aspire to a higher set of values.

It is interesting that although the Plutonians really have little interest in sex, and usually are rather cold and certainly very disciplined, they have thoroughly analyzed ordinary humanity's susceptibility at the level of both emotional or astral and physical sex. They therefore systematically stimulate humanity with sex motivation, moving into pornography, perversion and all types of degrading sex impulses when they see that the stimulus of normal sex is ceasing to be effective.

As a period of civilization becomes more decadent, the Plutonians resort to steeping humanity in brutality. Examples of this today are modern horror movies, much display of war horrors in movies and photographs, filming of executions on television, books on violence and brutality, playing up in the news of crime and violence. In this way they endeavor to bring the human race to a place where cruelty, torture, violence and brutality seem to be the norm.

By the above methods of constantly stimulating the astral bodies of humanity they exhaust humanity emotionally until the human kingdom becomes docile, weary and confused from emotional exhaustion, and the mind is unable to function. This method is a most effective technique, especially so when most of humanity is "I" conscious at the emotional level. This method also cripples the emotional vehicle.

At this point the teacher illustrated this with the biology experiment where you stimulate the nerve and muscle of the frog with an electrical stimulus until the frog no longer responds due to muscular or nervous fatigue. He said humanity suffers at this time from emotional fatigue, due to over-stimulation of the astral body. More and more intense stimulation is applied at such a stage.

A solution for mankind could lie in the teaming up of a triangle of abilities — Martian, Venusian and earth humanity. This team would be supported by the Neptunian, Jupiterian and Mercurian groups. It requires that at least the Venusians and Martians wake up to how the Plutonians work and who and what they are. Earth humanity will be slower to do this. Up to the present time the Venusians and the Martians have had a mutual friendliness toward each other as a group and a mutual respect, but not very much coordinated working together. Together with the Will Ray and the Love-Wisdom Ray, along with the concrete mind ability of the Martian, they could build clearcut and altruistic institutions and organizations, making the clearcut thoughtforms that are necessary to bring them into manifestation.

Here the idealism of the Neptunian could be extremely valuable, because the Neptunian is a channel for an inspired and high level of astral energy. He could channel this kind of energy to humanity and energize the fatigued astral bodies of mankind and this would also help to build more stable astral bodies. The Jupiterian could work with the concept of abundance, not as materialism and posessiveness about material things, but bringing to mankind the concept of the Son in the Father's House to whom all things belong. The Plutonian has fostered in man on this planet a fear that he will not have enough and that he must take and hold what belongs to others or he must have more than others in order to be important. The Mercurian then becomes the recorder and teacher of new values.

Earth humanity will respond to ideals, to a new kind
of value based on spiritual development, and to beauty,
if these are presented, and respond joyfully. At this point
in evolution the other five planetary types could move into a united teamwork for the welfare of the whole human
kingdom on the planet. This will be discussed further in
a future class.

### General Observations—Discussion (VPN/SK)

*Plutonians* are suspicious, ascribe motives to others
which they do not have. They have involved, suspicious
thought processes, a negative outlook, a great desire for
power and domination. They are insecure, and the majority seek lower, sensual satisfaction.

*Neptunians* are easy to fool, poor judges of people, expect fantastic intervention of divine force on their behalf,
expect to accomplish unusual and important things out
of line with their ability or the facts or circumstances. They
are unrealistic about life problems and have a lack of reality about money and finances.

# IX

# Prevision

## The New Age

*Why do we sit beside time's far highway*
*And weeping clutch the things*
*That have decayed,*
*Holding the shabby fragments of the forms*
*Already broken by the hands of men?*
*New bottles*
*For the golden wine of life.*
*New cities*
*For the children of the sun.*
*Mankind reborn to higher consciousness*
*Shall move with joy into tomorrow's day.*

# Symbols in Ancient Egypt

September 15, 1960
Night Class
Recalled by Viola Petitt Neal

The crux ansata, the serpent, the winged circle, the sphinx, the papyrus, the lotus, are some of the symbols. There is a series of temples under the sphinx carved into the rock about 150 feet down. There are papyrus scrolls there, carefuly preserved. The temples have colonnades with rooms and there is an underground stream flowing through. Columns are of a beautiful green stone and carved. There are even older green stone tablets with writing on them. These are very ancient. The temple rooms seem older than the Egyptian period we now know. The rooms are lined with lovely white alabaster with symbols and pictures in inlaid stone, lapis lazuli and gold. The Egyptians painted their walls. This is a center of the Schools of the Mysteries.

There is a tunnel under the great pyramid. It is a place for ceremonies of the mysteries — the pyramid. There are rooms not yet opened. The pyramid was built by the Priests of Atlantis more than 11,000 years ago. They used a method of levitation using the mind and astral energy. I am not told just how it is done.

In one of the rooms of the underground temple which represents the temple of the human body for the indwelling consciousness there is a caduceus on the wall. It is inlaid. One serpent of lapis lazuli, one serpent of a pink stone. The central rod of gold. Five coils as today in the symbol. The temple rooms are in the shape of the human body. That is, a group of them. There are others.

The symbol of the serpent is the symbol of the energy of matter that moves in a spiral or serpentine fashion. It represents not matter itself — this is the divine mother — but the life of matter. The life of matter moves to join the life aspect of mind, then to be joined to Spirit. Its movement through the human body or temple through many lifetimes is a cosmic ritual. The life of matter is represented by the serpent. The reptile kingdom is between the bird and the animal kingdom, the deva and animal group. The serpent at the forehead is the life of matter ascended into heaven and represents the initiate who has completed the ritual of the life of animal man aspect and achieved illumination — the second divine hermetic marriage — the marriage of Soul with Spirit or Monad.

These temples can be excavated in due course. There is an opening left of the sphinx about a hundred feet from a middle point of the body of the sphinx and 150 feet down, approximately, a slab and a stairway under the slab. The sphinx is also Atlantean. It guards a mystery. It is over the top of this series of temples and rooms of the mysteries. There are manuscripts here on healing and the secrets of the human body.

This was a field class.

# The Relationship of Light to Gold

January 14, 1961
Night Class
Recalled by Viola Petitt Neal

This was a field trip class. The students felt as though they were taken to a large cavelike opening — a cavern. Two hundred feet inside the cavern a door appeared made of bronze with ancient writings and designs. Inside the door there was a large room — a hall for scrolls. A large table was made of stones which seated fifteen to sixteen persons around it. Scrolls were taken out of the vaults in the wall and placed on tables where the people were working. One particular group consisted of fifteen students around a table with a teacher at the head. There were objects on the table but their purpose was not given.

The instructor began the discussion on the place of gold in the human culture and civilization on our planet. *Gold* is a symbol of a Love-Wisdom solar system; a symbol of consciousness or Soul. It was pointed out that we have a golden yellow sun in our solar system. On the planet earth gold is used as a measure of value in our economic system, and in truth gold is a measure of value. But the whole concept and use of it in our present earth civilization is wrong and confused and is in fact destructive. The ancient Incas and Aztecs did not mine the gold they had — they made

253

it from sunlight by an occult process known to the priests who were trained in occult esoteric knowledge. These individuals knew some of the secrets of how energy becomes substance and/or substance becomes energy.

*Light* is actually the midway point between Spirit and matter or energy and substance. That is why light puzzles scientists who find that in some ways light behaves like a wave frequency of energy and in other ways like particles of substance. There has been much controversy in the scientific field with regard to this problem.

Man on this planet is coming very close to a point where he will be able to manipulate energy and substance with great ease and gold will become an abundant metal and will be in daily use for the making of household objects. Gold has a frequency which is beneficial to man and it is interesting that it was withdrawn from circulation and paper money substituted in most countries of the world. Thus, the beneficent radiations of gold were withdrawn from many people. Circulation of gold money kept people in touch with its beneficent frequencies. Also the mining of gold was restricted and almost stopped. Even the gold in the earth was made from light aeons ago when this planet came into its second incarnation in its physical form at the time of the second incarnation of our Solar Logos who is the Cosmic Christ.

The Aryan or Fifth Root Race is destined to have a command of substance, very especially to make gold from sunlight not as a possession or money, but as a substance that should be in common use in household articles. This was the dream of the alchemist. This knowledge lies dormant in the consciousness of the Aryan Root Race of man. The alchemist touched the fringe of this knowledge but because of the wrong motivation, greed of the rulers, and the lack of wisdom in humanity at large, they were not permitted to realize this dream. There were a few who discovered how to make gold by a roundabout process of transmuting baser metals into gold. Actually, the salt, sulphur and mercury of the alchemist's formula were symbolical terms and not actual elements to be used.

At present, our solar system is moving at a tremendous rate through space and is moving into a vast ocean of frequencies and substances which is and will alter the life on all planets and increase the radiations of the physical sun as well as produce changes spiritually. One of the results of this will be a much more rapid growth of plants. There will be alterations in the physical bodies of man and animals and a closer link between the physical and etheric brains.

This lecture or field trip is actually an elementary lecture designed primarily to be thought provoking and to point out the nature of light and also the relationship of light to the element gold.

# The Crystal Temple of the Torch

June 1, 1961
Night Class
Recalled by Viola Petitt Neal

Over a thousand persons were present of the Fifth Kingdom, and disciples of the Human Kingdom. The individual officiating carried great power and authority and wore violet robes. There was a great deal of soft but brilliant light. He had tablets before Him. This had to deal with man's place in the order of things. Reading from the tablets:

"When the time of purification is finished, the clear light of a new day dawns upon our planet earth and man as the Fourth Creative Hierarchy expressing the throat center of the Logos, and therefore speaking the Word of God, will manifest a new and better society on earth very quickly.

"He will use a type of energy that does not befoul his cities with dust and smoke and the earth will provide him with food more suited for his body without the toil and stress of the aeons that are past. He will know that he lives to achieve a greater awareness of the mind and heart of God. The masses will receive constructive

256

leadership to bring them along in evolution. Those of the Fifth Kingdom will live among mankind, and friends from Mars and Venus will come in their ships to the planet earth.

"The flame of immortal consciousness will burn steadily in mankind and there will be greater beauty of nature than ever before.

"Man, himself, may initiate the beginning of the drastic day of purification by hurling the thunderbolts of God into the solar system. Those who know these things are to happen, and their order and sequence, will be able to be steadily burning lights in the midst of these things.

"In many parts of the world, groups of students and disciples are tuning in on the pattern of things, and have provided places of safety and work where they can be preparing for the emergence of the light after the darkness, for they will be tending the light of the world in the consciousness of man through the days of destruction and this is as it should be. Remember, all disciples of the world, your destiny in these days. Remember your responsibility and opportunity and do not be dismayed."

# Vortices of Good and Evil
# On the Planet

December 10, 1961
Night Class
Recalled by Viola Petitt Neal

National leaders sum up in themselves the life and attitude of a nation and people or race. For example, "Z"
sums up in himself the life and attitude of the American
people better than any other national leader, because he
is himself the epitome of the life and attitude of the
American people.

The American people are dynamic, but oscillating. They
like to be thought generous, but they also have a hard core
of selfishness and self-centeredness, in a sense, almost irresponsibility. They are like happy puppy dogs that are
very friendly, but will growl if anybody bothers their own
bone. American people like to be liked and as long as they
have plenty, they like to share it. But they have no basic
understanding of the principles that involve the life of the
human race on the planet and their desire to be liked
makes them oscillating.

This discussion about leaders or families in leadership,
summing up the life of the people, also went on to say that
you find within this particular family both the positive and
constructive forces, and the negative forces represented.
This is more apparent because they do act as the summing

up of the life of humanity. Leaders represent the people as the priests sum up and represent the spiritual aspiration of people in all religions in all times of history. In religions, both in the ancient and modern world, the priest or religious leader acts as a focal point for the religious or spiritual aspirations of the people. It is as if all their thoughts and energy were focused toward one center. The priest acts as the summing up of that energy, that aspiration, that attitude of the people. This is why the Pope means a great deal to the Catholic people in a subconscious way, which they do not understand in their conscious thinking. He is a focal point for Christendom and this is why the Catholic Church is a stronger church than the Protestant Church, which lacks a focal point of leadership. It is divided into many groups and sects.

However, much as the Protestants may like or not like this idea, it is the Catholic Church that holds the lines of Christendom. And it is the Catholic Church that is important in keeping a focus of the Christ energy in the world today. The Protestant Church is merely contributing. If Christendom depended upon the Protestant churches to hold the line of faith, the line of the focal power of the Christ energy, it would be broken very quickly. This is simply because there is not that organized focus of the Christ energy in the Protestant churches and this is not criticism of the Protestant churches—this is a discussion of principle.

This was a very interesting class on energies and focus of energies of all kinds—spiritual, material and physical energies.

One group on the planet sums up in itself the materialistic desire element of mankind, the desire for material things and sensation. These two desires go together. They are Lemurian and Atlantean. There is one group on the planet that focuses in itself desires for sensation, the lower types of sensation, which come under the word sensuality, pornography, etc., and the desire for material things for their own sake. It also desires to have power over most of the bodies and desires of people. This group focuses in itself and its leaders this type of energy and principle on the planet. For this reason, the leaders within this group would be found counter-clockwise or on the destructive arc. Remembering that clockwise and counter-clockwise simply represent left-hand path and right-hand path.

The political leaders of the world can be leaders only because they sum up in themselves the attitude and life of the people of a nation. We have the leaders that we deserve in America. Other nations have the leaders they deserve. These leaders can rise to power only because they have some elements in their character that make it possible for them to become a focal point for the life of the people. They have somehow evolved in the process of evolution so that they can become, you might say, the focal point of the sum of the people. Looking at the leaders in the world today, we can see how the human race is evolving, what its attitude and background and nature are.

The American people must face the forces of evil. They will see and will experience the swamps and the depths of evil and destruction in their own experience in this nation. This is perhaps the next great experience that the American people must go through. It will give them a great tempering and they will either with full conscious awareness choose the ways of good or go down in the forces of destruction. It is almost as if how America chooses, the human race on the planet will choose, because the people of this nation are made up of the most hardy elements of all of the nations of the world.

Since we have been a melting pot of all peoples, we as a nation in the world will go through great suffering and great stress. We will face the Dweller on the Threshold as

"Z" faced the vast evil in the area. The vortex in the ocean, the snakes and poison, the swamps, the heat and the evil. This was a projection in physical form of what the American nation must experience and go through in a more specific form in the jungles of the human consciousness.

I understood this so clearly as the teacher gave the lecture, but it was so difficult to express in outer consciousness. All of the steps of reasoning were so clearly picked up that one had a flash of understanding that encompassed the whole idea.

The vortex of Lemurian evil is in New Guinea. The vortex of Lemurian good is in Tahiti. The vortex of Atlantean evil is in South America — Brazil. In South America and the jungles of Brazil there is the vortex of Atlantean evil, destructiveness. The vortex of Atlantean good is in the Andes. Such a vortex does not mean that there has to be a vortex in the ocean, such as there is in New Guinea. There is one in New Guinea because the Lemurian Root Race was very physical, developing the physical vehicle through which humanity would express as a spiritual kingdom later. It is more an astral vortex in South America. There are not the evil physical forces in South America. Although you have the jungle, there are not the evil forces of the jungle that you find in New Guinea.

All that humanity accomplishes that is good and constructive on the astral level has a focus in the Andes mountains of South America and there is a center there where people live. I don't know anything about it, but there are people in it. These vortices of force attract certain activities to them and attract certain people to them.

The vortex of force in Brazil which is a negative vortex of Atlantean black magic and Atlantean destructiveness is a center for the activity of the materialistic forces, whereas, the one in the Andes mountains attracts the constructive forces of the Hierarchy.

Central Europe—the Balkan countries, Hungary—is the vortex of evil for the Fifth Root Race. North America, place not designated, is the vortex of good for the Fifth Root Race. The Fifth Root Race has been called the Aryan, but the word has been so misused by some people that we use Fifth Root Race to designate the present development of humanity on the planet, as this involves most of the human race. The people of North India belong to the Aryan or Fifth Root Race. There has been a good deal of intermixture there with the Atlanteans. The more advanced Atlanteans are the Chinese and Japanese.

There will be vortices of force in the Northern Hemisphere. Central Europe is a focus for negative and destructive forces. The exact location was not indicated, but a large portion of central Europe was shown on the map, including Switzerland. Several points were shown—one was in the mountains of Hungary. One was in the Balkan area of Bulgaria. One was in Switzerland. These three formed a triangle of energy which was negative and destructive. The people of Switzerland themselves are not destructive, but because the country is so surrounded by mountains, is small, and has enough political significance, it has been chosen as a center for the materialistic forces, the misuse of the gold of the world.

In the same way Tibet is a focus for a type of Atlantean destructiveness. He said there are two vortices in Tibet, one constructive and the other destructive. They are not as strong as these other power centers.

This is the summing up of a long lecture. Awareness was very clear and I have tried to give the highlights of it.

# Centers of World Upheaval

March 22, 1962
Night Class
Recalled by Viola Petitt Neal

There are four centers of world upheaval at present: The Middle East with its focus in Arabia; Southeast Asia with its focus in New Guinea; South America with its focus in Brazil; Europe with its focus in Switzerland.

There was a discussion in the class of the Book of Revelation. It was pointed out that the great whore of Babylon is a symbol for all sensual appeal to humanity through all the present channels of pornography and Freudian psychology. Freud was an evil person through whom the forces of evil, the Black Lodge, poured out a river of filth upon humanity. The whore was a prophetic symbol. At the moment, the astral plane on the planet is swarming with negative entities and negative thoughtforms and we are already in the midst of the things described in this Book.

The minds of men are shaken by totally irrational behavior of governments, which on any sane planet would be considered an insane and irrational pattern. Partly what keeps the rank and file of earth humanity stable is that they are so pinned on their everyday needs and activity they don't reason enough to see their irrationality. Those who do see it must hold steady on the mental plane because

263

forces of evil are warring against the fortress of the mind, seeking to shatter its rational integration and thereby sabotaging the human kingdom on the planet. The technique of reversal is a Plutonian technique for shaking the foundation of the mental faculty in man. This is their chief weapon against the mind.

If all disciples could see it and not be swayed by it, it would be their safeguard. You have to know who the enemy is and what their workings are and then you are protected. There are two weapons against humanity today: pornography for the masses and the technique of reversal for the intellectuals.

# The Temple of the Records

May 31, 1962
Night Class
Recalled by Viola Petitt Neal

VPN had great difficulty in recalling the details of this experience. She was not feeling physically strong. This is an abstract of the lecture.

From a depository in the Temple of the Records, records were taken which were written on sheets of gold and sealed. These records were laid upon the table with some ceremony. The seal was broken by One who works under the Laws of Karma.

(VPN thought to herself at the time that the letter of Fatima reminded her of this greater and bigger experience, the opening of the sealed records.)

The record was read to those present. A large group of the Fifth Kingdom individuals were present on one side of the hall and on the other side were over two hundred students from many parts of the world. Everyone was standing. He read:

"At the *third purification* of the planet, the physical planet earth will wrinkle its skin and continents and oceans will move. There will be purification by fire, water and wind.

265

"At first, there will be gradual warnings with earthquakes, shocks, and then things will happen quickly in a matter of days.

"Man will hasten the day by his own tampering with the forces of nature. *For man has seized the thunderbolts of God and flung them into the earth, the sea and air with the irresponsibility of children playing with toys without due consideration, without wisdom and without moral responsibility.*

"In this time there will be removed from the planet earth the men of the 'invader planet' who have corrupted earth and those of the Third Solar System who are still mired in substance. Those who go out of incarnation, earth humanity and other planetary groups, will return again. But many will remain in spite of the destruction.

"This also marks the purification of our solar system, and the etheric sun will cast out the 'invader planet' and a new harmony will be established in the solar system. On the planet earth, there will come a new day with a brighter and clearer atmosphere and the many who have survived will build a new society. This is not the end of the world but a purification and a renewal of the earth. The new day comes on quickly, even as destruction came quickly.

"The time is indicated for the period of purification, as perhaps—earth years. This depends to some extent on man himself. This is also an initiation for the Planetary Logos."

# Earth Changes — 1962-2000

January 18, 1962
Night Class
Recalled by Viola Petitt Neal

The changes that are coming about on the planet in human society, generally, from now to the end of the century have already begun. They were discussed under several headings.

*Changes in the Physical Appearance of the Planet*

There are movements in the earth crust all over the world and, as in the time of ancient Atlantis there were many warnings — earthquakes, changes in climate and volcanic eruptions, so today, for the last few years, especially the last year, there have been many earthquakes in different parts of the world which indicate the shift of continents and of the earth's crust.

The spin of the earth will change. Not in time of rotation, although there will be a disturbance in the time of rotation for a while. The axis of rotation will change. The North axis will move toward Siberia, the South axis into the South Pacific. This will cause considerable disturbance in the whole atmosphere which will produce storms and winds of great velocity and climate changes.

The Southern part of the United States, will move closer to the equator and the equator will move closer to the Southern part. The whole Pacific Coast will be changed right down through South America because of various sinking and rising of land. Much of California, quite a bit of it, can come down and there could be an island of California. A part of California will become a large island.

There will also be changes in the Atlantic including the St. Lawrence area and Maine. New York and Manhattan will be broken up. The rainfall will be different in various parts of the world. Many places that are deserts will become very fertile with plenty of rainfall. For example, the Sahara Desert in North Africa will become a very populous area and, with lots of rainfall and vegetation, will become more fertile.

The climate of Arabia will be colder, more temperate, but it will also be a more fertile country—Southern Arabia especially. There was a great map there or rather a globe of the world; from time to time places that have changed were indicated.

This will not come all at once. There is a gradual move up in the shifts here and there. There will come a time when there will be tremendous shifts at once and suddenly. This is not too far off, but it was not indicated how soon it would be. We seem to be already in this process of change.

## Human Society

Many individuals will go out of incarnation partly through war, but more of them will go out of incarnation through epidemics, changes of climate and fear that is engendered by the lack of ability to adapt which will make them vulnerable to any kind of disease or hardship.

Many people in this Life Wave who go in and out of incarnation on this planet will be removed to two other planets. Not in their physical bodies, of course, but they will be held over and will go into incarnation eventually on these other planets and will live on them. They will not reincarnate on the planet earth. Many of those who are from the planet Pluto will also be removed from this planet. They will share the destiny of their own planet.

Those who come back into incarnation will be more constructive people and eventually there will be a more constructive society. This will take place over the next period of thousands of years. The new society will begin to be manifest during the lifetime of many people now on the earth. There will be a different type of society. Those who learn the lessons through hardship and difficulties and through the impact of the forces of evil will be able to build a better society and a more constructive one as they reincarnate — or if they are now in incarnation begin to move towards it.

The present *economical picture* in the world is moving towards a very serious situation. There will be an economic collapse in the countries of the world. Great confusion. There will be new and temporary governments set up that will be dictator governments, that will distribute food according to their own idea of who should or should not have it. This will come pretty quickly. It is already beginning.

He mentioned the United States and said that our economic system is already out of the hands of the American people and that our money is totally worthless, although we do not know it. We will find that whatever we have or own as regards the necessities of life will be useful to us but our money will not be. This is true in England and France. It is true in all the civilized countries of the world.

Many people will die eventually from lack of food. Not because there is really a lack of food, but because of the breakdown of the distribution, the money system and the whole economic system of the world. Those who want the wealth and power of the world and power over people will themselves be in a state of chaos. They will have brought about a breakdown so enormous that they will not be able to handle it and they will also be in a state of panic.

For a time, there will be a temporary government set up known as the government of the antichrist which will be ruthless and violent and evil. Those that are in outlying areas and away from large concentrations of population will be able to maintain a certain amount of stability and integration focus. There are many groups like this all over the world who have been aware of this situation and they will be held together by help from the Planetary Hierarchy in the sense of encouragement to their leaders.

Our whole *solar system* is passing through an area in space for many thousands of years that will actually produce a more pleasant climate on the planet earth than other planets and will produce a condition where the earth will be more fertile. But there will be a bad upheaval in climatic conditions preceding this. The upheaval is due to changes in the planet rather than to our position in the solar system. The position of the solar system is very favorable; the immediate conditions of the climate on the planet not so favorable. However, this situation will right itself in a few years and gradually there will be a greater fertility of the soil, a quicker growing season and generally a more fertile planet as far as producing food and vegetation is concerned.

Also conditions will prevail which will be unfavorable to destructive things in the human body. In other words, the human body will not have as many enemies to its survival in the minute organisms that now cause disease and destruction. I'm not sure whether this meant the human body developed a greater resistance or whether it meant that these would not exist. I'm not quite clear about that.

There is a great star out there indicating the direction of the movement of our solar system in space. But this is simply for the purpose of indicating movement. It seems such a vast picture to get any kind of concept of it.

This was a class which included about one hundred persons.


August 29, 1962
Night Class
Recalled by Viola Petitt Neal

The lecture was given by a member of a Seventh Ray Ashram in the College of the Lamp. As the student went into the college there was at the gate the symbol of the Lamp. It seemed more substantial as a college on the mental plane than other colleges.

This college seems to deal with astronomy, geology, the mineral kingdom, earth changes, etc. There were many charts on the walls and the lecture dealt mainly with future earth changes to condition the students for what might be coming. *No exact timing was given* as to when the major earth changes would take place, but the teacher indicated that we are already in the beginning of this change. Many minor earthquakes are taking place daily and there will be more of them until the time when the major changes will take place in the crust of the earth. The geophysical year did find shifts in the earth's crust and some of this data has not yet been published. They did not wish to frighten the public and there was little they could do about it.

He indicated the following earth changes will be made: a large portion of the Coast of California will sink. Land masses will rise off the Coast of California. The whole of Japan will eventually sink. There will be land changes all around the Pacific Ocean, including Alaska and South America. There will also be changes on the East Coast of the United States, especially in the vicinity of New York. Some land will rise in the South Atlantic. There will be a great bay where the Mississippi River now is, practically dividing the United States in half. Some of the Great Lakes will be drained, especially Lake Superior and Lake Michigan. Some of England will sink. There will be great changes in the Mediterranean — earthquakes in Gibraltar and around Turkey.

The teacher explained that the whole crust of the earth right around the planet is in a state of nervous uneasiness with small temblors occurring all over the surface of the planet. There have been pressures and strains built up for thousands of years which will result in major cataclysms which are preceded by smaller tremors occurring daily at the present time. The changes will be so vast that there will really be "a new heaven and a new earth," as mentioned in the Book of Revelation.

The sky will have a somewhat different color from the past and we will talk about the violet sky instead of the blue sky. It is hoped that no bomb will be sent into the Van Allen belt. If one is fired into the Van Allen belt it will cause a coalescing of radioactive particles which will produce a rain of fireballs on the planet burning certain areas and causing radioactivity; also very high temperatures. This could result in much more destruction than the earth changes we have mentioned. He said vast numbers of the population would be killed and many more would die from disease and hunger.

In more ancient times, more than eighty percent of the world population was engaged in agriculture. This meant that in time of disaster many people knew how to raise and preserve food. Also, each city was supplied by farm lands immediately in its vicinity. Today, less than twenty percent of the world's population, especially in the civilized countries, knows anything about agriculture or is engaged in it. Food supplies are shipped long distances, packaged and processed by factories. Therefore, a major breakdown in distribution would mean that large populations would starve to death. We must also realize that those who survive famine would have to learn how to procure seeds and raise food. In more ancient times more people knew how to do this. Today very few people know how.

These earth changes will be accompanied by changes in the soil bacteria, which will cause plants to grow more quickly. People will discover that plants not only draw minerals from the soil, but they also eat bacteria from the soil in their growth process. There are already discoveries about this.

He said that we were not using methods that would be successful in getting into space, but that eventually we would get into space. He said that there would be some slight changes in the earth's orbit. During all this process the Plutonians will be removed from the planet as well as the Third Ray Solar System group.


November 16, 1963
Night Class
Recalled by Viola Petitt Neal

*Cosmic Energies and Their Effect*
*on the Planet Earth*

The class had to do with changes and conditions from the point of view of physical changes in the planet earth.

He began by saying that there are many changes taking place today in the physical constitution of the planet. These changes are more basic than just surface earthquakes or local weather changes.

During the time of Atlantis when the continent sank and practically the whole face of the planet was changed, there were impacts of cosmic energies which caused the earth to make a jump in its orbit. This meant that it was slightly farther away from the sun. This is somewhat like the jump of an electron in the orbit of the atom. There was also a shift of the poles and axis of rotation.

The *earth is not molten at its core* as is sometimes said. At present the solar system has moved into great streams of Cosmic energy in space. Some of these energies, striking through the surface of the earth, have the effect of melting certain substances and they do become molten, although ordinarily they may be in a solid state. It is as if these radiations from space kindle numerous fires under the surface of the earth and we have volcanic activity and also shifts at deep levels. The earth has many vast caverns far under its surface. It is not solid straight through. Therefore, when these fires are kindled by the penetration of cosmic radiations there is a flow and shift of masses which cause a vast number of small earthquakes all over the surface of the earth. These are increasing every day and will continue to increase because deep inside the earth much shifting and change is taking place. Wherever there are major fault lines or cracks closer to the surface it is expected that large major shifts will take place.

Numerous breakthroughs of molten substance are taking place in the floor of the Pacific Ocean and to some extent in the Atlantic. This is heating the water in local areas and disturbing deep sea life. The whole coastline of the Pacific will change. These major changes started with the vast earthquake in Chile in May, 1960. But as you will

note, there have been major earthquakes in widely separated areas — Agadir, Yugoslavia and Persia. The change
in the planet is total, not local. It hits local areas from time
to time where the stresses or fault lines receive too great
an impact.

We must explain a little more clearly how these cosmic
radiations affect the planet. You have a good example in
a recent discovery in science which will somewhat explain
the action of these radiations. The laser beam will instantly
make steel molten when it strikes it. The beam can travel
through space or the atmosphere without appearing hot,
but when it strikes steel, for example, it will burn a hole
in it instantly. This beam can also be directed for certain
kinds of surgery to do a specific job.

These cosmic radiations of energy are of many different
types. Some affect only certain minerals or solid substances
and not others. At this time, the solar system is moving
through a new area in space where great cosmic streams
and tides affect the sun and all the planets, first of all,
on the physical level. This has happened before in the
time of Atlantis approximately 25,000 years ago. These
changes come in cycles of about 24,000 years. It is a cosmic
spiral and cycle difficult for man to identify because he
has not been able to span in his awareness such vast reaches
of time. Much that is now considered to be authentic geology is not correct. However, it is the best man can achieve
by applying reasoning to what he is able to observe.

These radiations will raise the frequency of the planet
and affect consciousness. The actual substance, physical,
astral and mental, is even at the present moment being
raised. This means that the vehicles of expression for the
human kingdom will of necessity be built of substance of
a higher frequency. Therefore, automatically those Egos
(or Souls) at a lower state of evolution will be unable to
reincarnate. This will mean that for several thousand years

those of a more evolved level will come into incarnation. Possibly for the rest of this planetary life wave.

Today, the raising of astral substance is bringing about a great deal of upheaval in the human kingdom. The first result observable is more crime and more evil. We might say that the higher radiations of astral substance in the astral bodies of humanity are irritating and disturbing to those of a lower level of astral consciousness. Therefore, it stirs up the latent evil selfishness and greed in human beings. This is an initial effect but the long-range effect is to strengthen all that is good and constructive and more evolved in the astral life of humanity. The constructive people will become more definitely constructive, more discriminating and more ready to stand up for what is good.

The task of the disciples of the world will become easier, both in their own efforts to go forward in consciousness and in their efforts to bring about a better society.

These vast streams of cosmic radiation that have hit the planet have caused the molten conditions that produced the crystalline forms on the planet. Therefore, the diamond and other crystals are not just the result of some local volcanic action and pressure, but have been formed all over the earth at times when these streams of cosmic energy have brought major changes.

There will be great changes especially in the plant kingdom and a greater yield of food than in the past. This will make the problem of food of the right kind far less difficult, and will assist in building healthier physical vehicles.

There will also be changes in the animal kingdom. The domesticated animals will show a higher level of development.

December 15, 1963
Night Class
Recalled by Viola Petitt Neal

## Communication of the Will Energy

Instability of governments all over the world will undermine their sense of security. There is a great deal of trouble ahead for Germany and more so for the United States.

There will be more earthquakes in more populated areas. Changes will occur in the coastline of continents and there will be a rising of areas from the sea. There will be a shifting of the North Pole into Siberia and the South Pole farther north into the South Pacific. Canada and Alaska will become temperate in climate. The southern part of the United States will become tropical. The Equator will be through Central America.

Some of the civilizations in Europe will decline or be destroyed. Lemurian forms will be removed entirely. Atlantean forms will remain to a limited degree. Many now in Atlantean form will incarnate in the Fifth Root Race.

The Hierarchy will be among us to teach us and those from other planets who will wear our garment of frequency while among us.

Those who individualized on other planets will attend institutions of higher learning under teachers of their own planetary group. Many of the earth's humanity will also attend these higher schools of learning. The planet Pluto will be torn off our Solar System. Those from Pluto here on earth will be removed from this planet because their source of life is not our solar system.

The humanity on this planet has had the love-wisdom and intelligent activity aspects without the will or purpose aspect. So the forces of evil have used them to their will and purpose. Now that the will of life or Spirit energy will become a part of the makeup of earth humanity, earth humanity itself will direct its activity with purpose towards good instead of wandering and meandering along the pathway of illusion, a prey to the direction of the forces of evil. The decision regarding the planet earth is not only a decision of the Lord of the World, it is a planetary family decision and a decision of our Solar Logos, the Cosmic Christ.

To the class present it was stated that it is most important to keep informing and instructing humanity who are students and disciples on the Path to help them understand the events that will take and are taking place, and to hold steady and give leadership in times of seeming chaos and disaster.

On the planet earth the humanity, from its long struggle through darkness, its seemingly pointless wandering without purpose, its confused sleepwalking, will emerge into a clear light of consciousness. Humanity has been in the dark womb of substance for long ages, unaware of purpose or destiny. With these changes in its material environment which are, in fact, "birth pains," it will emerge from the confinement of the womb into the light of spiritual day. Not all individuals achieve this, but humanity as a Life Wave does so. It is because of this birth of humanity into the Divine Sonship that the Hierarchy, like a loving parent, comes to its assistance to train and direct it, and those from other planets, like delighted relatives, bring gifts and assist in its training and growth.

This is a major cosmic event in the solar system. The Christ foreshadowed it. A few of the human kingdom understood it because they individually had achieved this birth. These few have been puzzled and perplexed that they could not reach most of humanity still sleeping in the womb. The birth pangs of the planet earth are inevitable, but there is swift rejoicing to come when the child humanity is born.

Other great upheavals and changes on the planet earth have not resulted in such quick and wonderful changes because they have been crises as Mother Earth carried the child in its womb. The time of Atlantis was almost a miscarriage of the child humanity. Help was given the planet from high levels and a change made in the nurturing of humanity as one makes a change in the diet and care of a pregnant human mother.

May 11, 1962
Night Class
Recalled by Viola Petitt Neal

*Frequency Band of Experiences*

In the human kingdom you are in touch with certain limited bands of frequency and a certain limited band of experiences. In other words, you live in a world of experience which has been deliberately defined by the Lord of the World to nurture and to protect the human kingdom on His planet until a certain stage of growth and development has been reached. As you nurture and protect a child in the nursery, you must realize that outside this circumscribed sphere there are forces, experiences, entities and beings involved in the evolution of the planet who are totally beyond the range of human experience.

The constructive forces of this type seek to cooperate with the Lord of the World and to protect the human kingdom. The destructive forces seek to break through the protected sphere of the human nursery. As individuals in the human kingdom begin to evolve out of the nursery state, they begin to penetrate this "ring-pass-not" of the human sphere. If they are constructive and disciplined, they begin to make contact with the Forces of Light and go forward in their growth and development. Those who achieve a high stage of intellectual development and integration, but remain egotistically separative, naturally contact Black Forces and either cooperate with and become stronger on the left-hand path or become victims if they are weak.

The Black Forces do not tolerate weakness. They use and destroy the weak members of humanity who may stray outside the sphere of human protection. He said:

"At this point, you who are present here (about twenty-five) need to realize that there are many forces and beings who are involved in the planetary life who are endowed with power above that which you call human and their sphere is beginning to interpenetrate the human sphere.

"Very definitely, there are space people who come and go on your planet. Some of these are very constructive, as those from Venus and Mars. Some are destructive.

"More and more you will meet up with people who are being controlled consciously or not so consciously by individuals who are more than human and yet seem to be ordinary members of the human kingdom. Where any of these negative individuals are concerned, you have a kind of built-in protection. They do not understand the Soul and will evaluate you as personalities. Therefore, if you are wise and do not talk too much you can be in their presence and observe their activities and they will consider themselves totally undetected. You can always ask for Ashramic protection in the 'Name of The Christ.'

"This kind of knowledge would stagger the minds of ordinary humanity, and at times indi-

viduals who have accidentally stumbled upon
some of these things, specifically the negative
aspects, have become mentally deranged. This
is in case of people not well integrated and not
sufficiently evolved.

"This knowledge need not trouble you. The
reason for this class is simply to inform you and
reassure you that these things do exist. Take
them in your stride; observe and do not be
disturbed. The dabbling with the astral plane
which humanity does has nothing to do with
what is being discussed. Although occasionally
these negative forces do penetrate through the
astral plane of man's experience and manipulate
him if he dabbles with psychic phenomena. This
is fairly rare. It is a part of growth and training
to become aware of the world outside the sphere
of the human nursery."

# Panoramic View of
# Current Events—1972

January 7, 1972
Night Class
Recalled by Viola Petitt Neal

### The Five Masters of the Black Lodge

This was a crash program, but seemed to be a summing up of classes I have been attending for some time. It had to do with a panoramic view of what is happening on the planet and why. There are five Black* Masters in charge of five departments of activity on the planet. These work with Black initiates, adepts and disciples in well-planned and organized activity. The first lecture explained that up to a point these activities had to be allowed to go on as long as humanity has cooperated with them and until humanity on the planet was sufficiently uncomfortable to see what destructive forces were doing and to be ready and willing to cooperate with constructive forces. He also explained that it is important for students of the right-hand path to know what is happening because they can more

*The word "black" refers here to the quality of the life of the man and not to the color of his skin. Black Master means he who seeks the material aspect and lures humanity to that goal, away from the Spiritual search.

intelligently cooperate with the forces of light and not waste their energy where it would do no good. Knowledge is the power to understand causes and cooperate intelligently to save the humanity on this planet.

### The First Black Master Utilizes
### Elemental and Demoniac Forces

The five activities were then discussed, each by a separate lecturer. The first lecturer, who began with the above introduction, discussed the most dangerous of all the activities. One of the five Black Masters is in charge of releasing and using destructively elemental forces of the planet — the elemental fires, the kundalini elementals — on the involutionary path. These elemental lives are very potent and neither good nor bad. They maintain the balance of nature on the planet, its internal fire and all its energy. There are magical means by which these energies can be released and used destructively by a master of the Black Lodge. These elemental forces are directed to people to cause strange psychic phenomena not of the astral plane.

Witchcraft belongs to this kind of activity and people dabbling in witchcraft or working with this master, whether they know it or not, become small pipelines for these negative elemental forces, which in many places are causing people to do weird and inhuman things. The word "unhuman" is better. These forces cannot influence people who are constructive, but they do have an effect on people who through many incarnations have dabbled in these things and who have a resonant frequency to them.

This master is influencing and clouding the minds of scientists who work with atomic energy. These people are influenced to explode more bombs and every explosion is upsetting the internal fires of the planet and bringing us closer to cataclysm. Atomic reactors for atomic energy for energy uses are unwise and very dangerous. Something is happening which could be more dangerous than the immediate effects of an atomic war. There is a critical point when a certain number of atoms have been split which could start a chain reaction that would disintegrate the planet. This will not be allowed to happen, but at the moment the atomic bombs begin to be exploded and the atomic reactors and the radioactive wastes begin to be deposited deep in the earth and the ocean, we are moving in the direction of this critical point.

The recent explosion in Alaska set into activity the ring of fire around the Pacific which will gradually cause drastic earthquakes and volcanoes. It marked one minor critical point along this highway which points toward disintegration. Many of the scientists who are not concerned with altruism or with moral or ethical values are influenced and pushed to continue their work; however, there are dedicated Black disciples who keep this destructive activity moving.

This particular Black Master also handles and uses the demoniac forces of the astral plane. These are powerful destructive entities with a type of awareness and intelligence and malicious intent and purpose, against whom the doors have been closed since the time of Atlantis. The door has been opened by man's evil and by this particular Black Master. We must remember that man is always the key; that a sufficient number of human beings must desire and embrace and cooperate with evil consciously before a Black Master has any power over the human race. Even so he has no power over people with good and constructive outlets. But such people can find themselves in a society being overrun by these destructive forces. The larger group of humanity who do not really choose and who drift with the tide are pulled into the maelstrom of this evil and must wake up enough and suffer enough to make a choice. Until they do neither the Planetary Logos nor the White Lodge can help them.

The informed students and disciples and people of good will constitute a bulwark and a lighthouse against the evil and whether they know it or not are surrounded by the guardian of light and are the assistants of the White Lodge.

At this point I will explain that the human being on the astral plane and the human thoughtforms may to some degree be negative as well as constructive. These do not constitute a terrible danger to the human race and can be dealt with.

The demoniac forces are terribly destructive to the human race and at the ultimate limit can destroy the vehicles through which the soul expresses, and, therefore, cause failure of groups of individuals in this life wave.

The asteroids are the remains of a planet that exploded and disintegrated because of tampering with the elemental forces and kundalini fire of the planet. Our moon was thrown off from this planet and captured by the earth gravity. This was done so that those members of the human life wave on the asteroid planet would have a resonant frequency with our planet and could be transferred to our planet incarnating here for their further evolution. These are called "the people from the moon chain." Most of the humanity on that planet had its vehicles destroyed, but those who came through the experiences were incarnated on our planet.

When these individuals, who in many ways are more advanced than earth humanity, can achieve the Fifth Kingdom level, then the moon will no longer exist around our planet and will disappear. The demoniac beings on the astral plane are from this asteroid planet and are influenced by the moon. These demoniac beings will also be removed from the planet when the moon chain group of people achieve the Fifth Kingdom. They were the constructive people saved from the destruction of the asteroid planet.

The basic elemental forces of nature belong to a different plane and a different order than the demoniac forces of the astral plane. Remember that these elemental forces are neither good nor bad, just as electricity is neither good nor bad. They belong to the realm of substance or matter.

The demoniac forces of the astral plane are consciously and intentionally evil. They could never disturb human beings in a physical incarnation if there were no resonant frequency in human beings. There are members of the human kingdom who intentionally and consciously invoke these forces and consequently become victims and instruments of these demoniac beings. Individuals with a constructive outlook on life who do not dabble in things cannot be harmed by them. There is no resonant frequency.

The second lecture the same evening was with regard to the work of the second Black Master in physical incarnation.

## The Second Black Master Utilizes Narcotics, Psychedelics

This particular Black Master is in charge of promoting the use and distribution of narcotic, psychedelic and hallucinogenic drugs. This is organized for the whole planet from the producing of the drugs to the distribution and the recruiting of the users. It is not something that has just happened on the planet earth. The distributors are greedy people with no moral or ethical value who do not realize how highly organized this activity is and who do not realize that they are simply pawns in the game and always expendable. Greedy, crafty, cunning individuals always think they can win against the forces of light and that they can handle the forces of evil. Eventually, the forces of light win but the forces of evil use the greedy ones and toss them aside.

Those who are addicted to drugs are in no position, once addicted, to help themselves or the situation and they have to be helped when and if they will accept it by constructive people.

Humans are the key to evil on this planet. If they did not cooperate with evil, it could not harm or hurt them. Greed, selfishness, lust, in human beings create a resonant frequency with a whole powerful host of evil. Human beings thus oriented become channels for evil and victims of it.

These first two departments of organized and directed evil toward the human race on the planet have been discussed in the beginning because they are the most dangerous in the long run. The elemental and demoniac forces along with drug addiction can so completely damage the etheric vehicle that the Soul is deprived of its vehicle and the Monad must start over again in another life wave. Such individuals are lost to this life wave if the damage is severe enough, which means that this course of action is pursued without change or effort to get back to the right-hand Path. This is what happened to most of the moon chain of humanity.

There were more than three hundred people in the class, of many different nationalities.

### The Third Black Master Sabotages World Leaders

The third Black Master is in charge of an activity which is organized and directed to confusing, bemusing, blackmailing, bribing and otherwise sabotaging world leaders — especially in government, but also in other areas of leadership. The weaknesses of leaders are studied and methods for controlling them through their weaknesses. Their strengths and their virtues are studied and methods devised to appeal to these in ways that will be destructive to the human race, while leading the leaders to believe that they are doing what is wise and good. The lecturer turned to one national group and said, "Your country's leader has a Black disciple as adviser who plays upon the man's better points to divert his actions into negative and destructive channels."

This sabotage of leadership has left the world at the present time with almost no good leaders who are alert and aware and uninfluenced by these forces. The whole area of politics is systematically and scientifically corrupted and confused with planned intent and purpose by this particular Black Master.

### The Fourth Black Master Sabotages the Economy of the World

This particular Black Master is in danger of sabotaging the economy of all the nations of the world. Here again the greed of many individuals and the lethargy of a vast number facilitate the activity of this department. The resources of people, whether groups or nations, consist of the natural resources of the planet and the brains and the hands of the human race. In a well-organized economic structure the flow of material goods and services would be unimpeded and, like the flow of blood in the human body, would nourish and sustain the whole body of humanity. A measuring rod of money is excellent to facilitate this economic flow of goods and services. However, when the forces of evil take control of this measuring rod they can make havoc with the normal flow of goods and services. This has been a problem on the planet for many ages. Today, it is more acute for two reasons: there is a larger number of people in incarnation and a greater abundance of goods and services. Money is no longer a measure of the wealth of the human race, but an instrument to be manipulated against them.

## The Fifth Black Master Sabotages Education

The fifth Black Master is in charge of an organized group of initiates and Black disciples whose intent and purpose is to destroy the processes of education and to substitute in its place, through the channels which education has created, every possible method of corrupting the human race at an early age and through to the adult level. Remember this is organized. It doesn't just happen. It is specifically and definitely organized to reach education in all lands.

The White Lodge and its Hierarchy of Masters are prepared to move into the human kingdom with organized methods and procedures for a highly constructive and creative society in the world when humanity is ready. The problem for the White Lodge is that until humanity has suffered enough and seen a drastic-enough result of its choices there would be little or no cooperation with the efforts of the White Lodge. But that time is approaching and it is very useful and necessary that large groups of disciples should understand clearly what the problems of humanity are and what they have been.

The Black Lodge uses weak men, destructive men, selfish and greedy men as puppets to be their tools and instruments. Often such human beings have no idea of the vastness of the evil ways in which they are involved.

The White Lodge asks for the cooperation of informed and instructive disciples and people of goodwill who are taken into the confidence of the Forces of Light and invited to be a part of their creative effort for the human race. For this reason, at this time, the White Lodge is making every effort to give information or instruction to disciples and people of good will so that they will know and understand the problems confronting mankind and, therefore, be able to work in partnership with the Forces of Light.

# The Universal Alphabet

August 14, 1960
Night Class
Recalled by Viola Petitt Neal

Only the fragments of this night class were recalled. There was a discussion of how the three basic movements of the universe could be transformed into a form of an alphabetic language that could be understood by all nations. These three movements were represented thus:

a) *Rotary* or circular motion; O

b) *Progressive*, in the form of a straight line, moving both vertically and horizontally; — |

c) *Spiral* movement, either right or left.

From these three basic movements — rotary, progressive and spiral — the student was shown how an alphabet for any language could be designed.* The following is an illustration:

*In view of the coming age of computers, these three symbols could be combined in different ways by all nations to form the new script for the New Age. — SK

291

# X

# Consciousness

# The Tapestry of the Soul

We are sent from the far off country
    of the spirit
Into this workshop
    and we call it life
Earth clad we grapple
    with a world of atoms,
For we are sent to fashion
The stubborn stuff of earth
To forms of spirit
And sometimes we forget
    the glorious pattern;
And as we labour with
    this stuff of earth
There grows a tapestry
    we call the soul.
And who shall say we
    labour through one life or many.
Until that web shall be complete,
And all this potter's clay
    that we call earth
Be moulded into vessels
    for the Gods.

# Reincarnation

September 11, 1960
Night Class
Recalled by Viola Petitt Neal

There is very little technical information on reincarnation. Asia is familiar with the idea, but often does not understand its implications. The Western world is ready for the knowledge. More must be given out and written.

Each personality is a mathematical equation of energies which makes up that personality pattern for the Soul for the given incarnation. Sometimes certain soul qualities already developed are inhibited and others used in order to achieve what is needed. More can be understood about what the individual is doing and working out in a given lifetime and what activities will assist him. This could help greatly in assisting mankind. It is the only basis for the teaching of the moral law, energies, and cause and effect in a universe that works according to law and order.

So far man on this planet has made progress slowly with much pain and suffering. It does not need to be this way. Man should grow as the tree grows—in rhythmic cycles with order and beauty, and with far less suffering. But because he does not understand the cosmic laws of cause and effect, or how and why we grow, or for what end or reason, he stumbles blindly. He thinks he must be here to amass possessions. Often he knows no other goal. Or he struggles to be clothed and fed and sheltered, and barely does so. He does not know his divine destiny or the why or wherefore of existence in a physical body.

For the disciple and aspirant on the Path, there are four particular things which hinder progress in any given personality. It may be one or several of these things: materialism, self-centeredness or selfishness, pride, fear. Materialism separates from life, and at the mental level pride separates from life. Self-centeredness isolates and confines the life of the individual. At a somewhat higher level fear can isolate and confine the activities of the disciple. All other problems can be listed under these four. Sensuality and lust come under materialism, as does the desire for possessions. Fear isolates us from love.

Perfect love casts out fear, said the Christ. The more we realize that we are in a Love-Wisdom solar system where perfect love cares for and protects us the more will we overcome fear.

Pride is overcome by realizing that we are an intimate and necessary part of the life of God. That God is dependent upon us and we are dependent upon God. We cannot be isolated from Him. The Christ said, "In him we live and move and have our being." To know that we are dependent upon His life melts pride and isolation.

Self-centeredness is harder to get over. It is due to such a preoccupation with the personality self that the individual is unaware of the outside world. He may appear to be fully aware in ordinary life, but in fact he is spinning too fast in his own little orbit of life. Often only great suffering will break this rotary motion which has become static in that there is little or no forward motion.

# Meditation

July 23, 1980
Night Class
Recalled by Viola Petitt Neal

*Five results of meditation*:

(A repeated dream that I kept waking from, with the pressure to remember.)

(a) Illumination on the things studied.

(b) Insight into problems within ourselves which need to be handled.

(c) Creative ideas — new ways to do things — new discoveries — new inventions.

(d) Momentary at-one-ness of Soul and personality.

(e) Insight into the laws of nature.

# New Developments in Consciousness

September, 1960
Night Class
Recalled by Viola Petitt Neal

The disciple's abilities may be considered a mutation in the development of human abilities. Mutation in the organic kingdom is a sudden appearance in the life cycle of a new and different type of living form.

In consciousness, mutation will be almost sudden appearance of abilities of consciousness — new and astonishing ones. In the Theosophical teachings there is a picture of the root races in the form of a graph with a sudden upturn in mind. Humanity is at present at this point of the turn, thus making possible the appearance of new abilities. The word mutation is not a precise term, but has a connotation in consciousness which conveys the idea.

At the beginning of the discussion, the teacher said that he was not discussing so-called psychic abilities, but a new break in consciousness in the human kingdom which had to do with the Buddhic contact and the etheric brain.

The teacher was asked whether or not radioactivity had anything to do with these phenomena. He replied:

"There is more mutation in consciousness than in the physical organ.

"Radioactivity is pure spirit in the mineral kingdom and so it brings about a monadic light in the physical cells of the body which can be

298

harmful in large doses, but makes the vehicle
capable of handling mutation in consciousness."

VPN   Words used here were to convey a concept rather
than precise scientific data.

The world is flooded today with literature written by
"contactees"—by people "in touch with other worlds."
Much of this data is distorted; much of it is clothed in trail-
ing garments of astral glamour. This is a part of moving
up to new states of consciousness. They feel the impact of
a new era in consciousness and of necessity, if undisciplined
and untrained, it produces this type. Look for all the grains
of wheat in all the chaff of this phenomenon.

Disciples in classes of the First Ray Ashram were given
information and conditioning to handle this and because
of the rapid moving upward they were being pushed in
classes and with some attending dictation at times. Because
of this rapid growth of consciousness, many new things are
coming into our world—new information with healing—
new discoveries—new methods of education.

The discovery of atomic energy was premature, but it
was not an accident. Earth humanity was stuck in materialism and the only way to wake them up was to allow a
breakthrough of the physical plane, namely, splitting the
atom. Instead of a break coming in the consciousness level,
that is from above down, it had to come from below up.

The splitting of the atom, producing radioactive
substances, is producing a condition in the physical cells
of human bodies that makes the physical brain receptive
to a breakthrough in consciousness. Too much radio activity could destroy mankind. In some respect, it may be
a costly way of doing it. It is expected that many people
will go out of incarnation in what may seem to be strange
epidemics. This will probably remove the more
materialistic out of incarnation. One group in particular
which is most materialistic.

Radioactivity produces a certain amount of physical tension in the finer substance of the nervous system which is hard to identify. That is why, maybe, some people reach out for tranquilizers, which is not good. A certain amount of tension is focus and is related to a new type of focus in the brain and such focus up to a point is very good and makes humanity more receptive to this state of consciousness. It is an automatic building of a bridge or antahkarana between consciousness and the physical vehicle of humanity. (This is merely to convey an idea.)

In a sense humanity has let itself in for a new kind of experiment in the human kingdom on this planet, namely, using radioactivity to raise the frequencies of the physical cells of the body—by using physical means rather than the impact of consciousness. There will be casualties, but in the long run it may be a quick method of evolution. The caudate nucleus is a resonator to Consciousness. It is capable of resonating to the modulation of consciousness like a many-stringed harp.

September, 1960
Night Class
Recalled by Viola Petitt Neal

There are two aspects of an *idea*: Simply the idea—its body, and the life or spirit of an idea.

We can understand an idea purely intellectually with the concrete mental aspect and know what the words mean. However, we have the energy of the idea available to us only when we have achieved that inner understanding of the idea. Most people get only the *form* of an idea but not its *life*. When an idea really becomes dynamic, both of these components have been assimilated by the individual.

# The Creative Process

October 17, 1960
Night Class
Recalled by Viola Petitt Neal

We speak often of the creative process and of seeking ourselves to be creative. It is important to understand more clearly what the creative process is. We might explain it this way: Spirit, the one became the two—Spirit and Substance expressing as life and form. Between these two great opposite polarities the creative process takes place.

The creative process is the process of adapting life to form (insofar as the Cosmos or the Universe is concerned) in order to produce the flower of consciousness. Spirit and Matter—Father and Mother—work at building better forms for life so that more adequate consciousness may result.

To adapt life to forms and forms to life is the whole creative process with the end result in view of producing consciousness: at the form level—a solar system, a planet, a galaxy, a plant, a tree, a human being's vehicles—there is the effort ever to find more adequate forms, more beautiful forms, more flexible forms. At the life level there is the effort better to control and use the form. These efforts seek to achieve several things in the continuing

301

creative process: more rapid growth of the flower of consciousness, more perfect and more harmonious growth in consciousness.

In the busy workshops "studios" of universes many forms are tried. Some prove more adequate than others. Some produce better results than others. On the planet earth, growth through conflict and combat with evil producing a stronger and wiser kind of consciousness than some other planets may produce. More beauty in consciousness has lagged behind on this planet that must catch up.

Consciousness is the result of spirit's contact with form —its exploration of form, its experience in form. Consciousness is love because it holds an awareness of all relationship, all contact of life and form (in time — *All*). Consciousness is therefore the magnetic field of force which spirit and matter set up through their interrelationship. This is why the words *love* and *magnetic* are used almost interchangeably in the language. Consciousness is also wisdom. Wisdom denotes that meaning and value have come into existence and are recognized. Consciousness recognizes value and meaning in the contact of life with form.

You build a house and move into it. Life has moved into form. You achieve experience that has value and meaning. Life moves into the house of form and consciousness is the creative result.

The artist in the human kingdom is calling the attention of humanity to this vast creative process. The painter is seeking to make humanity realize that the life aspect is expressing through all forms. He is endeavoring, whether he knows it or not, to say form is not the ultimate reality. It exists so that the life may express through it and consciousness flower. This also is true of the sculptor. The painter must emphasize the life aspect, and the sculptor also. On the other hand, the architect is emphasizing the form side, beauty of form — form in its importance as the house for life. He builds the building to house a culture. In turn, his buildings have an effect upon the kind of life that can express in a culture.

The musician is speaking of qualities of consciousness. He is calling our attention to the consciousness aspect and to the nuances of quality at many levels — sound — music — is the scale of consciousness.

Religion should deal with the love aspect of consciousness and does, but could do so better. Religion deals with man's relationship to the total reality of spirit and matter. All religions speak of love. To give man an understanding of the love aspect of consciousness is the office of religion *per se*.

Science has the role (at present not realized) of giving man the understanding of the wisdom aspect of consciousness — value and meaning of the creative process; spirit's contact with matter. Science got lost in the externals of the form world. It will eventually achieve its real purpose. Religion and science will then assume their joint role of making man aware of himself as Love-Wisdom.

Literature in the creative field touches all three aspects of the creative process. Drama deals with the struggle of the life to work in and through the form and portrays the happy or tragic ending in producing consciousness. Literature generally deals with life, with form and with quality of consciousness. Literature will one day be seen as the synthesizing form in human culture and development in consciousness.

The creative process means adapting form to life and life to form. Man at a lower level identifies and points out this creative process in art, religion and science. In doing so, man is creative at a lesser level and achieves more rapid growth in consciousness the better he can do this.

# Chaos and Order

October, 1960
Night Class
Recalled by Viola Petitt Neal

As disciples on the path, we are seeking to see clearly the great issues on our planet so that we can cooperate with the Planetary Hierarchy and work constructively in the Plan. This is the only way of action that can bring us satisfaction, a sense of security and the growth in consciousness we seek. It is not easy to see the great Planetary Plan and purpose as it works out. Often the Black Lodge and the masters of evil speak as angels of light and appear so until and unless we challenge them in the name of the Christ.

We might say that the conflict on our planet is between chaos and order. Chaos and confusion are the great opponents of order — the negative and positive poles of manifestation. Matter alone is chaos without the power of Spirit to give order. Disease is the temporary victory of chaos. War and famine and pestilence seek to destroy order.

The world movement to make one faceless humanity of a zombie-like nature is the advance of chaos. It is a pulling of humanity back to the level of the animal kingdom, moved by one impulse, like migrating herds. Eventually either chaos wins or chaos is absorbed into order. The conflict between these two eventuates in growth and the tempering of man. For man must choose which side he is on. Man finds this outer conflict reflected in himself. In fact this great conflict reaches its height in man. It is in man that the balance of power and eventual victory of order must be attained.

In the kingdoms below man, matter reigns and spirit is imprisoned. In the kingdoms above man, spirit is in charge and matter has been dominated. Humanity is, therefore, the pivotal point of the battle in this solar system and on our planet as well as other planets. Man either joins the forces of chaos or the forces of order. It is in man that the battle rages most fiercely, but also it is in the human kingdom that the greatest achievement can be won. Man can truly win the crown of life in this battle. Man has most to gain or most to lose of all the kingdoms in nature.

Man is both a soldier in the army of the Logos and also himself a microcosmic logos of the seven principles which are his seven bodies and all the minute lives that constitute his personal universe. Man must first bring order in his own individual universe if he wishes to be an adequate soldier in the army of the Logos. This is why he is constantly told that he must control his vehicles of expression especially in the three worlds of the personality. As a result of this effort consciousness expands, will and love-wisdom and intelligent activity develop.

Through long ages man struggles for moral values which are law and order in the three worlds. Today the forces of chaos in our society are seeking to break down these values and hurl man back into the stages of savagery where there is no moral law. Chaos is the natural state of matter without the impact and impress of spirit. When spirit comes into contact with matter and builds it into forms for life expression, order ensues. Man becomes as the son, the custodian of order.

Man because he is a conscious son of God is the point where the battle is won or lost. He can choose. Man is the

epitome of the universe. He is the battleground. Man is
the victor when the battle is won. Humanity is the battle-
front and the testing place of the universe and this accounts
for the difficulty of human life. But man's reward is
tremendous beyond his imagination. He becomes the
master of matter and passes on into the Fifth Kingdom
and to vast fields of illumined experience in the universe.
Eventually order absorbs chaos and matter is exalted into
heaven.

Man finds all his capacities tested to the limit. Before
he becomes a disciple on the Path his problems are
primarily with the personal self, separativeness, selfishness,
preoccupation with the little personal desires. He suffers
because of his emotions and his selfish desires. As he
becomes the disciple on the Path, he finds that the great
effort is to have discrimination. He has won some degree
of control in the three worlds of the personality and is
reaching for the eternal spiritual values. At this point the
Black Forces seek to cloud his discrimination, to con-
fuse his goals and to get him to work for their goals under
words and terms that sound right. Here the great test is
discrimination.

Today, this life wave on this planet has come up to the
critical point in the battle of order against chaos. Will
humanity sink back into a faceless mob of slaves, to a
monster called the state — in a sense another name for the
antichrist — or will individualized sons of God rise to great
moral heights of order and beauty and justice and lead
humanity to these heights? The disciples of the world will
swing the battle if they hold steadily to the spiritual values
and goals which they see and know.

Let us ask for discrimination to know the difference between the antichrist and the Christ. The antichrist is the
lord of chaos; the Christ is the lord of order and truth and
beauty and justice and love. The antichrist would reduce

humanity to cattle, feeding on the material things of the world doled out by their masters, the slaves to matter. The Christ challenges mankind to become illumined sons of God and masters of the material world. You are either on top of the job or the job is on top of you. We must choose to be slaves of matter or masters of matter.

# Consciousness of the Human Race, by the Manu

February 24, 1961
Night Class of Viola Petitt Neal
Taped by SK

VPN   There are a number of students. It is not an ordinary classroom — more like a temple. There is a discussion on consciousness.

The teacher has on robes. Usually he doesn't wear robes. They are sort of ivory colored — some kind of a decorative trimming of violet. He is a teacher from a higher order than some of the others. But I think it is a First Ray Ashram — has to do with the consciousness of the human race on our planet at this time. He says:

"There has been quite a problem on our planet, because the life-wave on the planet has been slow in the unfoldment of the consciousness, especially unfoldment of the connection between Soul and personality. An effort is being made to speed up the development in consciousness. This requires a change in the substance aspect of the different bodies, especially the physical, etheric, astral and mental bodies of mankind. People are not able to carry the frequencies of consciousness. Consciousness is frequency, of course. The

308

substance must be able to carry the frequency of
energy.

"A new method is being undertaken, a new approach to the human race on our planet which
will especially involve those who are in a higher
stage of development — an effort to bring in
substance of a higher frequency."

VPN    It is a strange method; I am trying to understand
it — something very strange.

SK    What is strange about it?
VPN    I don't know how it is done. I think He will explain
it a little more presently. It is very strange, because it looks
as if it is substance. Substance from — not another planet
— it is interpenetrating substance that is moving into our
solar system. It is a great etheric cloud substance moving
into our solar system, reaching all the planets, but expe-
cially the planet earth.

This etheric substance is reacting and will react with the
radiations of our sun and other planets. It will cause a kind
of luminosity in our atmosphere around the earth. It is
already moving in a little — like what you might call a vast
etheric cloud — more than a hundred million miles across.
It's not just the method — the method being used didn't
originate on our planet. It is really from outside our solar
system, but it would be appropriated, He says. This particular thing which is happening to the solar system will
be appropriated to the uses of consciousness on our planet.

This is very serious. Not so much like a class. This is
a convocation. It's a very serious, a more profound occasion. There are many present. Many members of the
Ashrams are present and some of the students. We are on
one side of the room — not in the main part. It's like a small
auditorium, only it is more like a temple.

SK   How many do you think are present?
VPN   I think several hundred people.

SK   Where are you? Which part are you in? With the students?
VPN   Some of the students are on the right hand side of the room.

This etheric substance will interpenetrate the etheric substance of the etheric bodies of people on the planet. Those who are more evolved will be able to take it. They will have a great deal more understanding—a great deal more ability to see relationships, to see *why* things are on the planet. It is almost as if we lived in darkness and couldn't see. This substance interpenetrating the etheric bodies will help us to carry more of the etheric energy. We will understand more clearly than we do now. See more clearly. Some people won't be able to take it. It will be like an epidemic that takes them out of incarnation. Others just won't react to it at all, because it won't be able to penetrate the denser frequency. He says:

> "This is a good thing and constructive—helpful to the evolutionary process, and will help change some of the things on the planet more quickly. It will also affect the growth of things—plants; and they will grow more quickly and better."

VPN   This is like a report. It isn't a lecture in a class—it's a report that is being made to the Ashramic groups on what is to be expected and planned for. He says:

> "This is already beginning slightly. Just the very, very tenuous edge of this cloud of etheric substance has moved in to the area where we are in the solar system. It is also affecting the planet Venus. This is one reason that it seems so much

brighter. It's not just because it is closer to the earth, but it is also because of this etheric substance that is almost physical."

SK  Does He say from where this etheric cloud is coming?
VPN  He says:
"Our solar system is moving into it. It is moving toward us. There are two movements."

SK  Where is it coming from?
VPN  It is part of the vast reaches of space. One of those conditions far out in space that we encounter as we move through it. Sometimes vast aeons of time cross these patterns of energy or substance. All this is part of the Plan and purpose that has to do with the Solar Logos, but affects all life on all planets. He says.:
"We must not be frightened. It doesn't mean that there is any destruction and disaster to the solar system. Our solar system will continue in its evolution and progress, and our planet earth also. This is beneficial to those wo are students and who understand it and are not frightened or disturbed by it. This will bring adjustment in the physical, etheric, astral and mental vehicles much more quickly than could be done in a number of lifetimes.
"The Soul, the Self, will have a more clear and adequate and integrated vehicle more quickly. Those who are students and understand it, those who are evolved and integrated and are perhaps not students, will come to believe and understand it, and even for many of the people—good intelligent people, who are constructive in their outlook on life.

"Those who are negative, destructive—it will increase the darkness of substance and will make their vehicles less useful. It is a positive thing, in the sense of positive and constructive.

"There are climatic changes taking place all over the planet much more definite and specific and in some cases more drastic than the ordinary public has been told.

"The time of great change is almost upon us. These changes will make us more aware of ourselves as I the Soul."

VPN    Sitting here, you sense what he means. There is a sense of strength and integration and focus and awareness and knowledge that is continuous. Clear realization that one could be much more integrated—as if you gathered yourself together and knew yourself to be, I—the Soul, eternal and immortal. It is like standing in the light. There is a sense of clearness one does not have ordinarily. It is telepathic contact with knowledge, a quick understanding from higher levels, like the archetypal levels of awareness. It seems simple and not difficult, that kind of contact, but it is because one is in a certain atmosphere. Perhaps because one is in the frequency of the Ashram or members of the Ashram, I think the disciples and students are aware of this.

The speaker is not the ordinary teacher instructor. He is someone in authority on the Will Ray. Not the Master Jupiter, not the Master Morya. It is the Manu. The speaker is not speaking specifically to us actually, but to people senior to us in the Ashram.

SK    Have you ever seen Him lecture before?
VPN    I haven't seen Him before. He carries great power. That is why, perhaps, one has such a sense of clearness. In His light shall we see light.

There is strength—great strength and great wisdom—great clearness. It's a clearness you like. The Will Ray energy is not so strenuous as one thinks. I think the speaker gives one the feeling that the Will Ray energy is life. I know why this seems strange too. This is an effort or a method or a way by which there is a renewing of the etheric body, physical body. This is this etheric cloud coming in, without destructiveness, without having to destroy too much. It's a way of bringing in life to make it possible for the form to carry a greater voltage of energy without having to destroy the form, without groups of people having to go out of incarnation several times and come back and get adjusted. It is possible to accomplish a great deal more in a short time with the vehicles of expression.

There is a sense of the life force. Force isn't the word. Life energy—a sense of the life energy that is strong and resiliently clear. It is a different thing from what I have known before or experienced before. He says:

"You must have the courage to live. You must have the courage not to be disturbed or frightened by changes. Know and be from the center outward."

VPN   This is to the human kingdom. He says:

"This is why there are disciples in the human kingdom present. Know and be from the center of your self outward."

VPN   You sense what He means—if you can hold it. He says:

"The light of life is within you.

"The flame of life is within you, know this. And know evil and destructiveness cannot come nigh unto you.

"Know yourself to be the life.

*"You are the candles of God holding the eternal flame. Know this."*

VPN   Still trying to understand why this seems a very serious occasion. Perhaps it is because of the presence of the Manu. Because He carries a powerful light energy of the life aspect. I think all the disciples are trying to be aware of some aspect of consciousness or at least the meaning for human beings on the planet. You realize we do dwell in the twilight of consciousness most of the time, because the mind is so clear here. There is a clearness. Such a different perspective on life, such different orientation.

The Manu seems to sum up in Himself what the human race is on a planet. This is a very dynamic impact. It has a splendor about it — a splendor and a power. But a power that is truth and life and love — the opposite of the negative aspect.

There is an impact of energies here. I think they are wave frequencies that mean something to the awareness of those Ashramic — those at the higher levels in the Ashram. It is as if these frequencies were beamed to them and they understand them. We struggle to be aware of what they mean, because we don't have the same frequency or capacity — the disciples, the students. I know there is more I want to understand. He says:

"This information will be out in many groups. There will be rumors of it from the scientific levels, just a little bit said here and there in scientific reports, to condition people for some strange events. And if we look, we will find these references in newspapers and magazines. Some of the different esoteric groups will receive this information in one way or another through their leaders or through their own contact with it, and

many people will have a great deal more extrasensory perception because extrasensory is normal perception in certain stages of development."

VPN   It is very interesting to be aware of frequencies of
transmission which are beyond your own frequency band
and this band from the Ashramic level. But students, at
least, are getting the main points of what this convocation is about and why it is being held. He says:

"Very shortly there will be scientific murmur-
ings and mutterings about this phenomenon,
because this vast etheric cloud will very definitely
affect the astral material level, material substance of the planet and of the physical bodies
as well as the etheric bodies."

VPN   The instructor is with us and says that this is the
end of our part of the meeting. The disciples, the students,
are going out to something else. We are leaving the temple or the place where this meeting convocation is held.

# The Effect of Love on Consciousness

September 13, 1961
Night Class
Recalled by Viola Petitt Neal

Expansion of consciousness is a love activity. You see relatedness because you love. Love is a cohesive force that holds things in relatedness, so by seeing relationships you are participating in the love activity of the universe.

The Soul or love is the Christ aspect in the individual. In a sense we increase love energy in the Universe by seeing relationships. God needs our understanding of relationships. It rejoices God to see relationships as it rejoices the parent to see the child talk. As we expand in consciousness, we are more related to God. The more give and take there is between us and God, as with our friends, the more we understand Him. God needs our understanding of life. In a sense He will be lonely without it. He wants our comprehension of all He has created. A self-centered person is really destroying consciousness by narrowing his band of awareness.

316

# Radiatory State of the Planet Earth

September 5, 1962
Night Class
Recalled by Viola Petitt Neal

The life forms on this planet earth — that is, the mineral kingdom, the plant kingdom, the animal kingdom and the human kingdom — are at a stage of taking a step forward which can be defined in terms of radiation. Radiation is the life breaking through the form because the form is no longer adequate to express the life. There will be tremendous changes in all the four kingdoms, and coincident with this the changes in the physical body of the planet, in order to build new forms. It is true that areas of earth go under the ocean or become deserts for long ages of time to cleanse and to prepare them for a new stage of evolution. Just as a farmer must allow fields to lie fallow in order to grow a better crop later, so with earth changes.

What appears to be disaster is not actually, in the long run, a disaster. Looking at it from a specific point in time and space, from the point of view of human consciousness, world changes look like a total disaster and seem meaningless and cruel. If human beings had continuity of consciousness, they would not be utterly distressed and dismayed. Growth towards a high state of consciousness is always the purpose of these things.

317

The planet earth as a unit is moving toward a stepping up in consciousness. In fact, it is already in that process. This means a stepping up in all the kingdoms. This is why there will be new forms of plants, animals, and new developments in the mineral kingdom.

The upheavals of the earth will break the pattern of our modern culture and civilization which hold the mind of man at present firmly imprisoned. This was good as long as it produced growth in consciousness but not good when limited. A vast number of intelligent people today feel utterly frustrated, as though they were up against a stone wall. The form of civilization and culture in which they are living offers no further opportunity for development. We have reached the limit of the form's ability to express the life. The masses who are less evolved are satisfied with material things and weighed down with the anxieties of debt and insecurity. Within their narrow range of ability to grow, they too are utterly frustrated. This is what is meant when it is pointed out that the form no longer serves the life. People are without goal or purpose. A vast majority of them in all stages of evolution see no goal ahead and have no enthusiasm for further effort in living.

While in physical incarnation we have energy flowing in through the spleen from the planetary entity (the physical life of the planet) as though man were in the womb of substance and connected with the umbilical cord of life. The disciple needs to be consciousness-centered in his head in a point which is central in order to adjust to the flow of energy. The caudate nucleus is an organ for use in more advanced man, and it is not yet being used by ordinary humanity — and very slightly used by some disciples.

# Why Humanity Is the Fourth Creative Hierarchy

May 8, 1962
Night Class
Recalled by Viola Petitt Neal

In the Fifth Kingdom, man is referred to as the Mason or builder. By his emotions and feelings he sets up frequencies which draw to him the substances on the physical, etheric, astral and mental planes with which he builds a structure which is the human personality vehicle, the physical etheric, astral and mental bodies.

The quality of substance is determined by the frequency of his thoughts and emotions. A thoughtform was shown to the students in which the frequencies that a person sends out may be likened to a conveyor belt which brings in the building blocks. This could be presented in slides to the students with the analogy of building a house of adobe, bricks or alabaster. The kind of substance built into the structure also, in turn, determines the kind of frequency to which the vehicle is responsive. However, man, the thinker, the dweller in the house, has the power to change his thoughts and emotions and, therefore, to change the substance and structure. Because the etheric, astral and mental substances are much more fluidic types than dense physical, this is easier than building an actual physical structure. Man often takes a long time to do this, because he is slow in changing his mental and emotional frequency.

The energies which flow automatically into the centers are made up of all the ranges of frequencies, but the vehicles respond only to those ranges of frequencies to which they resonate. A good analogy is the string of the violin. The tension and thickness of the string determine the tone and frequency. The thicker the string the lower the note.

Although all frequencies of energies are available at all times, the individual has access to those frequencies to which the substance of his vehicles is resonant. This goes back to the quality of his thinking and emotions. Man, the thinker, the dweller in the house.

Thoughtforms were presented to illustrate this on a screen.

# The World of Meaning—
# Plan and Purpose

December 16, 1963
Night Class
Recalled by Viola Petitt Neal

The true meaning, the understanding of the world of
meaning, is really mathematical. It has to do with seeing
patterns of energies and their interplay on the planet. It
is seeing the relatedness of events to *Plan* and *Purpose*.

It is characteristic of humanity that they interpret events
emotionally—which means that for the most part events
have an emotional meaning to an individual nation or race
which may have no relatedness to actual meaning. They
see meaning at the level of the concrete mind on the basis
of the limited facts given at any given time. This again
is a limited approach to the world of meaning. This type
of seeing relationships usually has very little validity in the
larger world of energy patterns. They see meaning in relationship to their own selfish and circumscribed orbits of
activity.

The world of meaning has to do with how energies meet
and affect each other in relationship to overall Plan and
Purpose.

Events in themselves are end results of the intersection
of frequencies. One begins to understand meaning not by

321

interpreting the events but by examining the energies and meeting points which produce an event. At the higher level this could be seen as mathematical, like the beat frequency in radio phenomena.

Man's effort to ascribe meaning to events depends upon his point of view, which includes his background, training and prejudices. The same effect within these limitations will therefore have different meaning for different individuals or groups of individuals. For example, the American Declaration of Independence: to the English, the signers were the traitors; to the Americans, they were heroes. In the true world of meaning the human race had taken a step forward in the understanding of freedom which was important in the overall Plan and Purpose.

To approach the true world of meaning it is necessary to understand the evolutionary process, to have a knowledge of the Wisdom Teaching. One cannot be emotionally dominated or limited by the concrete mind. There must be students and disciples who can begin to understand this true world of meaning and to interpret it to humanity.

# Department of the Manu—
# Life, Form and Consciousness

August 9, 1964
Night Class
Recalled by Viola Petitt Neal

The universe moves in an evolution of life, form and consciousness. This could be symbolized in the caduceus, in which case the two spiral streams would represent life and form and the central rod would represent consciousness. In passing, remember that symbols have a seven-fold meaning always (in our seven-plane universe). At this point we will use a further symbol to create in your minds a better condition of awareness regarding the material to be represented.

Let us take the circle with a dot. The dot represents life; the circle represents substance. The cross represents consciousness. The triangle represents the manifested world of form, which as you can see, in order to be manifested, must have all three aspects. The purpose of the symbol is to flash a total of a pattern of concepts on the mind.

Now to move to the discussion for this class period. Life moving through substance is universal electricity which inevitably creates a magnetic field which is called consciousness. When life flows through pure undifferentiated substance, there is a universal and undifferentiated magnetic field. Therefore, the creative universe as such does not yet exist. Let us remember that this undifferentiated magnetic field is consciousness. We might call it a dreamy elementary state of consciousness.

Form arises because of consciousness. This is a very important point to remember. It is consciousness that needs form to achieve its evolution.

Life flowing into substance is involution. (Life involved into substance.) But immediately when consciousness moves into the path of evolution, consciousness needs diversified forms for its evolutionary purpose. Because it is magnetic, it draws substance into diversified forms. This begins with the basic elements: oxygen is a state of consciousness or a state of magnetism — gold is a state of consciousness or a state of magnetism. In the mineral kingdom the highest state of magnetism or consciousness is to be found in the crystals.

In each kingdom substance is built into more complex forms through which the life flows and the consciousness in those kingdoms grows and in turn modifies the form. Consciousness does not modify or change the life aspect itself. But by modifying the form through which life flows, consciousness continually achieves its own change and modification along those lines which it conceives to be desirable and creative. Self-consciousness marks the high level of achievement.

Man has almost infinite capacity to modify the forms. He does not modify basic substance but can build an infinite variety of forms from the basic blocks of substance. He modifies mineral forms, plant forms and animal forms and thereby modifies consciousness in the kingdoms below him. This is a very definite, exact statement. In many of the Holy Books of the world it is expressed as man being "given dominion" over the other kingdoms in nature. We might say that a human being is a stronger magnetic field than an animal.

At this point I want you to remember the principle of analogy—basically likeness of relationship. The principle of analogy is true because the universe is built on a pattern that is endlessly repeated on all levels. We can call it the Three/Four Principle. Briefly: *Life* flowing through *Substance*, produces magnetism or *Consciousness* (the three aspect). The diversified form-universe which is manifested is represented by the four because it has four dimensions.

At this point let us go to our principle of analogy which applies on all planes and on all levels. At the lowest physical level man has discovered electricity. He does not really know what it is, but he has discovered ways to use it. Let us look at electricity for a moment. We can say that electricity (life) flowing through a wire (substance) always produces a magnetic field (consciousness). This is the principle at a level of everyday thinking, understandable to man as an experience of his daily life.

In the field of electricity, man himself produces the electromagnet (consciousness). However, he discovered electricity by first discovering the magnetic field of the mineral (magnetic ore). It was perhaps logical that he would first discover the consciousness aspect, since he himself is self-consciousness. By manipulating the magnetic field he was able to harness and control the life which was continuously producing the magnetic field and in this way controlling the flow of the life aspect—and by modified forms, produce the manifestations which he desired. His control of this life aspect is what we call electricity. Remember that we are talking about this at its lowest physical level.

We want to get back to the concept that life flowing through substance produces consciousness which builds and modifies form. Life does not build and modify form. It flows through the forms that are provided by consciousness.

A Planetary Logos or a Solar Logos is an inconceivably high state of consciousness that modifies and builds innumerable forms through which life flows.

Energy is an aspect of life. Force or power is an aspect of consciousness. One might say that life has the purpose to flow—to give itself to substance; in doing so, it produces consciousness. Consciousness of necessity is magnetic for it binds and holds life and its relationship to substance. To the students present he said:

> "Your consciousness and that of all humanity is constantly modifying form, more so than ever before. This is being done basically through one point of your consciousness, the concrete mind. The concrete mind observes and analyzes the world of form, and manipulates and changes it. This has changed your civilization (overall consciousness aspect of a nation—humanity) because the change in forms affects how life flows through forms.
>
> "However, to you as students, I would say something further: it is possible for man's total, integrated and unified consciousness to have a direct effect upon form, or the material world. This is not just the concrete mind operating, but the total consciousness. Those at the Fifth Kingdom level have this capacity to directly affect form in the three worlds. This ability begins with a control of the material of the three personality vehicles.
>
> "Today as we move into the next sub-race which will be the beginning of the next root race, man will learn a little more about this more direct effect of magnetic consciousness upon form."

VPN   In answer to a question about magnetic healing, he said:

> "In simple terms this is a case of consciousness in some degree altering form. The healer does

not understand the principle and probably does not have an idea how he does this, but because of a development of his own consciousness, he is able to some degree to alter form to permit a more harmonious flow of life. This does not mean that he is necessarily a highly evolved person in his total development, but there has been as it were a sideline development that makes this phenomenon possible to a greater or lesser degree. There is actually a magnetic effect on the physical body which brings the form into a better alignment for the flow of the life aspect."

VPN  In answer to the question about sound, he said:

"This may sound abstract to you, but sound is the 'word' of consciousness by which form is built. It is sound which modifies undifferentiated substance and builds it into forms. In a sense the magnetic healer speaks the word. Man can learn how to use sound frequencies through his mechanical devices to modify the physical body and produce therefore a more harmonious flow of life, which we call health.

"The word of the Logos (sound), builds the form of our solar system. Man may be destructive with his sonic frequencies before he learns how to use them constructively. Riding the thunderbolts of force is a daring and dangerous feat, but one that ultimately a Son of God must master."

# Art and Architecture

July 27, 1980
Night Class
Recalled by Viola Petitt Neal

Segments of the night class were recalled and written down later by VPN.

Summing up the lecture at the end of the class: *The Art of Italy* (Renaissance) is exuberant, dynamic and beautiful.

*The Art of France* is sophisticated and elegant.

*The Art of England* is as dull as their food. They excel in literature — the art of words.

*The Art of Holland* is earthy, heavy, but charming.

*The Art of Russia* is mystical and sad.

*The Art and Architecture of Egypt* is ponderous and powerful.

*The Architecture of Greece* is graceful and symmetrical, and mathematically pleasing.

*The Architecture of Rome* is solid and strong.

*The Architecture of the Orient* is sensuous, prolific, exuberant, with an overtone of spirituality.

*The Architecture of Islam*, is strong, anchored to the earth, but with an upreach of spiritual aspiration.

*The Architecture of Europe* (Middle Ages, etc.) Christianity. Mystical, graceful, aspiring.

These are just my notes of what I recall of the summing up of the lecture which was given.

# The Great Musician

*The Great Musician at his console sat.*
*His organ notes*
*Rolled through the empty corridors of space;*
*And substance sleeping in the night of time*
*Awakened.*
*Worlds were formed,*
*And suns and stars and shining galaxies.*
*His life flowed through the soaring melody*
*And all things moved*
*The dance of Life began.*

# Substance and Spirit —
# A New Habit of Consciousness

September 18, 1960
Night Class of Viola Petitt Neal
Taped by SK

SK    What class are you attending?
VPN    I am just beginning my own class. I think about thirty students are present.

SK    Which one is this?
VPN    This is Master _____'s Ashram and the subject is Substance and Spirit.

We begin class with a full and shining globe of energies in the center of the room. It is clear, like clear water when it is silver in the sunlight. Energies move beautifully in this globe. It is a large one about three feet in diameter. It gives one a strange and interesting understanding because you know very clearly that the outer world of form is a phenomenon, but not the reality. It's the crystallized outer form of an inner play of energies. It isn't the real world. It's like coming — when you come into incarnation. When you are working in the world of form — it is like coming into a forest of dense trees and trying to make a path through it.

You come into this world of crystallized forms, you live in it every day and you try to make an impact on it. Most

331

of the time, it makes an impact on you. Very, very few
people ever make an impact on the world of form, in the
way in which they are supposed to, or at all. Most of the
time the world of form is making an impact on us. And
yet, we come into it with the intent and purpose of making an impact on it. We must do things in our daily world.

The teacher says that we must do things to shape and
alter the outer world of form. We must not let it form and
mold us, but we must form and mold it. We only do this
if we can act from the Soul level, as individuals or creative
entities or beings. There is joy in acting at the Soul level
and there is only fever and fret and bewilderment in being acted upon on the phenomenal level of the phenomenal
world.

This globe of crystal light is a moving globe of scintillating colors, which represents the real world in which
we live. If we were aware of it, the world of Maya or
phenomena (this is a good translation of the word) is the
crystallized outer shell of an inner reality. If we can become
centers or focal points for this life energy, it can flow out
into the phenomenal world and change it in many ways
that are more desirable.

This globe of light, although it is silver light, seems to
have all the colors latent in it that we know and speak of.
It is a thoughtform I am sure, projected by the teacher.
As you look at it, your mind opens up. You can see clearly
the world of energy or light. You can see a new relationship between life and form. If the form were more flexible, there would be a better relationship between life and
form, a more joyous and creative relationship, I guess is
the word. Each student is encouraged to look at the globe
of light and meditate on it and record his own impressions
before the teacher goes on with his discussion.

As you look at it, you find out that you are not really
on the outside looking at it, but you move into it. You
become the energy and the life. You become identified

with the life, the living individual, the high Soul and
Monad. You find out the teacher has placed this here to
help the student become himself a scintillating center of
the life force. To become one with this life, this energy
or light, and move with it, rejoice with it, sing the Song
of Life with it. The teacher says:

"The myriad songs of the Universe are the
Songs of Life. All the energies dancing through
the Universe and their interplay and movement
create a vast symphonic composition — mathematical in its precision, as music is mathematical — creative in its effect. And life and form
should find always a flexible interplay.

"Inertia is a characteristic of matter or substance, especially physical matter, as we know it,
and the law of inertia in physics is a very good
statement of that. This inertia causes the form
to crystallize so long as so much of the life can
flow through it, and there must be forms other
than that. The human being is the most flexible form of all."

VPN   Very interesting. He says:

"The human being on any planet is the most
flexible of all forms. He has the capacity to be
flexible or not, as he chooses, but he can be. We
can live three or four incarnations in one lifetime
if we are flexible in any given incarnation. Then
we are able to achieve a great deal more when we
can change our outlook and point of view and
accept a new one. We can go forward in our
growth and development, and achieve more.

"This is why it helps if the individual is open
minded. The disciple on the Path should be such
an individual and should be able to achieve a
great deal more in any given lifetime than is or-

dinarily expected. The human being, being the most flexible of all forms, is therefore a center for the life force, for the play of the vital life energy through his vehicles."

VPN    This beautiful globe of scintillating light also represents Man, the Initiate, the Initiate Consciousness. Not only is it a replica or representation of the Universe, there is also representation of Man, the Initiate.

SK    What is an Initiate Consciousness?

VPN    It is the second or the fourth initiation, the second at the Hierarchial level. When the disciple has passed through the second initiation, he has become an initiate aware of the life force flowing through him. The life of Spirit, the Monad, flowing through — and this speeded up frequency gives him a certain amount of command over matter or substance.

There is a state of consciousness that has a command over matter or substance, a command that can mold and change matter and substance in ways that the ordinary person cannot. This is an unusual thing because ordinary man is not able to do this. This is probably why it is called the Initiate Consciousness. The teacher says:

"More and more disciples must be able to become aware of this life that works in and through the form. In living consciousness, the disciples must be aware of the life side, as well as the form side. This is the middle Path for the disciple — holding in his consciousness the life side and the form side in doing this, he will be able to make that impact upon his environment which it is intended that the Son of God should do."

SK    How can a disciple become more conscious of the life aspect?

VPN In his waking consciousness if he will simply in the beginning stop and realize that every form—a tree, a plant, a bird, a dog—any living form of plant or animal, has a life pulsating through it and just be aware of this. Man has a habit of consciousness. The teacher says:

"This is a well-chosen phrase, *a habit of consciousness*, and man's habit of consciousness is to see the form and take it for the reality. If he could just change that habit of consciousness to being aware of the life aspect, at least briefly, every time he looks at a tree, or a flower, or an animal, or the grass, he would simply momentarily be aware and know that there is a life behind this form.

"You see it's a matter of the change of focus —like focusing your eyes on a near object or a far object. If you focus on the near object, you don't see the far object; you can look at the far object, and the near object sort of fades out of your focus and consciousness and you see the far object. It is as simple and as difficult as that. Change your habit of consciousness. At least, momentarily, be aware of the life behind the form."

VPN As we live in the phenomenal world, we must deal with forms. There is some simple secret of being more in command of one's environment. He says:

"This is an important secret for the disciples of the world to understand. Those who are earth-bound, sunk in materialism with their feet in the mud, are grabbing and holding material things, taking more than they need and taking from others who do need. They are endeavoring frantically to amass wealth or money or gold or possessions and today, mankind is the victim of this

group, the people who are still tied so completely
to the matter aspect. The solution for this problem of economy is in the consciousness of disciples
of the world, aspirants and accepted disciples and
initiates."

VPN   Let me understand this. This is an interesting statement. He says:

"The imposition of a higher frequency upon
the material world can move and change it and
command it. Man was not supposed to be the servant of the material world. Man was not supposed to grab and amass and possess the material
world. He was supposed to *command* it. When
he seeks to possess it, he becomes the servant of
it. And the material world is supposed to be his
servant. The material world is the clay for the
potter to mold into forms of beauty and art and
unsefulness and service, but if the potter forgets
his wheel and merely tries to amass vast mountains of clay, then he has lost his focus in the
world and his purpose in being. To be aware of
the life behind the form will help man to control the form. It is as simple as that.

"At first, you become aware of the life behind
the form world. The more you are aware of this,
the more you will be able to command the form
world, to shape and mold it — the outer world.
To have and to hold and possess the material
world is to have and hold and possess a dead
shell, but to know the life behind that form world
is to know the meaning and purpose of existence.

"Let the disciples of the world achieve a *new
habit of consciousness*."

VPN   He says to us:

"Begin with the first tree or plant you see when you start out for the day and briefly be aware of the life that flows through that plant or tree or animal. This is the beginning of seeing the life behind the form."

VPN   It is a concept here that is a little difficult to get. He, the teacher, is seeking to get across to us some basic concept in consciousness. He says:

"Man, astrally focused, is the victim of his desires, when his desires have been directed toward the having and holding of things. This has given the form world power over him. The Disciple on the Path must command the world of form, because he knows the life behind the form."

VPN   Now, again, here is this concept that the teacher is endeavoring to give us. He repeats this:

"The disciple can command the world of form because he knows clearly in consciousness and is aware of the life behind the form. This is why disciples on the Path often have a problem about material things. They are in a kind of no-man's land. The disciple gets up and departs from the world of material domination; he sets out upon the Journey from Form to Life. (He is trying to give this concept in another way now.) So, he sets out on the journey from form to life; from the land of the form of material things, like the prodigal son, who lives in the country where he eats the husks which the swine eat and the prodigal son says, 'I want to arise and go to my Father.'

"The prodigal son is mankind having departed from the Father's house and into the world of form. And when at last he says, 'I will arise and

go to my Father,' he is saying, in effect, 'I will
arise and go forth on the journey from the
domination of substance and material things to
the reality of the life or spirit.' And, on the way,
as he departs from the country of material
domination and has not yet arrived at the realization of life or spirit, he goes into a kind of no-
man's land where there is a lack. He is at that
kind of neutral point; the disciple often needs to
go forward on his journey to an understanding
of the life behind the form, and in doing so he
will discover that he has not only gained the life,
but, also, the command of the form, and he will
be able to use the form world or material world
wisely and well because he can command it."

VPN   There is some bridging point here. I don't know
what it is. The teacher says:

"Go out into the garden for a while and come
back and talk."

VPN   No, he will go on. He wants to make another
thoughtform.

SK   What is the other thoughtform?
VPN   I think it's a garden. There are columns of beautiful stone. Kind of violet colored stone. No, it isn't, it's
light. And the students—I think we have to go in again
and talk. Our teacher will talk.

There are two globes. One is the globe of scintillating
crystal light, like clear water with the sunlight sparkling
on it. And there is another globe of a kind of milky solid
substance. It seems these are the two polarities Spirit and
Matter, Life and Form. And there is an attraction of these
two, one for the other. They move into each other—Life
and Form. The cosmic marriage of Life and Form. It is
very beautiful, like the creation of the universe.

This larger globe of scintillating light moves into the other. The creative process begins. They are moving, revolving globes of light and substance moving out all over the room until the walls seem to move back and we find ourselves looking at a kind of moving picture of the creation of the universe. Stars and suns and galaxies and planets; there is a tremendous exhilaration and joy, a sense of light and life and divinity, a great sense of beauty. Yes, it's a demonstration of the Song or Symphony of the Universe. As if we were out in the Milky Way or somewhere. The teacher says:

"We must seek to understand this concept of life and form; we must know the joy of the creative process in the world of nature; knowing this in our consciousness will give us the command over form."

VPN   He doesn't use the word "power;" he says it is often misused—perhaps the word "command" conveys more clearly what he means. He says:

"Ordinarily, mankind is rather lost in the wilderness of the world, surrounded by what appears to be to him a meaningless maze. But the Disciple on the Path must see the order, and he sees it simply by getting this new 'habit of consciousness'—seeing the life behind the form."

VPN   I think, perhaps, the concepts sort of dawn on one's consciousness and yet, I think, I don't get it quite clearly, Sire. The teacher says:

"Come again to class until you get it. Don't be discouraged if you haven't understood it all at first."

VPN   And he says:

"Think on these things and they will rise in your consciousness like the sun after the night.

"Life go before you and follow after you. Let life be the Shining Light that dawns into a new day of consciousness.

"Know that you walk in life and light and peace. Dynamic peace — peace that is not stagnation, but harmony — vital and moving life. For the true definition of peace is not stagnation — the stagnation of no activity, but the true meaning of peace is the dance of life in perfect harmony. Dynamic creativeness.

"War is disorder and confusion — disharmony in the processes of the Universe.

"The state of peace is the state of dynamic and symmetrical and orderly movement of life toward creative ends.

"The end of disharmony is destruction.

"The purpose of peace is new creation.

"And so, oh Disciples, go forth in peace — knowing the true meaning of peace.

"Walk softly in your inner consciousness that you miss not this dawning of a new day in your own Soul. When a new day has dawned in your own Soul, also in that of other disciples, then also will a new day dawn in the world of mankind."

VPN   There is a great sense of deep joy, a sense of worship that is tremendous. This is an approach to an understanding of the Love of God at the heart of the universe. It's very wonderful. The teacher says:

"Oh Disciples, let your hearts rest in the love of the universe of God, the Father, the Spirit.

"There is conscious and Divine Love at the heart of the universe and this love holds your life and your development as dear and precious beyond all words and all comprehension.

"Be quietly aware of this love at the heart of the universe that seeks and does all things for your growth and your safety and your development. This love that seeks only your good without ceasing."

VPN   This is the end of the class.

I think we have to stay in the awareness of this great light and power.

# To the Wayfarer

*You are a jewel in the Hand of God*
*I gaze upon your beauty and behold*
*The many facets of the being that you are*
*And though the polishing be not complete*
*You are beloved of God;*
*For all you are,*
*And all you shall become*
*So are we all jewels of consciousness*
*Held lovingly with the Hand of God.*